John Donne

The Works of
John Donne

✣

with an Introduction and Bibliography

The Wordsworth Poetry Library

The paper in this book is produced from pure wood
pulp, without the use of chlorine or any other substance
harmful to the environment. The energy used in its
production consists almost entirely of hydroelectricity
and heat generated from waste materials, thereby
conserving fossil fuels and contributing little to the
greenhouse effect.

This edition published 1994 by Wordsworth Editions Ltd,
Cumberland House, Crib Street, Ware, Hertfordshire SG12 9ET.

ISBN 1-85326-400-8

Typeset in the UK by Antony Gray.
Printed and bound in Denmark by Nørhaven

INTRODUCTION

John Donne was born in 1572, only eight years after Shakespeare, yet the two poets seem to inhabit very different emotional and literary atmospheres. Donne, with his startling scientific images, his muscular, colloquial directness and his complex, even tortured intelligence, appears to us very much as a figure of the seventeenth century of scientific discoveries and philosophical rigour. Some of this emotional complexity and intellectual sophistication can be ascribed to the fact that most of his life was spent in London, around or aspiring to courtly circles, and that he was born into a Catholic family at a time when Catholics were severely restricted and often persecuted in the exercise of their faith. His mother was related to Sir Thomas More, and an uncle led the Jesuit mission in England. After the early death of Donne's father his mother married another Catholic. While still very young Donne attended both Oxford and Cambridge, but was precluded by his faith from taking a degree. In 1593 his brother died in prison, after having been caught harbouring a priest. Donne, it seems, renounced Catholicism at about this time. While this undoubtedly removed a barrier to his ambitions, it should not be seen simply as an opportunistic move: for Donne faith and creed were matters of the most profound seriousness, to be probed throughout his life – initially in Satyre III where we find those famous lines whose vigorous, mimetic complexity seems to describe Donne's own style:

> On a huge hill,
> Cragged, and steep, Truth stands, and hee that will
> Reach her, about must, and about must goe.

The fear of damnation, of a very real hell-fire, permeates much of his religious poetry, and scholars agree that the abandonment of his ancestral faith was not arrived at easily.

Like most ambitious young men of his day Donne needed aristocratic patrons to further his career, even to subsist. After buccaneering expeditions with Essex and Raleigh he became secretary to Sir Thomas Egerton.

However, in 1601 he wrecked his prospects by marrying Ann More, Lady Egerton's niece. This led to a brief imprisonment and fourteen years of poverty and anxiety, poignantly summed up in the little triplet, 'John Donne, / Ann Donne, / Undone' (which gives us the pronunciation of his name, something he used with majestic punning in 'Hymn to God the Father'). They were to have twelve children, before her death after the last birth in 1617. Eventually the efforts of friends and patrons commended him to the notice of James I, but the king insisted that Donne's advancement must be in the church, and an initially reluctant Donne was ordained in 1615. At first he held plural livings, then travelled to Germany as chaplain to a diplomatic mission, before the influence of high-placed friends elevated him to the Deanery of St Paul's. Here, for the last ten years of his life, he preached with a passion and eloquence which brought him renown and respect. He died in March 1631.

Today Donne's reputation stands high, but this is a comparatively recent phenomenon. Succeeding generations found his verse too odd, too rough, too 'incorrect' to be either pleasing or edifying, and his eroticism, playfulness and cynicism were repugnant to many in the nineteenth century. It was modernists like T. S. Eliot, who finding that his daring, his cerebral qualities and his rugged diction chimed with their own preoccupations, began his rehabilitation. Nowadays Donne is taught in schools, and many a bookish adolescent will have got his or her first intuition of joyous sexuality from the love poems:

> License my roaving hands, and let them go,
> Before, behind, between, above, below.
> O my America! my new-found-land . . .
>
> *Elegie XIX*

Readers should not be troubled by two of the terms frequently attached to Donne. One is that he was a 'metaphysical' poet, along with such contemporaries as Marvell, Herbert and Traherne. This has no connection with the philosophical school but was an epithet coined by a disapproving Dr Johnson for seventeenth-century writers who flaunted their learning and employed abstruse 'conceits' – the other difficult term. A conceit is simply a learned or far-fetched image, of which there are plenty to be found in Donne: a flea, in the eponymous poem, becomes both the fortunate ravisher of the obdurate beloved – an ancient poet's joke – and, having sucked the blood of both lover and beloved, their marriage bed. In the grave and tender 'A Valediction: Forbidding Mourning' the parted lovers' united souls are 'like gold to airy thinness beat', or

> If they be two, they are two so
>> As stiffe twin compasses are two . . .
>> Yet when the other far doth rome,
> It leanes, and hearkens after it,
>> And growes erect, as that comes home.

Rather more disturbing, though physically evocative is an image in the rapt love poem, 'The Extasie':

> Our eye-beams twisted, and did thred
> Our eyes, upon one double string.

Again and again readers will be arrested by startling turns of phrase, by pungent frankness or by the poet's imperious commands ('For Godsake hold your tongue and let me love'; 'Goe tell Court-huntsmen that the King will ride'; 'Batter my heart, three person'd God'; 'Death, be not proud'), and, it has to be said, puzzled by some unfathomable phrase or allusion. There is no evading the fact that Donne is a difficult poet. To this day scholars are scrapping over the exact significance of obscure references or quarrelling over some particularly convoluted piece of syntax.

Nevertheless, much of Donne is wonderfully accessible to modern readers. Most will start with the *Songs and Sonnets*, a large number of which are love poems. These were almost certainly written over a long period, many probably after his marriage to the beloved Ann. Though those nurtured on the poetry of the Romantics may be troubled by worry about his sincerity, there is no real difficulty here; it may be helpful to think of Donne as a supreme actor, giving voice to intense and passionate feelings which he understood well but did not attach to specific autobiographical events. The lyrics vary widely in tone, from the playful magic of 'Song' ('Goe, and catche a falling starre') through the jocund arrogance of 'The Sunne Rising' to the elegiac 'A Nocturnall upon S. Lucie's Day', written on the illness of his loved patroness, Lucy Countess of Bedford. However difficult some passages may be, each poem has an unmistakable voice which speaks directly across the centuries, and awakens an equally direct response. Such vigour and directness are quite as telling in the religious poems, whose power and, often, anguish can be felt even by readers who have little feeling for religion and no knowledge of seventeenth-century theology. Belief was integral to the lives of almost all Donne's contemporaries, and Donne's probable disquiet about his renunciation of Catholicism may augment his sense of having a 'blacke soule' and inspire Sonnet XVIII of the Divine Poems, 'Show me deare Christ, thy spouse, so bright and clear'.

The Epithalamions, once the reader becomes accustomed to the elaborate, hyperbolic diction, give a lively sense of aristocratic panoply and ceremony, and a tender evocation of marital eroticism. Like the poems addressed to patrons, these worked within a convention of homage and, in the case of women, courtly love, which was well understood by the recipients and by Donne's contemporaries.

Not all the poems are so accessible. Few but Donne specialists plough through the 'Anniversaries', written to commemorate the death of a fifteen-year-old girl Donne had never met, in the hope of continued patronage from her father. Information about their recipients is needed for some of the verse letters, and several of the Satyres and Elegies demand specialist knowledge. Others, however, leap off the page. In Elegie XVI the poet, after imploring his love not to follow him abroad disguised as his page, imagines her dreaming of him during his absence and waking terrified:

> Nurse, O my love is slaine, I saw him goe
> O'er the white Alps alone.

Such vividly strange moments gleam through Donne's poetry – 'This bed thy center is, these walls, thy spheare'; the baroque 'At the round earths imagin'd corners, blow / Your trumpets, Angells'; ' . . . cloysterd in these living walls of Jet; 'A bracelet of bright haire about the bone' – echoing down the centuries and haunting the reader. The vitality, the individuality, the paradoxical modernity of this complex seventeenth-century man speak with piercing directness to readers of the late twentieth century.

Editorial note:
Many scholars now doubt the attribution to Donne of Elegies XIII, XIV and XVII.

FURTHER READING
Donne, edited by John Hayward, Penguin
John Donne, *The Elegies* and *Songs and Sonnets*, edited by Helen Gardner, Oxford at the Clarendon Press, 1965
John Carey, *John Donne: Life, Mind and Art*, Faber & Faber, 1981
Izaak Walton, *Life of Donne*, 1640, World's Classics
R. C. Bald, *John Donne, A Life*, Oxford University Press, 1970
A. Alvarez, *The School of Donne*, Chatto & Windus, 1961
James Winny, *A Preface to Donne,* Longman, 1970
J. B. Leishman, *The Monarch of Wit*, Hutchinson University Library, 1967

CONTENTS

SONGS AND SONNETS

EPIGRAMS

ELEGIES

HEROICALL EPISTLE

EPITHALAMIONS, OR MARRIAGE SONGS

SATYRES

LETTERS TO SEVERALL PERSONAGES

AN ANATOMIE OF THE WORLD

OF THE PROGRESSE OF THE SOULE

EPICEDES AND OBSEQUIES

INFINITATI SACRUM

DIVINE POEMS

INDEX OF POEM TITLES

INDEX OF FIRST LINES

The Good-Morrow

I wonder by my troth, what thou, and I
Did, till we lov'd? were we not wean'd till then?
But suck'd on countrey pleasures, childishly?
Or snorted we in the seaven sleepers den?
T'was so; But this, all pleasures fancies bee.   5
If ever any beauty I did see,
Which I desir'd, and got, t'was but a dreame of thee.

And now good morrow to our waking soules,
Which watch not one another out of feare;
For love, all love of other sights controules,   10
And makes one little roome, an every where.
Let sea-discoverers to new worlds have gone,
Let Maps to other, worlds on worlds have showne,
Let us possesse one world, each hath one, and is one.

My face in thine eye, thine in mine appeares,   15
And true plaine hearts doe in the faces rest,
Where can we finde two better hemispheares
Without sharpe North, without declining West?
What ever dyes, was not mixt equally;
If our two loves be one, or, thou and I   20
Love so alike, that none doe slacken, none can die.

Song

Goe, and catche a falling starre,
    Get with child a mandrake roote,
Tell me where all past yeares are,
    Or who cleft the Divels foot,

Teach me to heare Mermaides singing,   5
   Or to keep off envies stinging,
      And finde
      What winde
Serves to advance an honest minde.

If thou beest borne to strange sights,   10
   Things invisible to see,
Ride ten thousand daies and nights,
   Till age snow white haires on thee,
Thou, when thou retorn'st, wilt tell mee
All strange wonders that befell thee,   15
      And sweare
      No where
Lives a woman true, and faire.

If thou findst one, let mee know,
   Such a Pilgrimage were sweet;   20
Yet doe not, I would not goe,
   Though at next doore wee might meet,
Though shee were true, when you met her,
And last, till you write your letter,
      Yet shee   25
      Will bee
False, ere I come, to two, or three.

Womans Constancy

Now thou hast lov'd me one whole day,
To morrow when thou leav'st, what wilt thou say?
Wilt thou then Antedate some new made vow?
     Or say that now
We are not just those persons, which we were?   5
Or, that oathes made in reverentiall feare
Of Love, and his wrath, any may forsweare?
Or, as true deaths, true maryages untie,
So lovers contracts, images of those,
Binde but till sleep, deaths image, them unloose?   10
     Or, your owne end to Justifie,

For having purpos'd change, and falsehood; you
Can have no way but falsehood to be true?
Vaine lunatique, against these scapes I could
      Dispute, and conquer, if I would,   15
      Which I abstaine to doe,
For by to morrow, I may thinke so too.

The Undertaking

    I have done one braver thing
      Then all the *Worthies* did,
    And yet a braver thence doth spring,
      Which is, to keepe that hid.

    It were but madnes now t'impart   5
      The skill of specular stone,
    When he which can have learn'd the art
      To cut it, can finde none.

    So, if I now should utter this,
      Others (because no more   10
    Such stuffe to worke upon, there is,)
      Would love but as before.

    But he who lovelinesse within
      Hath found, all outward loathes,
    For he who colour loves, and skinne,   15
      Loves but their oldest clothes.

    If, as I have, you also doe
      Vertue'attir'd in woman see,
    And dare love that, and say so too,
      And forget the Hee and Shee;   20

    And if this love, though placed so,
      From prophane men you hide,
    Which will no faith on this bestow,
      Or, if they doe, deride:

Then you have done a braver thing   25
    Then all the *Worthies* did;
And a braver thence will spring,
    Which is, to keepe that hid.

The Sunne Rising

Busie old foole, unruly Sunne,
    Why dost thou thus,
Through windowes, and through curtaines call on us?
Must to thy motions lovers seasons run?
        Sawcy pedantique wretch, goe chide   5
        Late schoole boyes, and sowre prentices,
    Goe tell Court-huntsmen, that the King will ride,
    Call countrey ants to harvest offices;
Love, all alike, no season knowes, nor clyme,
Nor houres, dayes, moneths, which are the rags of time.

Thy beames, so reverend, and strong
    Why shouldst thou thinke?
I could eclipse and cloud them with a winke,
But that I would not lose her sight so long:
        If her eyes have not blinded thine,   15
        Looke, and to morrow late, tell mee,
    Whether both the'India's of spice and Myne
    Be where thou leftst them, or lie here with mee.
Aske for those Kings whom thou saw'st yesterday,
And thou shalt heare, All here in one bed lay.   20

She'is all States, and all Princes, I,
    Nothing else is.
Princes doe but play us; compar'd to this,
All honor's mimique; All wealth alchimie.
        Thou sunne art halfe as happy'as wee,   25
        In that the world's contracted thus;
    Thine age askes ease, and since thy duties bee
    To warme the world, that's done in warming us.
Shine here to us, and thou art every where;
This bed thy center is, these walls, thy spheare.   30

The Indifferent

I can love both faire and browne,
Her whom abundance melts, and her whom want betraies,
Her who loves lonenesse best, and her who maskes and plaies,
Her whom the country form'd, and whom the town,
Her who beleeves, and her who tries,   5
Her who still weepes with spungie eyes,
And her who is dry corke, and never cries;
I can love her, and her, and you and you,
I can love any, so she be not true.

Will no other vice content you?   10
Will it not serve your turn to do, as did your mothers?
Or have you all old vices spent, and now would finde out
others?
Or doth a feare, that men are true, torment you?
Oh we are not, be not you so,
Let mee, and doe you, twenty know.   15
Rob mee, but binde me not, and let me goe.
Must I, who came to travaile thorow you,
Grow your fixt subject, because you are true?

Venus heard me sigh this song,
And by Loves sweetest Part, Variety, she swore,   20
She heard not this till now; and that it should be so no more.
She went, examin'd, and return'd ere long,
And said, alas, Some two or three
Poore Heretiques in love there bee,
Which thinke to stablish dangerous constancie.   25
But I have told them, since you will be true,
You shall be true to them, who'are false to you.

Loves Usury

For every houre that thou wilt spare mee now,
              I will allow,
Usurious God of Love, twenty to thee,
When with my browne, my gray haires equall bee;

Till then, Love, let my body raigne, and let   5
Mee travell, sojourne, snatch, plot, have, forget,
Resume my last yeares relict: thinke that yet
        We'had never met.

Let mee thinke any rivalls letter mine,
        And at next nine   10
Keepe midnights promise; mistake by the way
The maid, and tell the Lady of that delay;
Onely let mee love none, no, not the sport;
From country grasse, to comfitures of Court,
Or cities quelque choses, let report   15
        My minde transport.

This bargaine's good; if when I'am old, I bee
        Inflam'd by thee,
If thine owne honour, or my shame, or paine,
Thou covet most, at that age thou shalt gaine.   20
Doe thy will then, then subject and degree,
And fruit of love, Love I submit to thee,
Spare mee till then, I'll beare it, though she bee
        One that loves mee.

The Canonization

For Godsake hold your tongue, and let me love,
    Or chide my palsie, or my gout,
My five gray haires, or ruin'd fortune flout,
      With wealth your state, your minde with Arts improve,
        Take you a course, get you a place,   5
        Observe his honour, or his grace,
Or the Kings reall, or his stamped face
    Contemplate, what you will, approve,
    So you will let me love.

Alas, alas, who's injur'd by my love?   10
    What merchants ships have my sighs drown'd?
Who saies my teares have overflow'd his ground?
    When did my colds a forward spring remove?

When did the heats which my veines fill
   Adde one more to the plaguie Bill?   15
Soldiers finde warres, and Lawyers finde out still
   Litigious men, which quarrels move,
   Though she and I do love.

Call us what you will, wee are made such by love;
   Call her one, mee another flye,   20
We'are Tapers too, and at our owne cost die,
   And wee in us finde the'Eagle and the Dove.
    The Phœnix ridle hath more wit
    By us, we two being one, are it.
So, to one neutrall thing both sexes fit,   25
   Wee dye and rise the same, and prove
   Mysterious by this love.

Wee can dye by it, if not live by love,
   And if unfit for tombes and hearse
Our legend bee, it will be fit for verse;   30
   And if no peece of Chronicle wee prove,
    We'll build in sonnets pretty roomes;
    As well a well wrought urne becomes
The greatest ashes, as halfe-acre tombes,
   And by these hymnes, all shall approve   35
   Us *Canoniz'd* for Love:

And thus invoke us; You whom reverend love
   Made one anothers hermitage;
You, to whom love was peace, that now is rage;
   Who did the whole worlds soule contract, and drove
    Into the glasses of your eyes
    So made such mirrors, and such spies,
That they did all to you epitomize,
   Countries, Townes, Courts: Beg from above
   A patterne of your love!   45

The Triple Foole

I am two fooles, I know,
For loving, and for saying so
   In whining Poëtry;
But where's that wiseman, that would not be I,
   If she would not deny?   5
Then as th'earths inward narrow crooked lanes
Do purge sea waters fretfull salt away,
   I thought, if I could draw my paines,
Through Rimes vexation, I should them allay,
Griefe brought to numbers cannot be so fierce,   10
For, he tames it, that fetters it in verse.

   But when I have done so,
Some man, his art and voice to show,
   Doth Set and sing my paine,
And, by delighting many, frees againe   15
   Griefe, which verse did restraine.
To Love, and Griefe tribute of Verse belongs,
But not of such as pleases when'tis read,
   Both are increased by such songs:
For both their triumphs so are published,   20
And I, which was two fooles, do so grow three;
Who are a little wise, the best fooles bee.

Lovers Infinitenesse

If yet I have not all thy love,
Deare, I shall never have it all,
I cannot breath one other sigh, to move;
Nor can intreat one other teare to fall.
And all my treasure, which should purchase thee,   5
Sighs, teares, and oathes, and letters I have spent,
Yet no more can be due to mee,
Then at the bargaine made was ment,
If then thy gift of love were partiall,
That some to mee, some should to others fall,   10
   Deare, I shall never have Thee All.

Or if then thou gavest mee all,
All was but All, which thou hadst then,
But if in thy heart, since, there be or shall,
New love created bee, by other men,   15
Which have their stocks intire, and can in teares,
In sighs, in oathes, and letters outbid mee,
This new love may beget new feares,
For, this love was not vowed by thee.
And yet it was, thy gift being generall,   20
The ground, thy heart is mine, what ever shall
   Grow there, deare, I should have it all.

Yet I would not have all yet,
Hee that hath all can have no more,
And since my love doth every day admit   25
New growth, thou shouldst have new rewards in store;
Thou canst not every day give me thy heart,
If thou canst give it, then thou never gavest it:
Loves riddles are, that though thy heart depart,
It stayes at home, and thou with losing savest it: 30
But wee will have a way more liberall,
Then changing hearts, to joyne them, so wee shall
   Be one, and one anothers All.

Song

Sweetest love, I do not goe,
   For wearinesse of thee,
Nor in hope the world can show
   A fitter Love for mee;
     But since that I   5
Must dye at last, 'tis best,
To use my selfe in jest
   Thus by fain'd deaths to dye;

Yesternight the Sunne went hence,
   And yet is here to day,   10
He hath no desire nor sense,
   Nor halfe so short a way:

Then feare not mee,
But beleeve that I shall make
Speedier journeyes, since I take   15
    More wings and spurres then hee.

O how feeble is mans power,
    That if good fortune fall,
Cannot adde another houre,
    Nor a lost houre recall!   20
        But come bad chance,
And wee joyne to'it our strength,
And wee teach it art and length,
    It selfe o'r us to'advance.

When thou sigh'st, thou sigh'st not winde,   25
    But sigh'st my soule away,
When thou weep'st, unkindly kinde,
    My lifes blood doth decay.
        It cannot bee
That thou lov'st mee, as thou say'st,   30
If in thine my life thou waste,
    Thou art the best of mee.

Let not thy divining heart
    Forethinke me any ill,
Destiny may take thy part,   35
    And may thy feares fulfill;
        But thinke that wee
Are but turn'd aside to sleepe;
They who one another keepe
    Alive, ne'r parted bee.   40

The Legacie

When I dyed last, and, Deare, I dye
    As often as from thee I goe,
    Though it be but an houre agoe,
And Lovers houres be full eternity,

I can remember yet, that I   5
   Something did say, and something did bestow;
  Though I be dead, which sent mee, I should be
  Mine owne executor and Legacie.

I heard mee say, Tell her anon,
  That my selfe, (that is you, not I,)   10
   Did kill me, and when I felt mee dye,
I bid mee send my heart, when I was gone,
But I alas could there finde none,
  When I had ripp'd me, 'and search'd where hearts did lye;
It kill'd mee againe, that I who still was true,   15
In life, in my last Will should cozen you.

Yet I found something like a heart,
  But colours it, and corners had,
  It was not good, it was not bad,
It was intire to none, and few had part.   20
As good as could be made by art
  It seem'd; and therefore for our losses sad,
I meant to send this heart in stead of mine,
But oh, no man could hold it, for twas thine.

A Feaver

Oh doe not die, for I shall hate
  All women so, when thou art gone,
That thee I shall not celebrate,
  When I remember, thou wast one.

But yet thou canst not die, I know;   5
  To leave this world behinde, is death,
But when thou from this world wilt goe,
  The whole world vapors with thy breath.

Or if, when thou, the worlds soule, goest,
  It stay, tis but thy carkasse then,   10
The fairest woman, but thy ghost,
  But corrupt wormes, the worthyest men.

O wrangling schooles, that search what fire
   Shall burne this world, had none the wit
Unto this knowledge to aspire,   15
   That this her feaver might be it?

And yet she cannot wast by this,
   Nor long beare this torturing wrong,
For much corruption needfull is
   To fuell such a feaver long.   20

These burning fits but meteors bee,
   Whose matter in thee is soone spent.
Thy beauty,'and all parts, which are thee,
   Are unchangeable firmament.

Yet t'was of my minde, seising thee,   25
   Though it in thee cannot persever.
For I had rather owner bee
   Of thee one houre, then all else ever.

Aire and Angels

Twice or thrice had I loved thee,
Before I knew thy face or name,
So in a voice, so in a shapelesse flame,
Angells affect us oft, and worship'd bee;
   Still when, to where thou wert, I came,   5
Some lovely glorious nothing I did see.
   But since my soule, whose child love is,
Takes limmes of flesh, and else could nothing doe,
   More subtile then the parent is,
Love must not be, but take a body too,   10
   And therefore what thou wert, and who,
      I bid Love aske, and now
That it assume thy body, I allow,
And fixe it selfe in thy lip, eye, and brow.

Whilst thus to ballast love, I thought,   15
And so more steddily to have gone,
With wares which would sinke admiration,
I saw, I had loves pinnace overfraught,
   Ev'ry thy haire for love to worke upon
Is much too much, some fitter must be sought;   20
   For, nor in nothing, nor in things
Extreme, and scatt'ring bright, can love inhere;
   Then as an Angell, face, and wings
Of aire, not pure as it, yet pure doth weare,
   So thy love may be my loves spheare;
      Just such disparitie   25
As is twixt Aire and Angells puritie,
'Twixt womens love, and mens will ever bee.

Breake of Day

'Tis true, 'tis day; what though it be?
O wilt thou therefore rise from me?
Why should we rise, because 'tis light?
Did we lie downe, because 'twas night?
Love which in spight of darknesse brought us hether,   5
Should in despight of light keepe us together.

Light hath no tongue, but is all eye;
If it could speake as well as spie,
This were the worst, that it could say,
That being well, I faine would stay,   10
And that I lov'd my heart and honor so,
That I would not from him, that had them, goe.

Must businesse thee from hence remove?
Oh, that's the worst disease of love,
The poore, the foule, the false, love can   15
Admit, but not the busied man.
He which hath businesse, and makes love, doth doe
Such wrong, as when a maryed man doth wooe.

The Anniversarie

All Kings, and all their favorites,
  All glory of honors, beauties, wits,
The Sun it selfe, which makes times, as they passe,
Is elder by a yeare, now, then it was
When thou and I first one another saw: 5
All other things, to their destruction draw,
  Only our love hath no decay;
This, no to morrow hath, nor yesterday,
Running it never runs from us away,
But truly keepes his first, last, everlasting day.   10

Two graves must hide thine and my coarse,
  If one might, death were no divorce,
Alas, as well as other Princes, wee,
(Who Prince enough in one another bee,)
Must leave at last in death, these eyes, and eares,   15
Oft fed with true oathes, and with sweet salt teares;
  But soules where nothing dwells but love
(All other thoughts being inmates) then shall prove
This, or a love increased there above,   19
When bodies to their graves, soules from their graves
remove.

And then wee shall be throughly blest,
  But wee no more, then all the rest;
Here upon earth, we'are Kings, and none but wee
Can be such Kings, nor of such subjects bee;
Who is so safe as wee? where none can doe   25
Treason to us, except one of us two.
  True and false feares let us refraine,
Let us love nobly, and live, and adde againe
Yeares and yeares unto yeares, till we attaine
To write threescore: this is the second of our raigne.   30

A Valediction: of my Name, in the Window

I

My name engrav'd herein,
Doth contribute my firmnesse to this glasse,
   Which, ever since that charme, hath beene
   As hard, as that which grav'd it, was;
Thine eye will give it price enough, to mock   5
      The diamonds of either rock.

II

'Tis much that Glasse should bee
As all confessing, and through-shine as I,
   'Tis more, that it shewes thee to thee,
   And cleare reflects thee to thine eye.   10
But all such rules, loves magique can undoe,
      Here you see mee, and I am you.

III

As no one point, nor dash,
Which are but accessaries to this name,
   The showers and tempests can outwash,   15
   So shall all times finde mee the same;
You this intirenesse better may fulfill,
      Who have the patterne with you still.

IIII

Or if too hard and deepe
This learning be, for a scratch'd name to teach,   20
   It, as a given deaths head keepe,
   Lovers mortalitie to preach,
Or thinke this ragged bony name to bee
      My ruinous Anatomie.

V

Then, as all my soules bee,   25
Emparadis'd in you, (in whom alone
    I understand, and grow and see,),
    The rafters of my body, bone
Being still with you, the Muscle, Sinew, and Veine,
        Which tile this house, will come againe: 30

VI

Till my returne, repaire
And recompact my scattered body so.
    As all the vertuous powers which are
    Fix'd in the starres, are said to flow
Into such characters, as graved bee   35
        When these starres have supremacie:

VII

So since this name was cut
When love and griefe their exaltation had,
    No doore 'gainst this names influence shut;
    As much more loving, as more sad,   40
'Twill make thee; and thou shouldst, till I returne,
        Since I die daily, daily mourne.

VIII

When thy inconsiderate hand
Flings ope this casement, with my trembling name,
    To looke on one, whose wit or land,   45
    New battry to thy heart may frame,
Then thinke this name alive, and that thou thus
        In it offendst my Genius.

IX

And when thy melted maid,
Corrupted by thy Lover's gold, and page,   50
    His letter at thy pillow'hath laid,
    Disputed it, and tam'd thy rage,
And thou begin'st to thaw towards him, for this,
        May my name step in, and hide his.

X

And if this treason goe   55
To an overt act, and that thou write againe;
  In superscribing, this name flow
  Into thy fancy, from the pane.
So, in forgetting thou remembrest right,
        And unaware to mee shalt write.   60

XI

But glasse, and lines must bee,
No meanes our firme substantiall love to keepe;
  Neere death inflicts this lethargie,
  And this I murmure in my sleepe;
Impute this idle talke, to that I goe,   65
        For dying men talke often so.

Twicknam Garden

Blasted with sighs, and surrounded with teares
  Hither I come to seeke the spring,
  And at mine eyes, and at mine eares,
Receive such balmes, as else cure every thing;
  But O, selfe traytor, I do bring   5
The spider love, which transubstantiates all,
  And can convert Manna to gall,
And that this place may thoroughly be thought
  True Paradise, I have the serpent brought.

'Twere wholsomer for mee, that winter did   10
  Benight the glory of this place,
  And that a grave frost did forbid
These trees to laugh, and mocke mee to my face;
  But that I may not this disgrace
Indure, nor yet leave loving, Love let mee   15
  Some senslesse peece of this place bee;
Make me a mandrake, so I may groane here,
  Or a stone fountaine weeping out my yeare.

Hither with christall vyals, lovers come,
  And take my teares, which are loves wine,   20

And try your mistresse Teares at home,
For all are false, that tast not just like mine;
  Alas, hearts do not in eyes shine,
Nor can you more judge womans thoughts by teares,
  Then by her shadow, what she weares.   25
O perverse sexe, where none is true but shee,
  Who's therefore true, because her truth kills mee.

A Valediction: of the Booke

I'll tell thee now (deare Love) what thou shalt doe
  To anger destiny, as she doth us,
  How I shall stay, though she Esloygne me thus,
And how posterity shall know it too;
    How thine may out-endure   5
    Sybills glory, and obscure
    Her who from Pindar could allure,
  And her, through whose helpe *Lucan* is not lame,
And her, whose booke (they say) *Homer* did finde, and name.

Study our manuscripts, those Myriades   10
  Of letters, which have past twixt thee and mee,
  Thence write our Annals, and in them will bee
To all whom loves subliming fire invades,
    Rule and example found;
    There, the faith of any ground   15
    No schismatique will dare to wound,
  That sees, how Love this grace to us affords,
To make, to keep, to use, to be these his Records.

This Booke, as long-liv'd as the elements,
  Or as the worlds forme, this all-graved tome   20
  In cypher writ, or new made Idiome,
Wee for loves clergie only'are instruments:
    When this booke is made thus,
    Should againe the ravenous
    Vandals and Goths inundate us,   25
  Learning were safe; in this our Universe
Schooles might learne Sciences, Spheares Musick, Angels Verse.

Here Loves Divines, (since all Divinity
   Is love or wonder) may finde all they seek,
   Whether abstract spirituall love they like,   30
Their Soules exhal'd with what they do not see,
        Or, loth so to amuze
        Faiths infirmitie, they chuse
        Something which they may see and use;
For, though minde be the heaven, where love doth sit,   35
Beauty a convenient type may be to figure it.

Here more then in their bookes may Lawyers finde,
   Both by what titles Mistresses are ours,
   And how prerogative these states devours,
Transferr'd from Love himselfe, to womankinde,   40
        Who though from heart, and eyes,
        They exact great subsidies,
        Forsake him who on them relies,
   And for the cause, honour, or conscience give,
Chimeraes, vaine as they, or their prerogative.   45

Here Statesmen, (or of them, they which can reade,)
   May of their occupation finde the grounds:
   Love and their art alike it deadly wounds,
If to consider what 'tis, one proceed,
        In both they doe excell   50
        Who the present governe well,
        Whose weaknesse none doth, or dares tell;
   In this thy booke, such will their nothing see,
As in the Bible some can finde out Alchimy.

Thus vent thy thoughts; abroad I'll studie thee,   55
   As he removes farre off, that great heights takes;
   How great love is, presence best tryall makes,
But absence tryes how long this love will bee;
        To take a latitude
        Sun, or starres, are fitliest view'd   60
        At their brightest, but to conclude
   Of longitudes, what other way have wee,
But to marke when, and where the darke eclipses bee?

Communitie

Good wee must love, and must hate ill,
For ill is ill, and good good still,
　　But there are things indifferent,
Which wee may neither hate, nor love,
But one, and then another prove,　　　　　　　　5
　　As wee shall finde our fancy bent.

If then at first wise Nature had
Made women either good or bad,
　　Then some wee might hate, and some chuse,
But since shee did them so create,　　　　　　　10
That we may neither love, nor hate,
　　Onely this rests, All, all may use.

If they were good it would be seene,
Good is as visible as greene,
　　And to all eyes it selfe betrayes:　　　　　　15
If they were bad, they could not last,
Bad doth it selfe, and others wast,
　　So, they deserve nor blame, nor praise.

But they are ours as fruits are ours,
He that but tasts, he that devours,　　　　　　　20
　　And he that leaves all, doth as well:
Chang'd loves are but chang'd sorts of meat,
And when hee hath the kernell eate,
　　Who doth not fling away the shell?

Loves Growth

I scarce beleeve my love to be so pure
 As I had thought it was,
 Because it doth endure
Vicissitude, and season, as the grasse;
Me thinkes I lyed all winter, when I swore,   5
My love was infinite, if spring make'it more.

But if this medicine, love, which cures all sorrow
With more, not onely bee no quintessence,
But mixt of all stuffes, paining soule, or sense,
And of the Sunne his working vigour borrow,   10
Love's not so pure, and abstract, as they use
To say, which have no Mistresse but their Muse,
But as all else, being elemented too,
Love sometimes would contemplate, sometimes do.

And yet no greater, but more eminent,   15
 Love by the spring is growne;
 As, in the firmament,
Starres by the Sunne are not inlarg'd, but showne.
Gentle love deeds, as blossomes on a bough,
From loves awakened root do bud out now.   20

If, as in water stir'd more circles bee
Produc'd by one, love such additions take,
Those like so many spheares, but one heaven make,
For, they are all concentrique unto thee;
And though each spring doe adde to love new heate,   25
As princes doe in times of action get
New taxes, and remit them not in peace,
No winter shall abate the springs encrease.

Loves Exchange

Love, any devill else but you,
Would for a given Soule give something too.
At Court your fellowes every day,
Give th'art of Riming, Huntsmanship, or Play,
For them which were their owne before;   5
Onely I have nothing which gave more,
But am, alas, by being lowly, lower.

I aske no dispensation now
To falsifie a teare, or sigh, or vow,
I do not sue from thee to draw   10
A *non obstante* on natures law,
These are prerogatives, they inhere
In thee and thine; none should forsweare
Except that hee *Loves* minion were.

Give mee thy weaknesse, make mee blinde,   15
Both wayes, as thou and thine, in eies and minde;
Love, let me never know that this
Is love, or, that love childish is;
Let me not know that others know
That she knowes my paines, least that so   20
A tender shame make me mine owne new woe.

If thou give nothing, yet thou'art just,
Because I would not thy first motions trust;
Small townes which stand stiffe, till great shot
Enforce them, by warres law *condition* not.   25
Such in loves warfare is my case,
I may not article for grace,
Having put Love at last to shew this face.

This face, by which he could command
And change the Idolatrie of any land,   30
This face, which wheresoe'r it comes,
Can call vow'd men from cloisters, dead from tombes,
And melt both Poles at once, and store

Deserts with cities, and make more
Mynes in the earth, then Quarries were before.   35

For this, Love is enrag'd with mee,
Yet kills not. If I must example bee
To future Rebells; If th'unborne
Must learne, by my being cut up, and torne:
Kill, and dissect me, Love; for this   40
Torture against thine owne end is,
Rack't carcasses make ill Anatomies.

Confined Love

Some man unworthy to be possessor
Of old or new love, himselfe being false or weake,
    Thought his paine and shame would be lesser,
If on womankind he might his anger wreake,
            And thence a law did grow,   5
            One might but one man know;
            But are other creatures so?

Are Sunne, Moone, or Starres by law forbidden,
To smile where they list, or lend away their light?
    Are birds divorc'd, or are they chidden   10
If they leave their mate, or lie abroad a night?
            Beasts doe no joyntures lose
            Though they new lovers choose,
            But we are made worse then those.

Who e'r rigg'd faire ship to lie in harbors,   15
And not to seeke new lands, or not to deale withall?
    Or built faire houses, set trees, and arbors,
Only to lock up, or else to let them fall?
            Good is not good, unlesse
            A thousand it possesse,   20
            But doth wast with greedinesse.

The Dreame

Deare love, for nothing lesse then thee
Would I have broke this happy dreame,
  It was a theame
For reason, much too strong for phantasie,
Therefore thou wakd'st me wisely; yet   5
My Dreame thou brok'st not, but continued'st it,
Thou art so truth, that thoughts of thee suffice,
To make dreames truths; and fables histories;
Enter these armes, for since thou thoughtst it best,
Not to dreame all my dreame, let's act the rest.   10

As lightning, or a Tapers light,
Thine eyes, and not thy noise wak'd mee;
  Yet I thought thee
(For thou lovest truth) an Angell, at first sight,
But when I saw thou sawest my heart,   15
And knew'st my thoughts, beyond an Angells art,
When thou knew'st what I dreamt, when thou knew'st when
Excesse of joy would wake me, and cam'st then,
I must confesse, it could not chuse but bee
Prophane, to thinke thee any thing but thee.   20

Comming and staying show'd thee, thee,
But rising makes me doubt, that now,
  Thou art not thou.
That love is weake, where feare's as strong as hee;
'Tis not all spirit, pure, and brave,   25
If mixture it of *Feare, Shame, Honor,* have.
Perchance as torches which must ready bee,
Men light and put out, so thou deal'st with mee,
Thou cam'st to kindle, goest to come; Then I
Will dreame that hope againe, but else would die. 30

A Valediction: of Weeping

      Let me powre forth
My teares before thy face, whil'st I stay here,
For thy face coines them, and thy stampe they beare,
And by this Mintage they are something worth,
      For thus they bee   5
      Pregnant of thee;
Fruits of much griefe they are, emblemes of more,
When a teare falls, that thou falst which it bore,
So thou and I are nothing then, when on a divers shore.

      On a round ball   10
A workeman that hath copies by, can lay
An Europe, Afrique, and an Asia,
And quickly make that, which was nothing, *All*,
      So doth each teare,
      Which thee doth weare,   15
A globe, yea world by that impression grow,
Till thy teares mixt with mine doe overflow
This world, by waters sent from thee, my heaven dissolved so.

      O more then Moone,
Draw not up seas to drowne me in thy spheare,   20
Weepe me not dead, in thine armes, but forbeare
To teach the sea, what it may doe too soone;
      Let not the winde
      Example finde,
To doe me more harme, then it purposeth;   25
Since thou and I sigh one anothers breath,
Who e'r sighes most, is cruellest, and hasts the others death.

Loves Alchymie

Some that have deeper digg'd loves Myne then I,
Say, where his centrique happinesse doth lie:
          I have lov'd, and got, and told,
But should I love, get, tell, till I were old,
I should not finde that hidden mysterie;   5
          Oh, 'tis imposture all:
And as no chymique yet th'Elixar got,
          But glorifies his pregnant pot,
          If by the way to him befall
Some odoriferous thing, or medicinall,   10
 So, lovers dreame a rich and long delight,
 But get a winter-seeming summers night.

Our ease, our thrift, our honor, and our day,
Shall we, for this vaine Bubles shadow pay?
          Ends love in this, that my man,   15
Can be as happy'as I can; If he can
Endure the short scorne of a Bridegroomes play?
          That loving wretch that sweares,
'Tis not the bodies marry, but the mindes,
          Which he in her Angelique findes,   20
          Would sweare as justly, that he heares,
In that dayes rude hoarse minstralsey, the spheares.
 Hope not for minde in women; at their best
 Sweetnesse and wit, they'are but *Mummy*, possest.

The Flea

Marke but this flea, and marke in this,
How little that which thou deny'st me is;
It suck'd me first, and now sucks thee,
And in this flea, our two bloods mingled bee;
Thou know'st that this cannot be said   5
A sinne, nor shame, nor losse of maidenhead,
     Yet this enjoyes before it wooe,
     And pamper'd swells with one blood made of two,
     And this, alas, is more then wee would doe.

Oh stay, three lives in one flea spare, 10
Where wee almost, yea more then maryed are,
This flea is you and I, and this
Our mariage bed, and mariage temple is;
Though parents grudge, and you, w'are met,
And cloysterd in these living walls of Jet. 15
   Though use make you apt to kill mee,
    Let not to that, selfe murder added bee,
    And sacrilege, three sinnes in killing three.

Cruell and sodaine, hast thou since
Purpled thy naile, in blood of innocence? 20
Wherein could this flea guilty bee,
Except in that drop which it suckt from thee?
Yet thou triumph'st, and saist that thou
Find'st not thy selfe, nor mee the weaker now;
   'Tis true, then learne how false, feares bee; 25
    Just so much honor, when thou yeeld'st to mee,
    Will wast, as this flea's death tooke life from thee.

The Curse

Who ever guesses, thinks, or dreames he knowes
Who is my mistris, wither by this curse;
     His only, and only his purse
     May some dull heart to love dispose,
And shee yeeld then to all that are his foes; 5
   May he be scorn'd by one, whom all else scorne,
   Forsweare to others, what to her he'hath sworne,
   With feare of missing, shame of getting, torne:

Madnesse his sorrow, gout his cramp, may hee
Make, by but thinking, who hath made him such: 10
     And may he feele no touch
     Of conscience, but of fame, and bee
Anguish'd, not that 'twas sinne, but that 'twas shee:
   In early and long scarcenesse may he rot,
   For land which had been his, if he had not 15
   Himselfe incestuously an heire begot:

May he dreame Treason, and beleeve, that hee
Meant to performe it, and confesse, and die,
   And no record tell why:
   His sonnes, which none of his may bee,   20
Inherite nothing but his infamie:
 Or may he so long Parasites have fed,
 That he would faine be theirs, whom he hath bred,
 And at the last be circumcis'd for bread:

The venom of all stepdames, gamsters gall,   25
What Tyrans, and their subjects interwish,
   What Plants, Mynes, Beasts, Foule, Fish,
   Can contribute, all ill which all
Prophets, or Poets spake; And all which shall
 Be annex'd in schedules unto this by mee,   30
 Fall on that man; For if it be a shee
Nature before hand hath out-cursed mee.

The Message

      Send home my long strayd eyes to mee,
      Which (Oh) too long have dwelt on thee;
      Yet since there they have learn'd such ill,
          Such forc'd fashions,
          And false passions,   5
            That they be
            Made by thee
      Fit for no good sight, keep them still.

      Send home my harmlesse heart againe,
      Which no unworthy thought could staine;   10
      But if it be taught by thine
          To make jestings
          Of protestings,
            And crosse both
            Word and oath,   15
      Keepe it, for then 'tis none of mine.

Yet send me back my heart and eyes,
That I may know, and see thy lyes,
And may laugh and joy, when thou
  Art in anguish   20
  And dost languish
    For some one
    That will none,
Or prove as false as thou art now.

A Nocturnall upon S. Lucies day,
being the shortest day

'Tis the yeares midnight, and it is the dayes,
Lucies, who scarce seaven houres herself unmaskes,
 The Sunne is spent, and now his flasks
 Send forth light squibs, no constant rayes;
  The worlds whole sap is sunke: 5
The generall balme th'hydroptique earth hath drunk,
Whither, as to the beds-feet, life is shrunke,
Dead and enterr'd; yet all these seeme to laugh,
Compar'd with mee, who am their Epitaph.

Study me then, you who shall lovers bee   10
At the next world, that is, at the next Spring:
 For I am every dead thing,
 In whom love wrought new Alchimie.
  For his art did expresse
A quintessence even from nothingnesse,   15
From dull privations, and leane emptinesse:
He ruin'd mee, and I am re-begot
Of absence, darknesse, death; things which are not.

All others, from all things, draw all that's good,
Life, soule, forme, spirit, whence they beeing have; 20
 I, by loves limbecke, am the grave
 Of all, that's nothing. Oft a flood
  Have wee two wept, and so
Drown'd the whole world, us two; oft did we grow
To be two Chaosses, when we did show   25

Care to ought else; and often absences
Withdrew our soules, and made us carcasses.

But I am by her death, (which word wrongs her)
Of the first nothing, the Elixer grown;
  Were I a man, that I were one,   30
  I needs must know; I should preferre,
   If I were any beast,
Some ends, some means; Yea plants, yea stones detest,
And love; All, all some properties invest;
If I an ordinary nothing were,   35
As shadow, a light, and body must be here.

But I am None; nor will my Sunne renew.
You lovers, for whose sake, the lesser Sunne
  At this time to the Goat is runne
  To fetch new lust, and give it you,   40
   Enjoy your summer all;
Since shee enjoyes her long nights festivall,
Let mee prepare towards her, and let mee call
This houre her Vigill, and her Eve, since this
Both the yeares, and the dayes deep midnight is. 45

Witchcraft by a Picture

I fixe mine eye on thine, and there
  Pitty my picture burning in thine eye,
My picture drown'd in a transparent teare,
  When I looke lower I espie;
   Hadst thou the wicked skill   5
By pictures made and mard, to kill,
How many wayes mightst thou performe thy will?

But now I have drunke thy sweet salt teares,
  And though thou poure more I'll depart;
My picture vanish'd, vanish feares,   10
  That I can be endamag'd by that art;
   Though thou retaine of mee
One picture more, yet that will bee,
Being in thine owne heart, from all malice free.

The Baite

Come live with mee, and bee my love,
And we will some new pleasures prove
Of golden sands, and christall brookes,
With silken lines, and silver hookes.

There will the river whispering runne   5
Warm'd by thy eyes, more then the Sunne.
And there the'inamor'd fish will stay,
Begging themselves they may betray.

When thou wilt swimme in that live bath,
Each fish, which every channell hath,   10
Will amorously to thee swimme,
Gladder to catch thee, then thou him.

If thou, to be so seene, beest loath,
By Sunne, or Moone, thou darknest both,
And if my selfe have leave to see,   15
I need not their light, having thee.

Let others freeze with angling reeds,
And cut their legges, with shells and weeds,
Or treacherously poore fish beset,
With strangling snare, or windowie net: 20

Let coarse bold hands, from slimy nest
The bedded fish in banks out-wrest,
Or curious traitors, sleavesilke flies
Bewitch poore fishes wandring eyes.

For thee, thou needst no such deceit,   25
For thou thy selfe art thine owne bait;
That fish, that is not catch'd thereby,
Alas, is wiser farre then I.

The Apparition

When by thy scorne, O murdresse I am dead,
And that thou thinkst thee free
From all solicitation from mee,
Then shall my ghost come to thy bed,
And thee, fain'd vestall, in worse armes shall see;   5
Then thy sicke taper will begin to winke,
And he, whose thou art then, being tyr'd before,
Will, if thou stirre, or pinch to wake him, thinke
    Thou call'st for more,
And in false sleepe will from thee shrinke,   10
And then poore Aspen wretch, neglected thou
Bath'd in a cold quicksilver sweat wilt lye
    A veryer ghost then I;
What I will say, I will not tell thee now,
Lest that preserve thee'; and since my love is spent,   15
I'had rather thou shouldst painfully repent,
Then by my threatnings rest still innocent.

The Broken Heart

He is starke mad, who ever sayes,
    That he hath beene in love an houre,
Yet not that love so soone decayes,
    But that it can tenne in lesse space devour;
Who will beleeve mee, if I sweare   5
That I have had the plague a yeare?
    Who would not laugh at mee, if I should say,
    I saw a flaske of *powder burne a day?*

Ah, what a trifle is a heart,
    If once into loves hands it come!   10
All other griefes allow a part
    To other griefes, and aske themselves but some;
They come to us, but us Love draws,
Hee swallows us, and never chawes:
    By him, as by chain'd shot, whole rankes doe dye,   15
    He is the tyran Pike, our hearts the Frye.

If 'twere not so, what did become
    Of my heart, when I first saw thee?
I brought a heart into the roome,
    But from the roome, I carried none with mee: 20
If it had gone to thee, I know
Mine would have taught thine heart to show
    More pitty unto mee: but Love, alas,
    At one first blow did shiver it as glasse.

Yet nothing can to nothing fall,   25
    Nor any place be empty quite,
Therefore I thinke my breast hath all
    Those peeces still, though they be not unite;
And now as broken glasses show
A hundred lesser faces, so   30
    My ragges of heart can like, wish, and adore,
    But after one such love, can love no more.

A Valediction: Forbidding Mourning

As virtuous men passe mildly away,
    And whisper to their soules, to goe,
Whilst some of their sad friends doe say,
    The breath goes now, and some say, no:

So let us melt, and make no noise,   5
    No teare-floods, nor sigh-tempests move,
T'were prophanation of our joyes
    To tell the layetie our love.

Moving of th'earth brings harmes and feares,
    Men reckon what it did and meant,   10
But trepidation of the spheares,
    Though greater farre, is innocent.

Dull sublunary lovers love
    (Whose soule is sense) cannot admit
Absence, because it doth remove   15
    Those things which elemented it.

But we by a love, so much refin'd,
    That our selves know not what it is,
Inter-assured of the mind,
    Care lesse, eyes, lips, and hands to misse.   20

Our two soules therefore, which are one,
    Though I must goe, endure not yet
A breach, but an expansion,
    Like gold to ayery thinnesse beate.

If they be two, they are two so   25
    As stiffe twin compasses are two,
Thy soule the fixt foot, makes no show
    To move, but doth, if the'other doe.

And though it in the center sit,
    Yet when the other far doth rome,   30
It leanes, and hearkens after it,
    And growes erect, as that comes home.

Such wilt thou be to mee, who must
    Like th'other foot, obliquely runne;
Thy firmnes makes my circle just,   35
    And makes me end, where I begunne.

The Extasie

Where, like a pillow on a bed,
    A Pregnant banke swel'd up, to rest
The violets reclining head,
    Sat we two, one anothers best.
Our hands were firmely cimented   5
    With a fast balme, which thence did spring,
Our eye-beames twisted, and did thred
    Our eyes, upon one double string;
So to'entergraft our hands, as yet
    Was all the meanes to make us one,   10
And pictures in our eyes to get
    Was all our propagation.

As 'twixt two equal Armies, Fate
  Suspends uncertaine victorie,
Our soules, (which to advance their state,   15
  Were gone out,) hung 'twixt her, and mee.
And whil'st our soules negotiate there,
  Wee like sepulchrall statues lay;
All day, the same our postures were,
  And wee said nothing, all the day.   20
If any, so by love refin'd,
  That he soules language understood,
And by good love were growen all minde,
  Within convenient distance stood,
He (though he knew not which soule spake,   25
  Because both meant, both spake the same)
Might thence a new concoction take,
  And part farre purer then he came.
This Extasie doth unperplex
  (We said) and tell us what we love,   30
Wee see by this, it was not sexe,
  Wee see, we saw not what did move:
But as all severall soules containe
  Mixture of things, they know not what,
Love, these mixt soules doth mixe againe,   35
  And makes both one, each this and that.
A single violet transplant,
  The strength, the colour, and the size,
(All which before was poore, and scant,)
  Redoubles still, and multiplies.   40
When love, with one another so
  Interinanimates two soules,
That abler soule, which thence doth flow,
  Defects of lonelinesse controules.
Wee then, who are this new soule, know,   45
  Of what we are compos'd, and made,
For, th'Atomies of which we grow,
  Are soules, whom no change can invade.
But O alas, so long, so farre
  Our bodies why doe wee forbeare?   50
They'are ours, though they'are not wee, Wee are
  The intelligences, they the spheare.

We owe them thankes, because they thus,
    Did us, to us, at first convay,
Yeelded their forces, sense, to us,   55
    Nor are drosse to us, but allay.
On man heavens influence workes not so,
    But that it first imprints the ayre,
Soe soule into the soule may flow,
    Though it to body first repaire.   60
As our blood labours to beget
    Spirits, as like soules as it can,
Because such fingers need to knit
    That subtile knot, which makes us man:
So must pure lovers soules descend   65
    T'affections, and to faculties,
Which sense may reach and apprehend,
    Else a great Prince in prison lies.
To'our bodies turne wee then, that so
    Weake men on love reveal'd may looke;   70
Loves mysteries in soules doe grow,
    But yet the body is his booke.
And if some lover, such as wee,
    Have heard this dialogue of one,
Let him still marke us, he shall see   75
    Small change, when we'are to bodies gone.

Loves Deitie

I long to talke with some old lovers ghost,
    Who dyed before the god of Love was borne:
I cannot thinke that hee, who then lov'd most,
    Sunke so low, as to love one which did scorne.
But since this god produc'd a destinie,   5
And that vice-nature, custome, lets it be;
    I must love her, that loves not mee.

Sure, they which made him god, meant not so much,
    Nor he, in his young godhead practis'd it;
But when an even flame two hearts did touch,   10
    His office was indulgently to fit

Actives to passives. Correspondencie
Only his subject was; It cannot bee
  Love, till I love her, that loves mee.

But every moderne god will now extend   15
  His vast prerogative, as far as Jove.
To rage, to lust, to write to, to commend,
  All is the purlewe of the God of Love.
Oh were wee wak'ned by this Tyrannie
To ungod this child againe, it could not bee   20
  I should love her, who loves not mee.

Rebell and Atheist too, why murmure I,
  As though I felt the worst that love could doe?
Love might make me leave loving, or might trie
  A deeper plague, to make her love me too,   25
Which, since she loves before, I'am loth to see;
Falshood is worse then hate; and that must bee,
  If shee whom I love, should love mee.

Loves Diet

To what a combersome unwieldinesse
And burdenous corpulence my love had growne,
  But that I did, to make it lesse,
  And keepe it in proportion,
Give it a diet, made it feed upon   5
That which love worst endures, *discretion*.

Above one sigh a day I'allow'd him not,
Of which my fortune, and my faults had part;
  And if sometimes by stealth he got
  A she sigh from my mistresse heart,
And thought to feast on that, I let him see   10
'Twas neither very sound, nor meant to mee.

If he wroung from mee'a teare, I brin'd it so
With scorne or shame, that him it nourish'd not;
  If he suck'd hers, I let him know   15

'Twas not a teare, which hee had got,
His drinke was counterfeit, as was his meat;
For, eyes which rowle towards all, weepe not, but sweat.

What ever he would dictate, I writ that,
But burnt my letters; When she writ to me,   20
   And that that favour made him fat,
    I said, if any title bee
Convey'd by this, Ah, what doth it availe,
To be the fortieth name in an entaile?

Thus I reclaim'd my buzard love, to flye   25
At what, and when, and how, and where I chuse;
   Now negligent of sport I lye,
    And now as other Fawkners use,
I spring a mistresse, sweare, write, sigh and weepe:
And the game kill'd, or lost, goe talke, and sleepe.   30

The Will

Before I sigh my last gaspe, let me breath,
Great love, some Legacies; Here I bequeath
Mine eyes to Argus, if mine eyes can see,
If they be blinde, then Love, I give them thee;
My tongue to Fame; to'Embassadours mine eares;   5
   To women or the sea, my teares.
  Thou, Love, hast taught mee heretofore
By making mee serve her who'had twenty more,
That I should give to none, but such, as had too much before.

My constancie I to the planets give;   10
My truth to them, who at the Court doe live;
Mine ingenuity and opennesse,
To Jesuites; to Buffones my pensivenesse;
My silence to'any, who abroad hath beene;
   My mony to a Capuchin.   15
  Thou Love taught'st me, by appointing mee
To love there, where no love receiv'd can be,
Onely to give to such as have an incapacitie.

My faith I give to Roman Catholiques;
All my good works unto the Schismaticks   20
Of Amsterdam; my best civility
And Courtship, to an Universitie;
My modesty I give to souldiers bare;
   My patience let gamesters share.
  Thou Love taughtst mee, by making mee   25
Love her that holds my love disparity,
Onely to give to those that count my gifts indignity.

I give my reputation to those
Which were my friends; Mine industrie to foes;
To Schoolemen I bequeath my doubtfulnesse;   30
My sicknesse to Physitians, or excesse;
To Nature, all that I in Ryme have writ;
   And to my company my wit.
  Thou Love, by making mee adore
Her, who begot this love in mee before,   35
Taughtst me to make, as though I gave, when I did but
    restore.

To him for whom the passing bell next tolls,
I give my physick bookes; my writen rowles
Of Morall counsels, I to Bedlam give;
My brazen medals, unto them which live   40
In want of bread; To them which passe among
   All forrainers, mine English tongue.
  Thou, Love, by making mee love one
Who thinkes her friendship a fit portion
For yonger lovers, dost my gifts thus disproportion.   45

Therefore I'll give no more; But I'll undoe
The world by dying; because love dies too.
Then all your beauties will bee no more worth
Then gold in Mines, where none doth draw it forth;
And all your graces no more use shall have   50
   Then a Sun dyall in a grave.
  Thou Love taughtst mee, by making mee
Love her, who doth neglect both mee and thee,
To'invent, and practise this one way, to'annihilate all three.

The Funerall

Who ever comes to shroud me, do not harme
     Nor question much
That subtile wreath of haire, which crowns my arme;
The mystery, the signe you must not touch,
     For 'tis my outward Soule,   5
Viceroy to that, which then to heaven being gone,
     Will leave this to controule,
And keepe these limbes, her Provinces, from dissolution.

For if the sinewie thread my braine lets fall
     Through every part,   10
Can tye those parts, and make mee one of all;
These haires which upward grew, and strength and art
     Have from a better braine,
Can better do'it; Except she meant that I
     By this should know my pain,
As prisoners then are manacled, when they'are condemn'd to die.

What ere shee meant by'it, bury it with me,
     For since I am
Loves martyr, it might breed idolatrie,
If into others hands these Reliques came;   20
     As 'twas humility
To afford to it all that a Soule can doe,
     So, 'tis some bravery,
That since you would save none of mee, I bury some of you.

The Blossome

    Little think'st thou, poore flower,
     Whom I have watch'd six or seaven dayes,
And seene thy birth, and seene what every houre
Gave to thy growth, thee to this height to raise,
And now dost laugh and triumph on this bough,   5
     Little think'st thou
That it will freeze anon, and that I shall
To morrow finde thee falne, or not at all.

Little think'st thou poore heart
   That labour'st yet to nestle thee,   10
And think'st by hovering here to get a part
In a forbidden or forbidding tree,
And hop'st her stiffenesse by long siege to bow:
            Little think'st thou,
That thou to morrow, ere that Sunne doth wake,   15
Must with this Sunne, and mee a journey take.

But thou which lov'st to bee
   Subtile to plague thy selfe, wilt say,
Alas, if you must goe, what's that to mee?
Here lyes my businesse, and here I will stay: 20
You goe to friends, whose love and meanes present
            Various content
To your eyes, eares, and tongue, and every part.
If then your body goe, what need you a heart?

Well then, stay here; but know,   25
   When thou hast stayd and done thy most;
A naked thinking heart, that makes no show,
Is to a woman, but a kinde of Ghost;
How shall shee know my heart; or having none,
            Know thee for one?   30
Practise may make her know some other part,
But take my word, shee doth not know a Heart.

Meet mee at London, then,
   Twenty dayes hence, and thou shalt see
Mee fresher, and more fat, by being with men,   35
Then if I had staid still with her and thee.
For Gods sake, if you can, be you so too:
            I would give you
There, to another friend, whom wee shall finde
As glad to have my body, as my minde.   40

The Primrose, being at Mountgomery Castle, upon the hill, on which it is situate

<blockquote>

Upon this Primrose hill,
Where, if Heav'n would distill
A shoure of raine, each severall drop might goe
To his owne primrose, and grow Manna so;
And where their forme, and their infinitie   5
Make a terrestriall Galaxie,
As the small starres doe in the skie:
I walke to finde a true Love; and I see
That 'tis not a mere woman, that is shee,
But must, or more, or lesse then woman bee.   10

Yet know I not, which flower
I wish; a sixe, or foure;
For should my true-Love lesse then woman bee,
She were scarce any thing; and then, should she
Be more then woman, shee would get above   15
All thought of sexe, and thinke to move
My heart to study her, and not to love;
Both these were monsters; Since there must reside
Falshood in woman, I could more abide,
She were by art, then Nature falsify'd.   20

Live Primrose then, and thrive
With thy true number five;
And women, whom this flower doth represent,
With this mysterious number be content;
Ten is the farthest number; if halfe ten   25
Belonge unto each woman, then
Each woman may take halfe us men;
Or if this will not serve their turne, Since all
Numbers are odde, or even, and they fall
First into this, five, women may take us all.   30

</blockquote>

The Relique

When my grave is broke up againe
Some second ghest to entertaine,
(For graves have learn'd that woman-head
To be to more then one a Bed)
    And he that digs it, spies   5
A bracelet of bright haire about the bone,
    Will he not let'us alone,
And thinke that there a loving couple lies,
Who thought that this device might be some way
To make their soules, at the last busie day,   10
Meet at this grave, and make a little stay?

    If this fall in a time, or land,
    Where mis-devotion doth command,
    Then, he that digges us up, will bring
    Us, to the Bishop, and the King,   15
    To make us Reliques; then
Thou shalt be a Mary Magdalen, and I
    A something else thereby;
All women shall adore us, and some men;
And since at such time, miracles are sought,   20
I would have that age by this paper taught
What mirades wee harmelesse lovers wrought.

    First, we lov'd well and faithfully,
    Yet knew not what wee lov'd, nor why,
    Difference of sex no more wee knew,   25
    Then our Guardian Angells doe;
    Comming and going, wee
Perchance might kisse, but not between those meales;
    Our hands ne'r toucht the seales,
Which nature, injur'd by late law, sets free: 30
These miracles wee did; but now alas,
All measure, and all language, I should passe,
Should I tell what a miracle shee was.

The Dampe

When I am dead, and Doctors know not why,
     And my friends curiositie
Will have me cut up to survay each part,
When they shall finde your Picture in my heart,
     You thinke a sodaine dampe of love   5
     Will through all their senses move,
And worke on them as mee, and so preferre
Your murder, to the name of Massacre.

Poore victories! But if you dare be brave,
     And pleasure in your conquest have,   10
First kill th'enormous Gyant, your *Disdaine,*
And let th'enchantresse *Honor,* next be slaine,
     And like a Goth and Vandall rize,
     Deface Records, and Histories
Of your owne arts and triumphs over men,   15
And without such advantage kill me then.

For I could muster up as well as you
     My Gyants, and my Witches too,
Which are vast *Constancy,* and *Secretnesse,*
But these I neyther looke for, nor professe;   20
     Kill mee as Woman, let mee die
     As a meere man; doe you but try
Your passive valor, and you shall finde than,
In that you'have odds enough of any man.

The Dissolution

Shee'is dead; And all which die
To their first Elements resolve;
And wee were mutuall Elements to us,
     And made of one another.
     My body then doth hers involve,   5
And those things whereof I consist, hereby
In me abundant grow, and burdenous,
     And nourish not, but smother.

My fire of Passion, sighes of ayre,
Water of teares, and earthly sad despaire,   10
        Which my materialls bee,
But neere worne out by loves securitie,
Shee, to my losse, doth by her death repaire,
        And I might live long wretched so
But that my fire doth with my fuell grow.   15
            Now as those Active Kings
        Whose foraine conquest treasure brings,
Receive more, and spend more, and soonest breake:
This (which I am amaz'd that I can speake)
        This death, hath with my store   20
            My use encreas'd.
And so my soule more earnestly releas'd,
Will outstrip hers; As bullets flowen before
A latter bullet may o'rtake, the pouder being more.

A Jet Ring Sent

    Thou art not so black, as my heart,
  Nor halfe so brittle, as her heart, thou art;
What would'st thou say? shall both our properties
          by thee bee spoke,
  Nothing more endlesse, nothing sooner broke?

    Marriage rings are not of this stuffe;   5
  Oh, why should ought lesse precious, or lesse tough
Figure our loves? Except in thy name thou have bid it say,
  I'am cheap, and nought but fashion, fling me'away.

    Yet stay with mee since thou art come,
  Circle this fingers top, which did'st her thombe.   10
Be justly proud, and gladly safe, that thou dost dwell with me,
  She that, Oh, broke her faith, would soon breake thee.

Negative Love

I never stoop'd so low, as they
Which on an eye, cheeke, lip, can prey,
 Seldome to them, which soare no higher
 Then vertue or the minde to'admire,
For sense, and understanding may   5
 Know, what gives fuell to their fire:
My love, though silly, is more brave,
For may I misse, when ere I crave,
If I know yet, what I would have.

If that be simply perfectest   10
Which can by no way be exprest
 But *Negatives* my love is so.
 To All, which all love, I say no.
If any who deciphers best,
 What we know not, our selves, can know,   15
Let him teach mee that nothing; This
As yet my ease, and comfort is,
Though I speed not, I cannot misse.

The Prohibition

  Take heed of loving mee,
At least remember, I forbade it thee;
Not that I shall repaire my'unthrifty wast
Of Breath and Blood, upon thy sighes, and teares,
By being to thee then what to me thou wast;   5
But, so great Joy, our life at once outweares,
Then, least thy love, by my death, frustrate bee,
If thou love mee, take heed of loving mee.

  Take heed of hating mee,
Or too much triumph in the Victorie.   10
Not that I shall be mine owne officer,
And hate with hate againe retaliate;
But thou wilt lose the stile of conquerour,
If I, thy conquest, perish by thy hate.
Then, least my being nothing lessen thee,   15
If thou hate mee, take heed of hating mee.

Yet, love and hate mee too,
So, these extreames shall neithers office doe;
Love mee, that I may die the gentler way;
Hate mee, because thy love'is too great for mee;   20
Or let these two, themselves, not me decay;
So shall I, live, thy Stage, not triumph bee;
Lest thou thy love and hate and mee undoe,
To let mee live, O love and hate mee too.

The Expiration

So, so, breake off this last lamenting kisse,
    Which sucks two soules, and vapors Both away,
Turne thou ghost that way, and let mee turne this,
    And let our selves benight our happiest day,
We ask'd none leave to love; nor will we owe   5
    Any, so cheape a death, as saying, Goe;

Goe; and if that word have not quite kil'd thee,
    Ease mee with death, by bidding mee goe too.
Or, if it have, let my word worke on mee,
    And a just office on a murderer doe.   10
Except it be too late, to kill me so,
    Being double dead, going, and bidding, goe.

The Computation

For the first twenty yeares, since yesterday,
    I scarce beleev'd, thou could'st be gone away,
For forty more, I fed on favours past,
    And forty'on hopes, that thou would'st, they might last.
Teares drown'd one hundred, and sighes blew out two,
    A thousand, I did neither thinke, nor doe,
    Or not divide, all being one thought of you;
    Or in a thousand more, forgot that too.
Yet call not this long life; But thinke that I
Am, by being dead, Immortall; Can ghosts die?   10

The Paradox

No Lover saith, I love, nor any other
      Can judge a perfect Lover;
Hee thinkes that else none can, nor will agree
      That any loves but hee:
I cannot say I lov'd, for who can say   5
      Hee was kill'd yesterday?
Love with excesse of heat, more yong then old,
      Death kills with too much cold;
Wee dye but once, and who lov'd last did die,
      Hee that saith twice, doth lye: 10
For though hee seeme to move, and stirre a while,
      It doth the sense beguile.
Such life is like the light which bideth yet
      When the lights life is set,
Or like the heat, which fire in solid maker   15
      Leaves behinde, two houres after.
Once I lov'd and dy'd; and am now become
      Mine Epitaph and Tombe.
Here dead men speake their last, and so do I;
      Love-slaine, loe, here I lye.   20

Farewell to Love

      Whilst yet to prove,
I thought there was some Deitie in love
    So did I reverence, and gave
Worship, as Atheists at their dying houre
Call, what they cannot name, an unknowne power,   5
    As ignorantly did I crave:
      Thus when
Things not yet knowne are coveted by men,
    Our desires give them fashion, and so
As they waxe lesser, fall, as they sise, grow.   10

But, from late faire
His highnesse sitting in a golden Chaire,
   Is not lesse cared for after three dayes
By children, then the thing which lovers so
Blindly admire, and with such worship wooe;   15
   Being had, enjoying it decayes:
        And thence,
What before pleas'd them all, takes but one sense,
   And that so lamely, as it leaves behinde
A kinde of sorrowing dulnesse to the minde.   20

     Ah cannot wee,
As well as Cocks and Lyons jocund be,
   After such pleasures? Unlesse wise
Nature decreed (since each such Act, they say,
Diminisheth the length of life a day)   25
   This, as shee would man should despise
        The sport;
Because that other curse of being short,
   And onely for a minute made to be
Eager, desires to raise posterity.   30

     Since so, my minde
Shall not desire what no man else can finde,
   I'll no more dote and runne
To pursue things which had indammag'd me.
And when I come where moving beauties be,   35
   As men doe when the summers Sunne
        Growes great,
Though I admire their greatnesse, shun their heat;
   Each place can afford shadowes. If all faile,
'Tis but applying worme-seed to the Taile.   40

A Lecture upon the Shadow

Stand still, and I will read to thee
A Lecture, Love, in loves philosophy.
    These three houres that we have spent,
    Walking here, Two shadowes went
Along with us, which we our selves produc'd;   5
But, now the Sunne is just above our head,
   We doe those shadowes tread;
   And to brave clearnesse all things are reduc'd.
   So whilst our infant loves did grow,
   Disguises did, and shadowes, flow,   10
   From us, and our cares; but, now 'tis not so.

That love hath not attain'd the high'st degree,
Which is still diligent lest others see.

Except our loves at this noone stay,
We shall new shadowes make the other way.   15
    As the first were made to blinde
    Others; these which come behinde
Will worke upon our selves, and blind our eyes.
If our loves faint, and westwardly decline;
    To me thou, falsly, thine,   20
    And I to thee mine actions shall disguise.
   The morning shadowes weare away,
   But these grow longer all the day,
   But oh, loves day is short, if love decay.

Love is a growing, or full constant light;   25
And his first minute, after noone, is night.

Sonnet. The Token

Send me some token, that my hope may live,
   Or that my easelesse thoughts may sleep and rest;
Send me some honey to make sweet my hive,
   That in my passion I may hope the best.
I beg noe ribbond wrought with thine owne hands,   5
   To knit our loves in the fantastick straine

Of new-toucht youth; nor Ring to shew the stands
   Of our affection, that as that's round and plaine,
So should our loves meet in simplicity;
   No, nor the Coralls which thy wrist infold,   10
Lac'd up together in congruity,
   To shew our thoughts should rest in the same hold;
No, nor thy picture, though most gracious,
   And most desir'd, because best like the best;
Nor witty Lines, which are most copious,   15
   Within the Writings which thou hast addrest.

   Send me nor this, nor that, t'increase my store,
   But swear thou thinkst I love thee, and no more.

Selfe Love

He that cannot chuse but love,
And strives against it still,
Never shall my fancy move;
For he loves 'gaynst his will;
Nor he which is all his own,   5
And can att pleasure chuse,
When I am caught he can be gone,
And when he list refuse.
Nor he that loves none but faire,
For such by all are sought;   10
Nor he that can for foul ones care,
For his Judgement then is nought:
Nor he that hath wit, for he
Will make me his jest or slave;
Nor a fool, for when others . . . ,   15
He can neither . . .
Nor he that still his Mistresse payes,
For she is thrall'd therefore:
Nor he that payes not, for he sayes
Within, shee's worth no more.   20
Is there then no kinde of men
Whom I may freely prove?
I will vent that humour then
In mine owne selfe love.

EPIGRAMS

Hero and Leander

Both rob'd of aire, we both lye in one ground,
Both whom one fire had burnt, one water drownd.

Pyramus and Thisbe

Two, by themselves, each other, love and feare
Slaine, cruell friends, by parting have joyn'd here.

Niobe

By childrens births, and death, I am become
So dry, that I am now mine owne sad tombe.

A Burnt Ship

Out of a fired ship, which, by no way
But drowning, could be rescued from the flame,
Some men leap'd forth, and ever as they came
Neere the foes ships, did by their shot decay;
So all were lost, which in the ship were found,
    They in the sea being burnt, they in the burnt
        ship drown'd.

Fall of a Wall

Under an undermin'd, and shot-bruis'd wall
A too-bold Captaine perish'd by the fall,
Whose brave misfortune, happiest men envi'd,
That had a towne for tombe, his bones to hide.

A Lame Begger

I am unable, yonder begger cries,
To stand, or move; if he say true, hee *lies*.

Cales and Guyana

If you from spoyle of th'old worlds farthest end
To the new world your kindled valors bend,
What brave examples then do prove it trew
That one things end doth still beginne a new.

Sir John Wingefield

Beyond th'old Pillers many have travailed
Towards the Suns cradle, and his throne, and bed:
A fitter Piller our Earle did bestow
In that late Island; for he well did know
Farther then Wingefield no man dares to goe.

A Selfe Accuser

Your mistris, that you follow whores, still taxeth you:
'Tis strange that she should thus confesse it, though'it be true.

A Licentious Person

Thy sinnes and haires may no man equall call,
For, as thy sinnes increase, thy haires doe fall.

Antiquary

If in his Studie he hath so much care
To'hang all old strange things, let his wife beware.

Disinherited

Thy father all from thee, by his last Will,
Gave to the poore; Thou hast good title still.

Phryne

Thy flattering picture, *Phryne,* is like thee,
Onely in this, that you both painted be.

An Obscure Writer

Philo, with twelve yeares study, hath beene griev'd
To be understood; when will hee be beleev'd?

Klockius

Klockius so deeply hath sworne, ne'r more to come
In bawdie house, that hee dares not goe home.

Raderus

Why this man gelded *Martiall* I muse,
Except himselfe alone his tricks would use,
As *Katherine,* for the Courts sake, put downe Stewes.

Mercurius Gallo-Belgicus

Like *Esops* fellow-slaves, O *Mercury,*
Which could do all things, thy faith is; and I
Like *Esops* selfe, which nothing; I confesse
I should have had more faith, if thou hadst lesse;
Thy credit lost thy credit: 'Tis sinne to doe,
In this case, as thou wouldst be done unto,
To beleeve all: Change thy name: thou art like
Mercury in stealing, but lyest like a *Greeke.*

Ralphius

Compassion in the world againe is bred:
Ralphius is sick, the broker keeps his bed.

The Lier

Thou in the fields walkst out thy supping howers,
And yet thou swear'st thou hast supp'd like a king:
Like Nebuchadnezar perchance with grass and flowers,
    A sallet worse then Spanish dieting.

ELEGIES

Jealosie

Fond woman, which would'st have thy husband die,
And yet complain'st of his great jealousie;
If swolne with poyson, hee lay in'his last bed,
His body with a sere-barke covered,
Drawing his breath, as thick and short, as can   5
The nimblest crocheting Musitian,
Ready with loathsome vomiting to spue
His Soule out of one hell, into a new,
Made deafe with his poore kindreds howling cries,
Begging with few feign'd teares, great legacies,   10
Thou would'st not weepe, but jolly,'and frolicke bee,
As a slave, which to morrow should be free;
Yet weep'st thou, when thou seest him hungerly
Swallow his owne death, hearts-bane jealousie.
O give him many thanks, he'is courteous,   15
That in suspecting kindly warneth us.
Wee must not, as wee us'd, flout openly,
In scoffing ridles, his deformitie;
Nor at his boord together being satt,
With words, nor touch, scarce lookes adulterate.   20
Nor when he swolne, and pamper'd with great fare,
Sits downe, and snorts, cag'd in his basket chaire,
Must wee usurpe his owne bed any more,
Nor kisse and play in his house, as before.
Now I see many dangers; for that is   25
His realme, his castle, and his diocesse.
But if, as envious men, which would revile
Their Prince, or coyne his gold, themselves exile
Into another countrie,'and doe it there,
Wee play'in another house, what should we feare?   30
There we will scorne his houshold policies,
His seely plots, and pensionary spies,
As the inhabitants of Thames right side
Do Londons Major; or Germans, the Popes pride.

ELEGIE II

The Anagram

Marry, and love thy *Flavia,* for, shee
Hath all things, whereby others beautious bee,
For, though her eyes be small, her mouth is great,
Though they be Ivory, yet her teeth be jeat,
Though they be dimme, yet she is light enough,   5
And though her harsh haire fall, her skinne is rough;
What though her cheeks be yellow, her haire's red,
Give her thine, and she hath a maydenhead.
These things are beauties elements, where these
Meet in one, that one must, as perfect, please.   10
If red and white and each good quality
Be in thy wench, ne'r aske where it doth lye.
In buying things perfum'd, we aske; if there
Be muske and amber in it, but not where.
Though all her parts be not in th'usuall place,   15
She'hath yet an Anagram of a good face.
If we might put the letters but one way,
In the leane dearth of words, what could wee say?
When by the Gamut some Musitions make
A perfect song, others will undertake,   20
By the same Gamut chang'd, to equall it.
Things simply good, can never be unfit.
She's faire as any, if all be like her,
And if none bee, then she is singular.
All love is wonder; if wee justly doe   25
Account her wonderfull, why not lovely too?
Love built on beauty, soone as beauty, dies,
Chuse this face, chang'd by no deformities.
Women are all like Angels; the faire be
Like those which fell to worse; but such as shee,   30
Like to good Angels, nothing can impaire:
'Tis lesse griefe to be foule, then to'have beene faire.
For one nights revels, silke and gold we chuse,
But, in long journeyes, cloth, and leather use.
Beauty is barren oft; best husbands say,   35
There is best land, where there is foulest way.

Oh what a soveraigne Plaister will shee bee,
If thy past sinnes have taught thee jealousie!
Here needs no spies, nor eunuches; her commit
Safe to thy foes; yea, to a Marmosit.   40
When Belgiaes citties, the round countries drowne,
That durty foulenesse guards, and armes the towne:
So doth her face guard her; and so, for thee,
Which, forc'd by businesse, absent oft must bee,
Shee, whose face, like clouds, turnes the day to night,
Who, mightier then the sea, makes Moores seem white,
Who, though seaven yeares, she in the Stews had laid,
A Nunnery durst receive, and thinke a maid,
And though in childbeds labour she did lie,
Midwifes would sweare,'twere but a tympanie,   50
Whom, if shee accuse her selfe, I credit lesse
Then witches, which impossibles confesse,
Whom Dildoes, Bedstaves, and her Velvet Glasse
Would be as loath to touch as Joseph was:
One like none, and lik'd of none, fittest were,   55
For, things in fashion every man will weare.

ELEGIE III

Change

Although thy hand and faith, and good workes too,
Have seal'd thy love which nothing should undoe,
Yea though thou fall backe, that apostasie
Confirme thy love; yet much, much I feare thee.
Women are like the Arts, forc'd unto none,   5
Open to'all searchers, unpriz'd, if unknowne.
If I have caught a bird, and let him flie,
Another fouler using these meanes, as I,
May catch the same bird; and, as these things bee,
Women are made for men, not him, nor mee.   10
Foxes and goats; all beasts change when they please,
Shall women, more hot, wily, wild then these,
Be bound to one man, and did Nature then
Idly make them apter to'endure then men?

They'are our clogges, not their owne; if a man bee   15
Chain'd to a galley, yet the galley'is free;
Who hath a plow-land, casts all his seed corne there,
And yet allowes his ground more corne should beare;
Though Danuby into the sea must flow,
The sea receives the Rhene, Volga, and Po.   20
By nature, which gave it, this liberty
Thou lov'st, but Oh ! canst thou love it and mee?
Likenesse glues love: and if that thou so doe,
To make us like and love, must I change too?
More then thy hate, I hate'it, rather let mee   25
Allow her change, then change as oft as shee,
And soe not teach, but force my'opinion
To love not any one, nor every one.
To live in one land, is captivitie,
To runne all countries, a wild roguery;   30
Waters stincke soone, if in one place they bide,
And in the vast sea are more putrifi'd:
But when they kisse one banke, and leaving this
Never looke backe, but the next banke doe kisse,
Then are they purest; Change'is the nursery   35
Of musicke, joy, life, and eternity.

ELEGIE IV

The Perfume

Once, and but once found in thy company,
All thy suppos'd escapes are laid on mee;
And as a thiefe at barre, is question'd there
By all the men, that have beene rob'd that yeare,
So am I, (by this traiterous meanes surpriz'd)   5
By thy Hydroptique father catechiz'd.
Though he had wont to search with glazed eyes,
As though he came to kill a Cockatrice,
Though hee hath oft sworne, that hee would remove
Thy beauties beautie, and food of our love,   10
Hope of his goods, if I with thee were seene,
Yet close and secret, as our soules, we'have beene.

Though thy immortall mother which doth lye
Still buried in her bed, yet will not dye,
Takes this advantage to sleepe out day-light,   15
And watch thy entries, and returnes all night,
And, when she takes thy hand, and would seeme kind,
Doth search what rings, and armelets she can finde,
And kissing notes the colour of thy face,
And fearing least thou'art swolne, doth thee embrace;   20
To trie if thou long, doth name strange meates,
And notes thy palenesse, blushing, sighs, and sweats;
And politiquely will to thee confesse
The sinnes of her owne youths ranke lustinesse;
Yet love these Sorceries did remove, and move   25
Thee to gull thine owne mother for my love.
Thy little brethren, which like Faiery Sprights
Oft skipt into our chamber, those sweet nights,
And kist, and ingled on thy fathers knee,
Were brib'd next day, to tell what they did see: 30
The grim eight-foot-high iron-bound serving-man,
That oft names God in oathes, and onely than,
He that to barre the first gate, doth as wide
As the great Rhodian Colossus stride,
Which, if in hell no other paines there were,   35
Makes mee feare hell, because he must be there:
Though by thy father he were hir'd to this,
Could never witnesse any touch or kisse.
But Oh, too common ill, I brought with mee
That, which betray'd mee to my enemie: 40
A loud perfume, which at my entrance cryed
Even at thy fathers nose, so were wee spied.
When, like a tyran King, that in his bed
Smelt gunpowder, the pale wretch shivered.
Had it beene some bad smell, he would have thought   45
That his owne feet, or breath, that smell had wrought.
But as wee in our Ile emprisoned,
Where cattell onely,'and diverse dogs are bred,
The pretious Unicornes, strange monsters call,
So thought he good, strange, that had none at all.   50
I taught my silkes, their whistling to forbeare,
Even my opprest shoes, dumbe and speechlesse were,

Onely, thou bitter sweet, whom I had laid
Next mee, mee traiterously hast betraid,
And unsuspected hast invisibly   55
At once fled unto him, and staid with mee.
Base excrement of earth, which dost confound
Sense, from distinguishing the sicke from sound;
By thee the seely Amorous sucks his death
By drawing in a leprous harlots breath;   60
By thee, the greatest staine to mans estate
Falls on us, to be call'd effeminate;
Though you be much lov'd in the Princes hall,
There, things that seeme, exceed substantiall;
Gods, when yee fum'd on altars, were pleas'd well,   65
Because you'were burnt, not that they lik'd your smell;
You'are loathsome all, being taken simply alone,
Shall wee love ill things joyn'd, and hate each one?
If you were good, your good doth soone decay;
And you are rare, that takes the good away.   70
All my perfumes, I give most willingly
To'embalme thy fathers corse; What? will hee die?

ELEGIE V

His Picture

Here take my Picture; though I bid farewell,
Thine, in my heart, where my soule dwels, shall dwell.
'Tis like me now, but I dead, 'twill be more
When wee are shadowes both, then 'twas before.
When weather-beaten I come backe; my hand,   5
Perhaps with rude oares torne, or Sun beams tann'd,
My face and brest of haircloth, and my head
With cares rash sodaine stormes, being o'rspread,
My body'a sack of bones, broken within,
And powders blew staines scatter'd on my skinne;   10
If rivall fooles taxe thee to'have lov'd a man,
So foule, and course, as, Oh, I may seeme than,
This shall say what I was: and thou shalt say,
Doe his hurts reach mee? doth my worth decay?

Or doe they reach his judging minde, that hee   15
Should now love lesse, what hee did love to see?
That which in him was faire and delicate,
Was but the milke, which in loves childish state
Did nurse it: who now is growne strong enough
To feed on that, which to disused tasts seemes tough.   20

ELEGIE VI

Oh, Let Mee not Serve So

Oh, let mee not serve so, as those men serve
Whom honours smoakes at once fatten and sterve;
Poorely enrich't with great mens words or lookes;
Nor so write my name in thy loving bookes
As those Idolatrous flatterers, which still   5
Their Princes stiles, with many Realmes fulfill
Whence they no tribute have, and where no sway.
Such services I offer as shall pay
Themselves, I hate dead names: Oh then let mee
Favorite in Ordinary, or no favorite bee.   10
When my Soule was in her owne body sheath'd,
Nor yet by oathes betroth'd, nor kisses breath'd
Into my Purgatory, faithlesse thee,
Thy heart seem'd waxe, and steele thy constancie:
So carelesse flowers strow'd on the waters face,   15
The curled whirlepooles suck, smack, and embrace,
Yet drowne them; so, the tapers beamie eye
Amorously twinkling, beckens the giddie flie,
Yet burnes his wings; and such the devill is,
Scarce visiting them, who are intirely his.   20
When I behold a streame, which, from the spring,
Doth with doubtfull melodious murmuring,
Or in a speechlesse slumber, calmely ride
Her wedded channels bosome, and then chide
And bend her browes, and swell if any bough   25
Do but stoop downe, or kisse her upmost brow;
Yet, if her often gnawing kisses winne
The traiterous banke to gape, and let her in

She rusheth violently, and doth divorce
Her from her native, and her long-kept course,   30
And rores, and braves it, and in gallant scorne,
In flattering eddies promising retorne,
She flouts the channell, who thenceforth is drie;
Then say I; that is shee, and this am I.
Yet let not thy deepe bitternesse beget   35
Carelesse despaire in mee, for that will whet
My minde to scorne; and Oh, love dull'd with paine
Was ne'r so wise, nor well arm'd as disdaine.
Then with new eyes I shall survay thee,'and spie
Death in thy cheekes, and darknesse in thine eye.   40
Though hope bred faith and love; thus taught, I shall
As nations do from Rome, from thy love fall.
My hate shall outgrow thine, and utterly
I will renounce thy dalliance: and when I
Am the Recusant, in that resolute state,   45
What hurts it mee to be'excommunicate?

ELEGIE VII

Natures Lay Ideot

Natures lay Ideot, I taught thee to love,
And in that sophistrie, Oh, thou dost prove
Too subtile: Foole, thou didst not understand
The mystique language of the eye nor hand:
Nor couldst thou judge the difference of the aire   5
Of sighes, and say, this lies, this sounds despaire:
Nor by the'eyes water call a maladie
Desperately hot, or changing feaverously.
I had not taught thee then, the Alphabet
Of flowers, how they devisefully being set   10
And bound up, might with speechlesse secrecie
Deliver arrands mutely, and mutually.
Remember since all thy words us'd to bee
To every suitor; I, if my friends agree;
Since, household charmes, thy husbands name to teach, 15
Were all the love trickes, that thy wit could reach;

And since, an houres discourse could scarce have made
One answer in thee, and that ill arraid
In broken proverbs, and torne sentences.
Thou art not by so many duties his,   20
That from the worlds Common having sever'd thee,
Inlaid thee, neither to be seene, nor see,
As mine: who have with amorous delicacies
Refin'd thee'into a blis-full Paradise.
Thy graces and good words my creatures bee;   25
I planted knowledge and lifes tree in thee,
Which Oh, shall strangers taste? Must I alas
Frame and enamell Plate, and drinke in Glasse?
Chafe waxe for others seales? breake a colts force
And leave him then, beeing made a ready horse?   30

ELEGIE VIII

The Comparison

As the sweet sweat of Roses in a Still,
As that which from chaf'd muskats pores doth trill,
As the Almighty Balme of th'early East,
Such are the sweat drops of my Mistris breast,
And on her neck her skin such lustre sets,   5
They seeme no sweat drops, but pearle coronets.
Ranke sweaty froth thy Mistresse's brow defiles,
Like spermatique issue of ripe menstruous boiles,
Or like the skumme, which, by needs lawlesse law
Enforc'd, Sanserra's starved men did draw   10
From parboild shooes, and bootes, and all the rest
Which were with any soveraigne fatnes blest,
And like vile lying stones in saffrond tinne,
Or warts, or wheales, they hang upon her skinne.
Round as the world's her head, on every side,   15
Like to the fatall Ball which fell on Ide,
Or that whereof God had such jealousie,
As, for the ravishing thereof we die.
Thy *head is* like a rough-hewne statue of jeat,
Where marks for eyes, nose, mouth, are yet scarce set;   20

Like the first Chaos, or flat seeming face
Of Cynthia, when th'earths shadowes her embrace.
Like Proserpines white beauty-keeping chest,
Or Joves best fortunes urne, is her faire brest.
Thine's like worme eaten trunkes, cloth'd in seals skin,   25
Or grave, that's dust without, and stinke within.
And like that slender stalke, at whose end stands
The wood-bine quivering, are her armes and hands.
Like rough bark'd elmboughes, or the russet skin
Of men late scurg'd for madnes, or for sinne,   30
Like Sun-parch'd quarters on the citie gate,
Such is thy tann'd skins lamentable state.
And like a bunch of ragged carrets stand
The short swolne fingers of thy gouty hand.
Then like the Chymicks masculine equall fire,   35
Which in the Lymbecks warme wombe doth inspire
Into th'earths worthlesse durt a soule of gold,
Such cherishing heat her best lov'd part doth hold.
Thine's like the dread mouth of a fired gunne,
Or like hot liquid metalls newly runne   40
Into clay moulds, or like to that Ætna
Where round about the grasse is burnt away.
Are not your kisses then as filthy, and more,
As a worme sucking an invenom'd sore?
Doth not thy fearefull hand in feeling quake,   45
As one which gath'ring flowers, still feares a snake?
Is not your last act harsh, and violent,
As when a Plough a stony ground doth rent?
So kisse good Turtles, so devoutly nice
Are Priests in handling reverent sacrifice,   50
And such in searching wounds the Surgeon is
As wee, when wee embrace, or touch, or kisse.
Leave her, and I will leave comparing thus,
She, and comparisons are odious.

ELEGIE IX

The Autumnall

No *Spring*, nor *Summer* Beauty hath such grace,
  As I have seen in one *Autumnall* face.
Yong *Beauties* force our love, and that's a *Rape*,
  This doth but *counsaile*, yet you cannot scape.
If t'were a *shame* to love, here t'were no *shame*,   5
  Affection here takes *Reverences* name.
Were her first yeares the *Golden Age*; That's true,
  But now shee's *gold* oft tried, and ever new.
That was her torrid and inflaming time,
  This is her tolerable *Tropique clyme*.   10
Faire eyes, who askes more heate then comes from hence,
  He in a fever wishes pestilence.
Call not these wrinkles, *graves*; If *graves* they were,
  They were *Loves graves*; for else he is no where.
Yet lies not Love *dead* here, but here doth sit   15
  Vow'd to this trench, like an *Anachorit*.
And here, till hers, which must be his *death*, come,
  He doth not digge a *Grave*, but build a *Tombe*.
Here dwells he, though he sojourne ev'ry where,
  In *Progresse*, yet his standing house is here.   20
Here, where still *Evening* is; not *noone*, nor *night*;
  Where no *voluptuousnesse*, yet all *delight*.
In all her words, unto all hearers fit,
  You may at *Revels, you* at *Counsaile,* sit.
This is loves timber, youth his under-wood;   15
  There he, as wine in *June,* enrages blood,
Which then comes seasonabliest, when our tast
  And appetite to other things, is past.
Xerxes strange *Lydian* love, the *Platane* tree,
  Was lov'd for age, none being so large as shee,   30
Or else because, being yong, nature did blesse
  Her youth with ages glory, *Barrennesse.*
If we love things long sought, *Age* is a thing
  Which we are fifty yeares in compassing.
If transitory things, which soone decay,   35
  Age must be lovelyest at the latest day.

But name not *Winter-faces,* whose skin's slacke;
    Lanke, as an unthrifts purse; but a soules sacke;
Whose *Eyes* seeke light within, for all here's shade;
    Whose *mouthes* are holes, rather worne out, then made;
Whose every tooth to a severall place is gone,
    To vexe their soules at *Resurrection;*
Name not these living *Deaths-heads* unto mee,
    For these, not *Ancient,* but *Antique* be.
I hate extreames; yet I had rather stay   45
    With *Tombs,* then *Cradles,* to weare out a day.
Since such loves naturall lation is, may still
    My love descend, and journey downe the hill,
Not panting after growing beauties, so,
    I shall ebbe out with them, who home-ward goe.   50

ELEGIE X

The Dreame

Image of her whom I love, more then she,
    Whose faire impression in my faithfull heart,
Makes mee her *Medall,* and makes her love mee,
    As Kings do coynes, to which their stamps impart
The value: goe, and take my heart from hence,   5
    Which now is growne too great and good for me:
Honours oppresse weake spirits, and our sense
    Strong objects dull; the more, the lesse wee see.
When you are gone, and *Reason* gone with you,
    Then *Fantasie is* Queene and Soule, and all;   10
She can present joyes meaner then you do;
    Convenient, and more proportionall.
So, if I dreame I have you, I have you,
    For, all our joyes are but fantasticall.
And so I scape the paine, for paine is true;   15
    And sleepe which locks up sense, doth lock out all.
After a such fruition I shall wake,
    And, but the waking, nothing shall repent;
And shall to love more thankfull Sonnets make,
    Then if more *honour, teares,* and *paines* were spent.   20

But dearest heart, and dearer image stay;
    Alas, true joyes at best are *dreame* enough;
Though you stay here you passe too fast away:
    For even at first lifes *Taper* is a snuffe.
Fill'd with her love, may I be rather grown   25
    Mad with much *heart,* then *ideott* with none.

ELEGIE XI

The Bracelet
Upon the losse of his Mistresses Chaine, for
which he made satisfaction.

Not that in colour it was like thy haire,
For Armelets of that thou maist let me weare:
Nor that thy hand it oft embrac'd and kist,
For so it had that good, which oft I mist:
Nor for that silly old moralitie,   5
That as these linkes were knit, our love should bee:
Mourne I that I thy seavenfold chaine have lost;
Nor for the luck sake; but the bitter cost.
    O, shall twelve righteous Angels, which as yet
No leaven of vile soder did admit;   10
Nor yet by any way have straid or gone
From the first state of their Creation;
Angels, which heaven commanded to provide
All things to me, and be my faithfull guide;
To gaine new friends, t'appease great enemies;   15
To comfort my soule, when I lie or rise;
Shall these twelve innocents, by thy severe
Sentence (dread judge) my sins great burden beare?
Shall they be damn'd, and in the furnace throwne,
And punisht for offences not their owne?   20
They save not me, they doe not ease my paines,
When in that hell they'are burnt and tyed in chains.
    Were they but Crownes of France, I cared not,
For, most of these, their naturall Countreys rot
I think possesseth, they come here to us,   25
So pale, so lame, so leane, so ruinous;

And howsoe'r French Kings most Christian be,
Their Crownes are circumcis'd most Jewishly.
Or were they Spanish Stamps, still travelling,
That are become as Catholique as their King,   30
Those unlickt beare-whelps, unfil'd pistolets
That (more than Canon shot) availes or lets;
Which negligently left unrounded, looke
Like many angled figures, in the booke
Of some great Conjurer that would enforce   35
Nature, as these doe justice, from her course;
Which, as the soule quickens head, feet and heart,
As streames, like veines, run through th'earth's every part,
Visit all Countries, and have slily made
Gorgeous *France,* ruin'd, ragged and decay'd;   40
Scotland, which knew no State, proud in one day:
And mangled seventeen-headed *Belgia.*
Or were it such gold as that wherewithall
Almighty *Chymiques* from each minerall,
Having by subtle fire a soule out-pull'd;   45
Are dirtely and desperately gull'd:
I would not spit to quench the fire they'are in,
For, they are guilty of much hainous Sin.
But, shall my harmlesse angels perish? Shall
I lose my guard, my ease, my food, my all?   50
Much hope which they should nourish will be dead,
Much of my able youth, and lustyhead
Will vanish; if thou love let them alone,
For thou will love me lesse when they are gone.

        And be content that some lowd squeaking Cryer 55
Well-pleas'd with one leane thred-bare groat, for hire,
May like a devill roare through every street;
And gall the finders conscience, if they meet.
Or let mee creepe to some dread Conjurer,
That with phantastique scheames fils full much paper; 60
Which hath divided heaven in tenements,
And with whores, theeves, and murderers stuft his rents,
So full, that though hee passe them all in sinne,
He leaves himselfe no roome to enter in.
But if, when all his art and time is spent,   65
Hee say 'twill ne'r be found; yet be content;

Receive from him that doome ungrudgingly,
Because he is the mouth of destiny.
     Thou say'st (alas) the gold doth still remaine,
Though it be chang'd, and put into a chaine;   70
So in the first falne angels, resteth still
Wisdome and knowledge; but,'tis turn'd to ill:
As these should doe good works; and should provide
Necessities; but now must nurse thy pride.
And they are still bad angels; Mine are none;   75
For, forme gives being, and their forme is gone:
Pitty these Angels; yet their dignities
Passe Vertues, Powers, and Principalities.
     But, thou art resolute; Thy will be done!
Yet with such anguish, as her onely sonne   80
The Mother in the hungry grave doth lay,
Unto the fire these Martyrs I betray.
Good soules, (for you give life to every thing)
Good Angels, (for good messages you bring)
Destin'd you might have beene to such an one,   85
As would have lov'd and worship'd you alone:
One that would suffer hunger, nakednesse,
Yea death, ere he would make your number lesse.
But, I am guilty of your sad decay;
May your few fellowes longer with me stay.   90
     But Oh thou wretched finder whom I hate
So, that I almost pitty thy estate:
Gold being the heaviest metal amongst all,
May my most heavy curse upon thee fall:
Here fetter'd, manacled, and hang'd in chains,   95
First mayst thou bee; then chaind to hellish paines;
Or be with forraine gold brib'd to betray
Thy Countrey, and faile both of that and thy pay.
May the next thing thou stoop'st to reach, containe
Poyson, whose nimble fume rot thy moist braine;   100
Or libels, or some interdicted thing,
Which negligently kept, thy ruine bring.
Lust-bred diseases rot thee; and dwell with thee
Itching desire, and no abilitie.
May all the evils that gold ever wrought;   105
All mischiefes that all devils ever thought;

Want after plenty; poore and gouty age;
The plagues of travellers; love; marriage
Afflict thee, and at thy lives last moment,
May thy swolne sinnes themselves to thee present.   110
  But, I forgive; repent thee honest man:
Gold is Restorative, restore it then:
But if from it thou beest loath to depart,
Because 'tis cordiall, would twere at thy heart.

ELEGIE XII

His Parting from Her

Since she must go, and I must mourn, come Night,
Environ me with darkness, whilst I write:
Shadow that hell unto me, which alone
I am to suffer when my Love is gone.
Alas the darkest Magick cannot do it,   5
Thou and greate Hell to boot are shadows to it.
Should *Cinthia* quit thee, *Venus,* and each starre,
It would not forme one thought dark as mine are.
I could lend thee obscureness now, and say,
Out of my self, There should be no more Day,   10
Such is already my felt want of sight,
Did not the fires within me force a light.
      Oh Love, that fire and darkness should be mixt,
Or to thy Triumphs soe strange torments fixt?
Is't because thou thy self art blind, that wee   15
Thy Martyrs must no more each other see?
Or tak'st thou pride to break us on the wheel,
And view old Chaos in the Pains we feel?
Or have we left undone some mutual Right,
Through holy fear, that merits thy despight?   20
No, no. The falt was mine, impute it to me,
Or rather to conspiring destinie,
Which (since I lov'd for forme before) decreed,
That I should suffer when I lov'd indeed:
And therefore now, sooner then I can say,   25
I saw the golden fruit, 'tis rapt away.

Or as I had watcht one drop in a vast stream,
And I left wealthy only in a dream.
Yet Love, thou'rt blinder then thy self in this,
To vex my Dove-like friend for my amiss: 30
And, where my own sad truth may expiate
Thy wrath, to make her fortune run my fate:
So blinded Justice doth, when Favorites fall,
Strike them, their house, their friends, their followers all.
Was't not enough that thou didst dart thy fires   35
Into our blouds, inflaming our desires,
And made'st us sigh and glow, and pant, and burn,
And then thy self into our flame did'st turn?
Was't not enough, that thou didst hazard us
To paths in love so dark, so dangerous: 40
And those so ambush'd round with houshold spies,
And over all, thy husbands towring eyes
That flam'd with oylie sweat of jealousie:
Yet went we not still on with Constancie?
Have we not kept our guards, like spie on spie?   45
Had correspondence whilst the foe stood by?
Stoln (more to sweeten them) our many blisses
Of meetings, conference, embracements, kisses?
Shadow'd with negligence our most respects?
Varied our language through all dialects,   50
Of becks, winks, looks, and often under-boards
Spoak dialogues with our feet far from our words?
Have we prov'd all these secrets of our Art,
Yea, thy pale inwards, and thy panting heart?
And, after all this passed Purgatory,   55
Must sad divorce make us the vulgar story?
First let our eyes be rivited quite through
Our turning brains, and both our lips grow to:
Let our armes clasp like Ivy, and our fear
Freese us together, that we may stick here,   60
Till Fortune, that would rive us, with the deed
Strain her eyes open, and it make them bleed:
For Love it cannot be, whom hitherto
I have accus'd, should such a mischief doe.
    Oh Fortune, thou'rt not worth my least exclame,
And plague enough thou hast in thy own shame.

Do thy great worst, my friend and I have armes,
Though not against thy strokes, against thy harmes.
Rend us in sunder, thou canst not divide
Our bodies so, but that our souls are ty'd,   70
And we can love by letters still and gifts,
And thoughts and dreams; Love never wanteth shifts.
I will not look upon the quickning Sun,
But straight her beauty to my sense shall run;
The ayre shall note her soft, the fire most pure;   75
Water suggest her clear, and the earth sure.
Time shall not lose our passages; the Spring
How fresh our love was in the beginning;
The Summer how it ripened in the eare;
And Autumn, what our golden harvests were.   80
The Winter I'll not think on to spite thee,
But count it a lost season, so shall shee.

    And dearest Friend, since we must part, drown night
With hope of Day, burthens well born are light.
Though cold and darkness longer hang somewhere,   85
Yet *Phoebus* equally lights all the Sphere.
And what he cannot in like Portions pay,
The world enjoyes in Mass, and so we may.
Be then ever your self, and let no woe
Win on your health, your youth, your beauty: so   90
Declare your self base fortunes Enemy,
No less by your contempt then constancy:
That I may grow enamoured on your mind,
When my own thoughts I there reflected find.
For this to th'comfort of my Dear I vow,   95
My Deeds shall still be what my words are now;
The Poles shall move to teach me ere I start;
And when I change my Love, I'll change my heart;
Nay, if I wax but cold in my desire,
Think, heaven hath motion lost, and the world, fire: 100
Much more I could, but many words have made
That, oft, suspected which men would perswade;
Take therefore all in this: I love so true,
As I will never look for less in you.

ELEGIE XIII

Julia

Harke newes, Oh envy, thou shalt heare descry'd
My *Julia*; who as yet was ne'r envy'd.
To vomit gall in slander, swell her vaines
With calumny, that hell it selfe disdaines,
Is her continuall practice; does her best,   5
To teare opinion even out of the brest
Of dearest friends, and (which is worse than wilde)
Sticks jealousie in wedlock; her owne childe
Scapes not the showres of envie, To repeate
The monstrous fashions, how, were, alive, to eate   10
Deare reputation. Would to God she were
But halfe so loath to act vice, as to heare
My milde reproofe. Liv'd *Mantuan* now againe,
That fœmall Mastix, to limme with his penne
This she *Chymera*, that hath eyes of fire,   15
Burning with anger, anger feeds desire;
Tongued like the night-crow, whose ill boding cries
Give out for nothing but new injuries,
Her breath like to the juice in *Tenarus*
That blasts the springs, though ne'r so prosperous,   20
Her hands, I know not how, us'd more to spill
The food of others, then her selfe to fill.
But oh her minde, that *Orcus,* which includes
Legions of mischiefs, countlesse multitudes
Of formlesse curses, projects unmade up,   25
Abuses yet unfashion'd, thoughts corrupt,
Mishapen Cavils, palpable untroths,
Inevitable errours, self-accusing oaths:
These, like those Atoms swarming in the Sunne,
Throng in her bosome for creation.   30
I blush to give her halfe her due; yet say,
No poyson's halfe so bad as *Julia*.

ELEGIE XIV

A Tale of a Citizen and his Wife

I sing no harme good sooth to any wight,
To Lord or foole, Cuckold, begger or knight,
To peace-teaching Lawyer, Proctor, or brave
Reformed or reduced Captaine, Knave,
Officer, Jugler, or Justice of peace,   5
Juror or Judge; I touch no fat sowes grease,
I am no Libeller, nor will be any,
But (like a true man) say there are too many.
I feare not *ore tenus;* for my tale,
Nor Count nor Counsellour will redd or pale.   10
    A Citizen and his wife the other day
Both riding on one horse, upon the way
I overtooke, the wench a pretty peate,
And (by her eye) well fitting for the feate.
I saw the lecherous Citizen turne backe   15
His head, and on his wifes lip steale a smacke,
Whence apprehending that the man was kinde,
Riding before, to kisse his wife behinde,
To get acquaintance with him I began
To sort discourse fit for so fine a man: 20
I ask'd the number of the Plaguy Bill,
Ask'd if the Custome Farmers held out still,
Of the Virginian plot, and whether Ward
The traffique of the Midland seas had marr'd,
Whether the Brittaine *Bourse* did fill apace,   25
And likely were to give th'Exchange disgrace;
Of new-built *Algate,* and the *More-field* crosses,
Of store of Bankerouts, and poore Merchants losses
I urged him to speake; But he (as mute
As an old Courtier worne to his last suite)   30
Replies with onely yeas and nayes; At last
(To fit his element) my theame I cast
On Tradesmens gaines; that set his tongue agoing:
    Alas, good sir (quoth he) *There is no doing
In Court nor City now;* she smil'd and I,   35
And (in my conscience) both gave him the lie

In one met thought: but he went on apace,
And at the present time with such a face
He rail'd, as fray'd me; for he gave no praise,
To any but my Lord of *Essex* dayes;   40
Call'd those the age of action; true (quoth Hee)
There's now as great an itch of bravery,
And heat of taking up, but cold lay downe,
For, put to push of pay, away they runne;
Our onely City trades of hope now are   45
Bawd, Tavern-keeper, Whore and Scrivener;
The much of Privileg'd kingsmen, and the store
Of fresh protections make the rest all poore;
In the first state of their Creation,
Though many stoutly stand, yet proves not one   50
A righteous pay-master. Thus ranne he on
In a continued rage: so void of reason
Seem'd his harsh talke, I sweat for feare of treason.
        And (troth) how could I lesse? when in the prayer
For the protection of the wise Lord Major,   55
And his wise brethrens worships, when one prayeth,
He swore that none could say Amen with faith.
To get him off from what I glowed to heare,
(In happy time) an Angel did appeare,
The bright Signe of a lov'd and wel-try'd Inne,   60
Where many Citizens with their wives have bin
Well us'd and often; here I pray'd him stay,
To take some due refreshment by the way.
Looke how hee look'd that hid the gold (his hope)
And at's returne found nothing but a Rope,   65
So he on me, refus'd and made away,
Though willing she pleaded a weary day:
I found my misse, struck hands, and praid him tell
(To hold acquaintance still) where he did dwell;
He barely nam'd the street, promis'd the Wine,   70
But his kinde wife gave me the very Signe.

ELEGIE XV

The Expostulation

To make the doubt cleare, that no woman's true,
    Was it my fate to prove it strong in you?
Thought I, but one had breathed purest aire,
    And must she needs be false because she's faire?
Is it your beauties marke, or of your youth,   5
    Or your perfection, not to study truth?
Or thinke you heaven is deafe, or hath no eyes?
    Or those it hath, smile at your perjuries?
Are vowes so cheape with women, or the matter
    Whereof they are made, that they are writ in water,   10
And blowne away with winde? Or doth their breath
    (Both hot and cold at once) make life and death?
Who could have thought so many accents sweet
    Form'd into words, so many sighs should meete
As from our hearts, so many oathes, and teares   15
    Sprinkled among, (all sweeter by our feares
And the divine impression of stolne kisses,
    That seal'd the rest) should now prove empty blisses?
Did you draw bonds to forfet? signe to breake?
    Or must we reade you quite from what you speake,   20
And finde the truth out the wrong way? or must
    Hee first desire you false, would wish you just?

O I prophane, though most of women be
    This kinde of beast, my thought shall except thee;
My dearest love, though froward jealousie,   25
    With circumstance might urge thy'inconstancie,
Sooner I'll thinke the Sunne will cease to cheare
    The teeming earth, and *that* forget to beare,
Sooner that rivers will runne back, or Thames
    With ribs of Ice in June would bind his streames,   30
Or Nature, by whose strength the world endures,
    Would change her course, before you alter yours.

But O that treacherous breast to whom weake you
   Did trust our Counsells, and wee both may rue,
Having his falshood found too late, 'twas hee   35
   That made me *cast* you guilty, and you me,
Whilst he, black wretch, betray'd each simple word
   Wee spake, unto the cunning of a third.
Curst may hee be, that so our love hath slaine,
   And wander on the earth, wretched as *Cain,*   40
Wretched as hee, and not deserve least pitty;
   In plaguing him, let misery be witty;
Let all eyes shunne him, and hee shunne each eye,
   Till hee be noysome as his infamie;
May he without remorse deny God thrice,   45
   And not be trusted more on his Soules price;
And after all selfe torment, when hee dyes,
   May Wolves teare out his heart, Vultures his eyes,
Swine eate his bowels, and his falser tongue
   That utter'd all, be to some Raven flung,   50
And let his carrion coarse be a longer feast
   To the Kings dogges, then any other beast.

Now have I curst, let us our love revive;
   In mee the flame was never more alive;
I could beginne againe to court and praise,   55
   And in that pleasure lengthen the short dayes
Of my lifes lease; like Painters that do take
   Delight, not in made worke, but whiles they make;
I could renew those times, when first I saw
   Love in your eyes, that gave my tongue the law   60
   To like what you lik'd; and at maskes and playes
Commend the selfe same Actors, the same wayes;
   Aske how you did, and often with intent
Of being officious, be impertinent;
   All which were such soft pastimes, as in these   65
   Love was as subtilly catch'd, as a disease;
But being got it is a treasure sweet,
   Which to defend is harder then to get:
And ought not be prophan'd on either part,
   For though 'tis got by *chance,* 'tis kept by *art.*   70

ELEGIE XVI

On his Mistris

By our first strange and fatall interview,
By all desires which thereof did ensue,
By our long starving hopes, by that remorse
Which my words masculine perswasive force
Begot in thee, and by the memory   5
Of hurts, which spies and rivals threatned me,
I calmly beg: But by thy fathers wrath,
By all paines, which want and divorcement hath,
I conjure thee, and all the oathes which I
And thou have sworne to seale joynt constancy,   10
Here I unsweare, and overswear them thus,
Thou shalt not love by wayes so dangerous.
Temper, oh faire Love, loves impetuous rage,
Be my true Mistris still, not my faign'd Page;
I'll goe, and, by thy kinde leave, leave behinde   15
Thee, onely worthy to nurse in my minde,
Thirst to come backe; oh if thou die before,
My soule from other lands to thee shall soare.
Thy (else Almighty) beautie cannot move
Rage from the Seas, nor thy love teach them love,   20
Nor tame wilde Boreas harshnesse; Thou hast reade
How roughly hee in peeces shivered
Faire Orithea, whom he swore he lov'd.
Fall ill or good, 'tis madnesse to have prov'd
Dangers unurg'd; Feed on this flattery,   25
That absent Lovers one in th'other be.
Dissemble nothing, not a boy, nor change
Thy bodies habite, nor mindes; bee not strange
To thy selfe onely; All will spie in thy face
A blushing womanly discovering grace;   30
Richly cloath'd Apes, are call'd Apes, and as soone
Ecclips'd as bright we call the Moone the Moone.
Men of France, changeable Camelions,
Spittles of diseases, shops of fashions,
Loves fuellers, and the rightest company   35
Of Players, which upon the worlds stage be,

Will quickly know thee, and no lesse, alas!
Th'indifferent Italian, as we passe
His warme land, well content to thinke thee Page,
Will hunt thee with such lust, and hideous rage,   40
As *Lots* faire guests were vext. But none of these
Nor spungy hydroptique Dutch shall thee displease,
If thou stay here. O stay here, for, for thee
England is onely a worthy Gallerie,
To walke in expectation, till from thence   45
Our greatest King call thee to his presence.
When I am gone, dreame me some happinesse,
Nor let thy lookes our long hid love confesse,
Nor praise, nor dispraise me, nor blesse nor curse
Openly loves force, nor in bed fright thy Nurse   50
With midnights startings, crying out, oh, oh
Nurse, oh my love is slaine, I saw him goe
O'r the white Alpes alone; I saw him I,
Assail'd, fight, taken, stabb'd, bleed, fall, and die.
Augure me better chance, except dread *Jove*   55
Thinke it enough for me to'have had thy love.

ELEGIE XVII

Variety

The heavens rejoyce in motion, why should I
Abjure my so much lov'd variety,
And not with many youth and love divide?
Pleasure is none, if not diversifi'd:
The sun that sitting in the chaire of light   5
Sheds flame into what else so ever doth seem bright,
Is not contented at one Signe to Inne,
But ends his year and with a new beginnes.
All things doe willingly in change delight,
The fruitfull mother of our appetite: 10
Rivers the clearer and more pleasing are,
Where their fair spreading streames run wide and farr;
And a dead lake that no strange bark doth greet,
Corrupts it self and what doth live in it.

Let no man tell me such a one is faite,   15
And worthy all alone my love to share.
Nature in her hath done the liberall part
Of a kinde Mistresse, and imploy'd her art
To make her loveable, and I aver
Him not humane that would turn back from her: 20
I love her well, and would, if need were, dye
To doe her service. But followes it that I
Must serve her onely, when I may have choice
Of other beauties, and in change rejoice?
The law is hard, and shall not have my voice.   25
The last I saw in all extreames is faire,
And holds me in the Sun-beames of her haire,
Her nymph-like-features such agreements have
That I could venture with her to the grave:
Another's brown, I like her not the worse,   30
Her tongue is soft and takes me with discourse.
Others, for that they well descended are,
Do in my love obtain as large a share;
And though they be not fair, 'tis much with mee
To win their love onely for their degree.   35
And though I faile of my required ends,
The attempt is glorious and it self commends.
How happy were our Syres in ancient times,
Who held plurality of loves no crime!
With them it was accounted charity   40
To stirre up race of all indifferently;
Kindreds were not exempted from the bands:
Which with the Persian still in usage stands
Women were then no sooner asked then won,
And what they did was honest and well done.   45
But since this title honour hath been us'd,
Our weake credulity hath been abus'd;
The golden laws of nature are repeald,
Which our first Fathers in such reverence held;
Our liberty's revers'd, our Charter's gone,   50
And we're made servants to opinion,
A monster in no certain shape attir'd,
And whose originall is much desir'd,
Formlesse at first, but growing on it fashions,

And doth prescribe manners and laws to nations. 55
Here love receiv'd immedicable harmes,
And was dispoiled of his daring armes.
A greater want then is his daring eyes,
He lost those awfull wings with which he flies;
His sinewy bow, and those immortall darts 60
Wherewith he'is wont to bruise resisting hearts
Onely some few strong in themselves and free
Retain the seeds of antient liberty,
Following that part of Love although deprest,
And make a throne for him within their brest, 65
In spight of modern censures him avowing
Their Soveraigne, all service him allowing.
Amongst which troop although I am the least,
Yet equall in perfection with the best,
I glory in subjection of his hand, 70
Nor ever did decline his least command:
For in whatever forme the message came
My heart did open and receive the same.
But time will in his course a point discry
When I this loved service must deny, 75
For our allegiance temporary is,
With firmer age returnes our liberties.
What time in years and judgement we repos'd,
Shall not so easily be to change dispos'd,
Nor to the art of severall eyes obeying; 80
But beauty with true worth securely weighing,
Which being found assembled in some one,
Wee'l love her ever, and love her alone.

ELEGIE XVIII

Loves Progress

Who ever loves, if he do not propose
The right true end of love, he's one that goes
To sea for nothing but to make him sick:
Love is a bear-whelp born, if we o're lick
Our love, and force it new strange shapes to take, 5

We erre, and of a lump a monster make.
Were not a Calf a monster that were grown
Face'd like a man, though better then his own?
Perfection is in unitie: preferr
One woman first, and then one thing in her.   10
I, when I value gold, may think upon
The ductilness, the application,
The wholsomness, the ingenuitie,
From rust, from soil, from fire ever free:
But if I love it, 'tis because 'tis made   15
By our new nature (Use) the soul of trade.
        All these in women we might think upon   1
(If women had them) and yet love but one.
Can men more injure women then to say
They love them for that, by which they're not they?   20
Makes virtue woman? must I cool my bloud
Till I both be, and find one wise and good?
May barren Angels love so. But if we
Make love to woman; virtue is not she,
As beauty'is not nor wealth: He that strayes thus   25
From her to hers, is more adulterous,
Then if he took her maid. Search every spheare
And firmament, our *Cupid* is not there:
He's an infernal god and under ground,
With *Pluto* dwells, where gold and fire abound: 30
Men to such Gods, their sacrificing Coles
Did not in Altars lay, but pits and holes.
Although we see Celestial bodies move
Above the earth, the earth we Till and love:
So we her ayres contemplate, words and heart,   35
And virtues; but we love the Centrique part.
        Nor is the soul more worthy, or more fit
For love, then this, as infinite as it.
But in attaining this desired place
How much they erre; that set out at the face?   40
The hair a Forest is of Ambushes,
Of springes, snares, fetters and manacles:
The brow becalms us when 'tis smooth and plain,
And when 'tis wrinckled, shipwracks us again.
Smooth, 'tis a Paradice, where we would have   45

Immortal stay, and wrinkled 'tis our grave
The Nose (like to the first Meridian) runs
Not 'twixt an East and West, but 'twixt two suns;
It leaves a Cheek, a rosie Hemisphere
On either side, and then directs us where   50
Upon the Islands fortunate we fall,
Not faynte *Canaries,* but *Ambrosiall)*
Her swelling lips; To which when wee are come,
We anchor there, and think our selves at home,
For they seem all: there Syrens songs, and there   55
Wise Delphick Oracles do fill the ear;
There in a Creek where chosen pearls do swell,
The Remora, her cleaving tongue doth dwell.
These, and the glorious Promontory, her Chin
Ore past; and the streight *Hellespont* betweene   60
The *Sestos* and *Abydos* of her breasts,
(Not of two Lovers, but two Loves the neasts)
Succeeds a boundless sea, but yet thine eye
Some Island moles may scattered there descry;
And Sailing towards her *India,* in that way   65
Shall at her fair Atlantick Navell stay;
Though thence the Current be thy Pilot made,
Yet ere thou be where thou wouldst be embay'd,
Thou shalt upon another Forest set,
Where many Shipwrack, and no further get.   70
When thou art there, consider what this chace
Mispent by thy beginning at the face.
      Rather set out below; practice my Art,
Some Symetry the foot hath with that part
Which thou dost seek, and is thy Map for that   75
Lovely enough to stop, but not stay at:
Least subject to disguise and change it is;
Men say the Devil never can change his.
It is the Emblem that hath figured
Firmness; 'tis the first part that comes to bed.   80
Civilitie we see refin'd: the kiss
Which at the face began, transplanted is,
Since to the hand, since to the Imperial knee,
Now at the Papal foot delights to be:
If Kings think that the nearer way, and do   85

Rise from the foot, Lovers may do so too;
For as free Spheres move faster far then can
Birds, whom the air resists, so may that man
Which goes this empty and Ætherial way,
Then if at beauties elements he stay.   90
Rich Nature hath in women wisely made
Two purses, and their mouths aversely laid:
They then, which to the lower tribute owe,
That way which that Exchequer looks, must go:
He which doth not, his error is as great,   95
As who by Clyster gave the Stomack meat.

ELEGIE XIX

Going to Bed

Come, Madam, come, all rest my powers defie,
Until I labour, I in labour lie.
The foe oft-times having the foe in sight,
Is tir'd with standing though he never fight.
Off with that girdle, like heavens Zone glittering,   5
But a far fairer world incompassing.
Unpin that spangled breastplate which you wear,
That th'eyes of busie fooles may be stopt there.
Unlace your self, for that harmonious chyme,
Tells me from you, that now it is bed time.   10
Off with that happy busk, which I envie,
That still can be, and still can stand so nigh.
Your gown going off, such beautious state reveals,
As when from flowry meads th'hills shadow steales.
Off with that wyerie Coronet and shew   15
The haiery Diademe which on you doth grow:
Now off with those shooes, and then safely tread
In this loves hallow'd temple, this soft bed.
In such white robes, heaven's Angels us'd to be
Receavd by men; Thou Angel bringst with thee   20
A heaven like Mahomets Paradise; and though
Ill spirits walk in white, we easly know,
By this these Angels from an evil sprite,
Those set our hairs, but these our flesh upright.

    Licence my roaving hands, and let them go,   25
Before, behind, between, above, below.
O my America! my new-found-land,
My kingdome, safeliest when with one man man'd,
My Myne of precious stones, My Emperie,
How blest am I in this discovering thee!   30
To enter in these bonds, is to be free;
Then where my hand is set, my seal shall be.
    Full nakedness! All joyes are due to thee,
As souls unbodied, bodies uncloth'd must be,
To taste whole joyes. Gems which you women use   35
Are like Atlanta's balls, cast in mens views,
That when a fools eye lighteth on a Gem,
His earthly soul may covet theirs, not them.
Like pictures, or like books gay coverings made
For lay-men, are all women thus array'd;   40
Themselves are mystick books, which only wee
(Whom their imputed grace will dignifie)
Must see reveal'd. Then since that I may know;
As liberally, as to a Midwife, shew
Thy self: cast all, yea, this white lynnen hence,   45
There is no pennance due to innocence.
    To teach thee, I am naked first; why than
What needst thou have more covering then a man.

ELEGIE XX

Loves Warre

Till I have peace with thee, warr other men,
And when I have peace, can I leave thee then?
All other Warrs are scrupulous; Only thou
O fayr free Citty, maist thyselfe allowe
To any one: In Flanders, who can tell   5
Whether the Master presse; or men rebell?
Only we know, that which all Ideots say,
They beare most blows which come to part the fray.
France in her lunatique giddiness did hate
Ever our men, yea and our God of late;   10
Yet she relyes upon our Angels well,

Which nere returne; no more then they which fell.
Sick Ireland is with a strange warr possest
Like to an Ague; now raging, now at rest;
Which time will cure: yet it must doe her good   15
If she were purg'd, and her head vayne let blood.
And Midas joyes our Spanish journeys give,
We touch all gold, but find no food to live.
And I should be in the hott parching clyme,
To dust and ashes turn'd before my time.   20
To mew me in a Ship, is to inthrall
Mee in a prison, that weare like to fall;
Or in a Cloyster; save that there men dwell
In a calme heaven, here in a swaggering hell.
Long voyages are long consumptions,   25
And ships are carts for executions.
Yea they are Deaths; Is't not all one to flye
Into an other World, as t'is to dye?
Here let mee warr; in these armes lett mee lye;
Here lett mee parlee, batter, bleede, and dye.   30
Thyne armes imprison me, and myne armes thee;
Thy hart thy ransome is; take myne for mee.
Other men war that they their rest may gayne;
But wee will rest that wee may fight agayne.
Those warrs the ignorant, these th'experienc'd love,   35
There wee are always under, here above.
There Engins farr off breed a just true feare,
Neere thrusts, pikes, stabs, yea bullets hurt not here.
There lyes are wrongs; here safe uprightly lye;
There men kill men, we'will make one by and by.   40
Thou nothing; I not halfe so much shall do
In these Warrs, as they may which from us two
Shall spring. Thousands wee see which travaile not
To warrs; But stay swords, armes, and shott
To make at home; And shall not I do then   45
More glorious service, staying to make men?

HEROICALL EPISTLE

Sapho to Philænis

Where is that holy fire, which *Verse* is said
  To have? is that inchanting force decai'd?
Verse that drawes *Natures* workes, from *Natures* law,
  Thee, her best worke, to her worke cannot draw.
Have my teares quench'd my old *Poetique* fire;   5
  Why quench'd they not as well, that of *desire?*
Thoughts, my mindes creatures, often are with thee,
  But I, their maker, want their libertie.
Onely thine image, in my heart, doth sit,
  But that is waxe, and fires environ it.   10
My fires have driven, thine have drawne it hence;
  And I am rob'd of *Picture, Heart,* and *Sense.*
Dwells with me still mine irksome *Memory,*
  Which, both to keepe, and lose, grieves equally.
That tells me'how faire thou art: Thou art so faire,   15
  As, *gods,* when *gods* to thee I doe compare,
Are grac'd thereby; And to make blinde men see,
  What things *gods* are, I say they'are like to thee.
For, if we justly call each silly *man*
  A *litle world,* What shall we call thee than?   20
Thou art not soft, and cleare, and strait, and faire,
  As *Down,* as *Stars, Cedars,* and *Lillies* are,
But thy right hand, and cheek, and eye, only
  Are like thy other hand, and cheek, and eye.
Such was my *Phao* awhile, but shall be never,   25
  As thou, wast, art, and, oh, maist be ever.
Here lovers sweare in their *Idolatrie,*
  That I am such; but *Griefe* discolors me.
And yet I grieve the lesse, least *Griefe* remove
  My beauty, and make me'unworthy of thy love.   30
Plaies some soft boy with thee, oh there wants yet
  A mutuall feeling which should sweeten it.
His chinne, a thorny hairy unevennesse
  Doth threaten, and some daily change possesse.

Thy body is a naturall *Paradise,*   35
    In whose selfe, unmanur'd, all pleasure lies,
Nor needs *perfection;* why shouldst thou than
    Admit the tillage of a harsh rough man?
Men leave behinde them that which their sin showes,
    And are as theeves trac'd, which rob when it snows. 40
But of our dallyance no more signes there are,
    Then *fishes* leave in streames, or *Birds* in aire.
And betweene us all sweetnesse may be had;
    All, all that *Nature* yields, or Art can adde.
My two lips, eyes, thighs, differ from thy two,   45
    But so, as thine from one another doe;
And, oh, no more; the likenesse being such,
    Why should they not alike in all parts touch?
Hand to strange hand, lippe to lippe none denies;
    Why should they brest to brest, or thighs to thighs?
Likenesse begets such strange selfe flatterie,
    That touching my selfe, all seemes done to thee.
My selfe I embrace, and mine owne hands I kisse,
    And amorously thanke my selfe for this.
Me, in my glasse, I call thee; But, alas,
    When I would kisse, teares dimme mine *eyes,* and *glasse.*
O cure this loving madnesse, and restore
    Me to mee; thee, my *halfe,* my *all,* my *more.*
So may thy cheekes red outweare scarlet dye,
    And their white, whitenesse of the *Galaxy,*   60
So may thy mighty, amazing beauty move
    Envy'in all *women,* and in all *men, love,*
And so be *change,* and *sicknesse,* farre from thee,
    As thou by comming neere, keep'st them from me.

EPITHALAMIONS, OR MARRIAGE SONGS

*An Epithalamion, or Mariage Song on the Lady Elizabeth,
and Count Palatine being married on St. Valentines Day.*

I

Haile Bishop Valentine, whose day this is,
    All the Aire is thy Diocis,
    And all the chirping Choristers
And other birds are thy Parishioners,
    Thou marryest every yeare   5
The Lirique Larke, and the grave whispering Dove,
The Sparrow that neglects his life for love,
The household Bird, with the red stomacher,
    Thou mak'st the black bird speed as soone,
As doth the Goldfinch, or the Halcyon;   10
The husband cocke lookes out, and straight is sped,
And meets his wife, which brings her feather-bed.
This day more cheerfully then ever shine,
This day, which might enflame thy self, Old Valentine.

II

Till now, Thou warmd'st with multiplying loves   15
    Two larkes, two sparrowes, or two Doves,
    All that is nothing unto this,
For thou this day couplest two Phœnixes;
    Thou mak'st a Taper see
What the sunne never saw, and what the Arke   20
(Which was of foules, and beasts, the cage, and park,)
Did not containe, one bed containes, through Thee,
    Two Phœnixes, whose joyned breasts
Are unto one another mutuall nests,
Where motion kindles such fires, as shall give   25
Yong Phœnixes, and yet the old shall live.
Whose love and courage never shall decline,
But make the whole year through, thy day, O Valentine.

III

Up then faire Phœnix Bride, frustrate the Sunne,
      Thy selfe from thine affection   30
      Takest warmth enough, and from thine eye
All lesser birds will take their Jollitie.
        Up, up, faire Bride, and call,
Thy starres, from out their severall boxes, take
Thy Rubies, Pearles, and Diamonds forth, and make   35
Thy selfe a constellation, of them All,
        And by their blazing, signifie,
That a Great Princess falls, but doth not die;
Bee thou a new starre, that to us portends
Ends of much wonder; And be Thou those ends.   40
Since thou dost this day in new glory shine,
May all men date Records, from this thy Valentine.

IIII

Come forth, come forth, and as one glorious flame
      Meeting Another, growes the same,
      So meet thy Fredericke, and so   45
To an unseparable union growe.
        Since separation
Falls not on such things as are infinite,
Nor things which are but one, can disunite,
You'are twice inseparable, great, and one;   50
        Goe then to where the Bishop staies,
To make you one, his way, which divers waies
Must be effected; and when all is past,
And that you'are one, by hearts and hands made fast,
You two have one way left, your selves to'entwine,   55
Besides this Bishops knot, or Bishop Valentine.

V

But oh, what ailes the Sunne, that here he staies,
      Longer to day, then other daies?
      Staies he new light from these to get?
And finding here such store, is loth to get?   60
        And why doe you two walke,
So slowly pac'd in this procession?
Is all your care but to be look'd upon,

And be to others spectacle, and talke?
       The feast, with gluttonous delaies,   65
Is eaten, and too long their meat they praise,
The masquers come too late, and'I thinke, will stay,
Like Fairies, till the Cock crow them away.
Alas, did not Antiquity assigne
A night, as well as day, to thee, O Valentine?   70

VI

They did, and night is come; and yet wee see
     Formalities retarding thee.
     What meane these Ladies, which (as though
They were to take a clock in peeces,) goe
      So nicely about the Bride;   75
A Bride, before a good night could be said,
Should vanish from her cloathes, into her bed,
As Soules from bodies steale, and are not spy'd.
      But now she is laid; What though shee bee?
Yet there are more delayes, For, where is he?   80
He comes, and passes through Spheare after Spheare,
First her sheetes, then her Armes, then any where.
Let not this day, then, but this night be thine,
Thy day was but the eve to this, O Valentine.

VII

Here lyes a shee Sunne, and a hee Moone here,   85
     She gives the best light to his Spheare,
     Or each is both, and all, and so
They unto one another nothing owe,
     And yet they doe, but are
So just and rich in that coyne which they pay,   90
That neither would, nor needs forbeare, nor stay;
Neither desires to be spar'd, nor to spare,
     They quickly pay their debt, and then
Take no acquittances, but pay again;
They pay, they give, they lend, and so let fall   95
No such occasion to be liberall.
More truth, more courage in these two do shine,
Then all thy turtles have, and sparrows, Valentine.

VIII

And by this act of these two Phœnixes
      Nature againe restored is,   100
      For since these two are two no more,
Ther's but one Phœnix still, as was before.
      Rest now at last, and wee
As Satyres watch the Sunnes uprise, will stay
Waiting, when your eyes opened, let out day,   105
Onely desir'd, because your face wee see;
      Others neare you shall whispering speake,
And wagers lay, at which side day will breake,
And win by'observing, then, whose hand it is
That opens first a curtaine, hers or his;
This will be tryed to morrow after nine,
Till which houre, wee thy day enlarge, O Valentine.

Epithalamion made at Lincolnes Inne

The Sun-beames in the East are spred,
Leave, leave, faire Bride, your solitary bed,
   No more shall you returne to it alone,
It nourseth sadnesse, and your bodies print,
Like to a grave, the yielding downe doth dint;   5
   You and your other you meet there anon;
   Put forth, put forth that warme balme-breathing thigh,
Which when next time you in these sheets wil smother,
   There it must meet another,
     Which never was, but must be, oft, more nigh;   10
Come glad from thence, goe gladder then you came,
To day put on perfection, and a womans name.

Daughters of London, you which bee
Our Golden Mines, and furnish'd Treasurie,
   You which are Angels, yet still bring with you   15
Thousands of Angels on your mariage daies,
Help with your presence and devise to praise
   These rites, which also unto you grow due;
   Conceitedly dresse her, and be assign'd,
By you, fit place for every flower and jewell,   20
   Make her for love fit fewell

As gay as Flora, and as rich as Inde;
So may shee faire, rich, glad, and in nothing lame,
To day put on perfection, and a womans name.

And you frolique Patricians,   25
Sonnes of these Senators, wealths deep oceans,
    Ye painted courtiers, barrels of others wits,
Yee country men, who but your beasts love none,
Yee of those fellowships whereof hee's one,
    Of study and play made strange Hermaphrodits,   30
    Here shine; This Bridegroom to the Temple bring.
Loe, in yon path which store of straw'd flowers graceth,
    The sober virgin paceth;
        Except my sight faile, 'tis no other thing;
Weep not nor blush, here is no griefe nor shame,   35
To day put on perfection, and a womans name.

Thy two-leav'd gates faire Temple unfold,
And these two in thy sacred bosome hold,
Till, mystically joyn'd, but one they bee;
Then may thy leane and hunger-starved wombe   40
Long time expect their bodies and their tombe,
    Long after their owne parents fatten thee.
    All elder claimes, and all cold barrennesse,
All yeelding to new loves bee far for ever,
    Which might these two dissever,   45
        All wayes all th'other may each one possesse;
For, the best Bride, best worthy of praise and fame,
To day puts on perfection, and a womans name.

Oh winter dayes bring much delight,
Not for themselves, but for they soon bring night;   50
    Other sweets wait thee then these diverse meats,
Other disports then dancing jollities,
Other love tricks then glancing with the eyes,
    But that the Sun still in our halfe Spheare sweates;
    Hee flies in winter, but he now stands still.   55
Yet shadowes turne; Noone point he hath attain'd,
    His steeds nill bee restrain'd,
        But gallop lively downe the Westerne hill;
Thou shalt, when he hath runne the worlds half frame,
To night put on perfection, and a womans name.   60

The amorous evening starre is rose,
Why then should not our amorous starre inclose
   Her selfe in her wish'd bed? Release your strings
Musicians, and dancers take some truce
With these your pleasing labours, for great use   65
   As much wearinesse as perfection brings;
   You, and not only you, but all toyl'd beasts
Rest duly; at night all their toyles are dispensed;
   But in their beds commenced
      Are other labours, and more dainty feasts;   70
She goes a maid, who, least she turne the same,
To night puts on perfection, and a womans name.

Thy virgins girdle now untie,
And in thy nuptiall bed (loves altar) lye
   A pleasing sacrifice; now dispossesse   75
Thee of these chaines and robes which were put on
T'adorne the day, not thee; for thou, alone,
   Like vertue'and truth, art best in nakednesse;
   This bed is onely to virginitie
A grave, but, to a better state, a cradle;   80
   Till now thou wast but able
      To be what now thou art; then that by thee
No more be said, I *may bee,* but, *I am,*
To night put on perfection, and a womans name.

Even like a faithfull man content,   85
That this life for a better should be spent,
   So, shee a mothers rich stile doth preferre,
And at the Bridegroomes wish'd approach doth lye,
Like an appointed lambe, when tenderly
   The priest comes on his knees t'embowell her;   90
   Now sleep or watch with more joy; and O light
Of heaven, to morrow rise thou hot, and early;
   This Sun will love so dearely
      Her rest, that long, long we shall want her sight;
Wonders are wrought, for shee which had no maime,   95
To night puts on perfection, and a womans name.

Ecclogue
1613. December 26

Allophanes finding Idios in the country in Christmas time,
reprehends his absence from court, at the mariage Of the Earle of
Sommerset; Idios gives an account of his purpose therein, and of his
absence thence.

Allophanes
Unseasonable man, statue of ice,
    What could to countries solitude entice
Thee, in this yeares cold and decrepit time?
    Natures instinct drawes to the warmer clime
Even small birds, who by that courage dare,   5
    In numerous fleets, saile through their Sea, the aire.
What delicacie can in fields appeare,
    Whil'st Flora'herselfe doth a freeze jerkin weare?
Whil'st windes do all the trees and hedges strip
    Of leafes, to furnish roddes enough to whip   10
Thy madnesse from thee; and all springs by frost
    Have taken cold, and their sweet murmures lost;
If thou thy faults or fortunes would'st lament
    With just solemnity, do it in Lent;
At Court the spring already advanced is,   15
    The Sunne stayes longer up; and yet not his
The glory is, farre other, other fires
    First, zeale to Prince and State; then loves desires
Burne in one brest, and like heavens two great lights
    The first doth governe dayes, the other nights.   20
And then that early light, which did appeare
    Before the Sunne and Moone created were
The Princes favour is defus'd o'r all
    From which all Fortunes, Names, and Natures fall;
Then from those wombes of starres, the Brides bright eyes,
    At every glance, a constellation flyes,
And sowes the Court with starres, and doth prevent
    In light and power, the all-ey'd firmament;
First her eyes kindle other Ladies eyes,
    Then from their beames their jewels lusters rise,   30
And from their jewels torches do take fire,
    And all is warmth, and light, and good desire;

Most other Courts, alas, are like to hell,
   Where in darke plotts, fire without light doth dwell:
Or but like Stoves, for lust and envy get   35
   Continuall, but artificiall heat;
Here zeale and love growne one, all clouds disgest,
   And make our Court an everlasting East.
And can'st thou be from thence?

Idios   No, I am there.
   As heaven, to men dispos'd, is every where,   40
So are those Courts, whose Princes animate,
   Not onely all their house, but all their State.
Let no man thinke, because he is full, he hath all,
   Kings (as their patterne, God) are liberall
Not onely in fulnesse, but capacitie,   45
   Enlarging narrow men, to feele and see,
And comprehend the blessings they bestow.
   So, reclus'd hermits often times do know
More of heavens glory, then a worldling can.
   As man is of the world, the heart of man,   50
Is an epitome of Gods great booke
   Of creatures, and man need no farther looke;
So is the Country of Courts, where sweet peace doth,
   As their one common soule, give life to both,
I am not then from Court.

Allophanes   Dreamer, thou art.   55
   Think'st thou fantastique that thou hast a part
In the East-Indian fleet, because thou hast
   A little spice, or Amber in thy taste?
Because thou art not frozen, art thou warme?
   Seest thou all good because thou seest no harme?   60
The earth doth in her inward bowels hold
   Stuffe well dispos'd, and which would faine be gold,
But never shall, except it chance to lye,
   So upward, that heaven gild it with his eye;
As, for divine things, faith comes from above,   65
   So, for best civil use, all tinctures move
From higher powers; From God religion springs,

Wisdome, and honour from the use of Kings.
Then unbeguile thy selfe, and know with mee,
   That Angels, though on earth employd they bee,   70
Are still in heav'n, so is hee still at home
   That doth, abroad, to honest actions come.
Chide thy selfe then, O foole, which yesterday
   Might'st have read more then all thy books bewray;
Hast thou a history, which doth present   75
   A Court, where all affections do assent
Unto the Kings, and that, that Kings are just?
   And where it is no levity to trust?
Where there is no ambition, but to'obey,
   Where men need whisper nothing, and yet may;   80
Where the Kings favours are so plac'd, that all
   Finde that the King therein is liberall
To them, in him, because his favours bend
   To vertue, to the which they all pretend?
Thou hast no such; yet here was this, and more,   85
   An earnest lover, wise then, and before.
Our little Cupid hath sued Livery,
   And is no more in his minority,
Hee is admitted now into that brest
   Where the Kings Counsells and his secrets rest.   90
What hast thou lost, O ignorant man?

Idios   I knew
   All this, and onely therefore I withdrew.
To know and feele all this, and not to have
   Words to expresse it, makes a man a grave
Of his owne thoughts; I would not therefore stay   95
   At a great feast, having no Grace to say.
And yet I scap'd not here; for being come
   Full of the common joy, I utter'd some;
Reade then this nuptiall song, which was not made
   Either the Court or mens hearts to invade,   100
But since I'am dead, and buried, I could frame
   No Epitaph, which might advance my fame
So much as this poore song, which testifies
   I did unto that day some sacrifice.

EPITHALAMION

The Time of the Mariage

Thou art repriv'd old yeare, thou shalt not die,   105
    Though thou upon thy death bed lye,
    And should'st within five dayes expire,
Yet thou art rescu'd by a mightier fire,
    Then thy old Soule, the Sunne,
When he doth in his largest circle runne.   110
The passage of the West or East would thaw,
And open wide their easie liquid jawe
To all our ships, could a Promethean art
Either unto the Northerne Pole impart
The fire of these inflaming eyes, or of this loving heart.   115

Equality of Persons

But undiscerning Muse, which heart, which eyes,
    In this new couple, dost thou prize,
    When his eye as inflaming is
As hers, and her heart loves as well as his?
    Be tryed by beauty, and than   120
The bridegroome is a maid, and not a man.
If by that manly courage they be tryed,
Which scornes unjust opinion; then the bride
Becomes a man. Should chance or envies Art
Divide these two, whom nature scarce did part?   125
Since both have both th'enflaming eyes, and both the loving heart.

Raysing of the Bridegroome

Though it be some divorce to thinke of you
    Singly, so much one are you two,
    Yet let me here contemplate thee,
First, cheerfull Bridegroome, and first let mee see,   130
How thou prevent'st the Sunne
And his red foming horses dost outrunne,
How, having laid downe in thy Soveraignes brest
All businesses, from thence to reinvest
Them, when these triumphs cease, thou forward art   135
To shew to her, who doth the like impart,
The fire of thy inflaming eyes, and of thy loving heart.

Raising of the Bride

But now, to Thee, faire Bride, it is some wrong,
   To thinke thou wert in Bed so long,
    Since Soone thou lyest downe first, tis fit   140
Thou in first rising should'st allow for it.
     Pouder thy Radiant haire,
Which if without such ashes thou would'st weare,
Thou, which to all which come to looke upon,
Art meant for Phœbus, would'st be Phaëton.   145
For our ease, give thine eyes th'unusual part
Of joy, a Teare; so quencht, thou maist impart,
To us that come, thy inflaming eyes, to him, thy loving heart.

Her Apparrelling

Thus thou descend'st to our infirmitie,
   Who can the Sun in water see.   150
   Soe dost thou, when in silke and gold,
Thou cloudst thy selfe; since wee which doe behold,
    Are dust, and wormes, 'tis just
Our objects be the fruits of wormes and dust;
Let every Jewell be a glorious starre,   155
Yet starres are not so pure, as their spheares are.
And though thou stoope, to'appeare to us in part,
Still in that Picture thou intirely art,
Which thy inflaming eyes have made within his loving heart.

Going to the Chappell

Now from your Easts you issue forth, and wee,   160
   As men which through a Cipres see
   The rising sun, doe thinke it two,
Soe, as you goe to Church, doe thinke of you,
    But that vaile being gone,
By the Church rites you are from thenceforth one.   165
The Church Triumphant made this match before,
And now the Militant doth strive no more;
Then, reverend Priest, who Gods Recorder art,
Doe, from his Dictates, to these two impart   169
All blessings, which are seene, or thought, by Angels eye or heart.

The Benediction

Blest payre of Swans, Oh may you interbring
      Daily new joyes, and never sing,
       Live, till all grounds of wishes faile,
Till honor, yea till wisedome grow so stale,
         That, new great heights to trie,   175
It must serve your ambition, to die;
Raise heires, and may here, to the worlds end, live
Heires from this King, to take thankes, you, to give,
Nature and grace doe all, and nothing Art.
May never age, or error overthwart   180
With any West, these radiant eyes, with any North, this heart.

Feasts and Revels

But you are over-blest. Plenty this day
      Injures; it causeth time to stay;
       The tables groane, as though this feast
Would, as the flood, destroy all fowle and beast.   185
And were the doctrine new
        That the earth mov'd, this day would make it true;
For every part to dance and revell goes.
They tread the ayre, and fal not where they rose.
Though six houres since, the Sunne to bed did part,   190
The masks and banquets will not yet impart
A sunset to these weary eyes, A Center to this heart.

The Brides going to Bed

What mean'st thou Bride, this companie to keep?
      To sit up, till thou faine wouldst sleep?
       Thou maist not, when thou art laid, doe so.   195
Thy selfe must to him a new banquet grow,
       And you must entertaine
And doe all this daies dances o'r againe.
Know that if Sun and Moone together doe
Rise in one point, they doe not set so too;   200
Therefore thou maist, faire Bride, to bed depart,
Thou art not gone, being gone; where e'r thou art,
Thou leav'st in him thy watchfull eyes, in him thy loving heart

The Bridegroomes comming

As he that sees a starre fall, runs apace,
    And findes a gellie in the place,   205
      So doth the Bridegroome hast as much,
Being told this starre is falne, and findes her such.
      And as friends may looke strange,
By a new fashion, or apparrells change,
Their soules, though long acquainted they had beene,   210
These clothes, their bodies, never yet had seene;
Therefore at first shee modestly might start,
But must forthwith surrender every part,
As freely, as each to each before, gave either eye or heart.

The Good-Night

Now, as in Tullias tombe, one lampe burnt cleare,   215
    Unchang'd for fifteene hundred yeare,
      May these love-lamps we here enshrine,
In warmth, light, lasting, equall the divine.
      Fire ever doth aspire,
And makes all like it selfe, turnes all to fire,   220
But ends in ashes, which these cannot doe,
For none of these is fuell, but fire too.
This is joyes bonfire, then, where loves strong Arts
Make of so noble individuall parts
One fire of foure inflaming eyes, and of two loving hearts.

Idios
As I have brought this song, that I may doe
    A perfect sacrifice, I'll burne it too.
Allophanes
No Sir. This paper I have justly got,
  For, in burnt incense, the perfume is not
His only that presents it, but of all;   230
  What ever celebrates this Festivall
Is common, since the joy thereof is so.
  Nor may your selfe be Priest: But let me goe,
Backe to the Court, and I will lay'it upon
  Such Altars, as prize your devotion.   235

SATYRES

Satyre I

Away thou fondling motley humorist,
Leave mee, and in this standing woodden chest,
Consorted with these few bookes, let me lye
In prison, and here be coffin'd, when I dye;
Here are Gods conduits, grave Divines; and here   5
Natures Secretary, the Philosopher;
And jolly Statesmen, which teach how to tie
The sinewes of a cities mistique bodie;
Here gathering Chroniclers, and by them stand
Giddie fantastique Poëts of each land.   10
Shall I leave all this constant company,
And follow headlong, wild uncertaine thee?
First sweare by thy best love in earnest
(If thou which lov'st all, canst love any best)
Thou wilt not leave mee in the middle street,   15
Though some more spruce companion thou dost meet,
Not though a Captaine do come in thy way
Bright parcell gilt, with forty dead mens pay,
Not though a briske perfum'd piert Courtier
Deigne with a nod, thy courtesie to answer.   20
Nor come a velvet Justice with a long
Great traine of blew coats, twelve, or fourteen strong,
Wilt thou grin or fawne on him, or prepare
A speech to Court his beautious sonne and heire!
For better or worse take mee, or leave mee: 25
To take, and leave mee is adultery.
Oh monstrous, superstitious puritan,
Of refin'd manners, yet ceremoniall man,
That when thou meet'st one, with enquiring eyes
Dost search, and like a needy broker prize   30
The silke, and gold he weares, and to that rate
So high or low, dost raise thy formall hat:
That wilt consort none, untill thou have knowne

What lands hee hath in hope, or of his owne,
As though all thy companions should make thee   35
Jointures, and rnarry thy deare company.
Why should'st thou (that dost not onely approve,
But in ranke itchie lust, desire, and love
The nakednesse and barenesse to enjoy,
Of thy plumpe muddy whore, or prostitute boy)   40
Hate vertue, though shee be naked, and bare?
At birth, and death, our bodies naked are;
And till our Soules be unapparrelled
Of bodies, they from blisse are banished.
Mans first blest state was naked, when by sinne   45
Hee lost that, yet hee was cloath'd but in beasts skin,
And in this course attire, which I now weare,
With God, and with the Muses I conferre.
But since thou like a contrite penitent,
Charitably warn'd of thy sinnes, dost repent   50
These vanities, and giddinesses, loe
I shut my chamber doore, and come, lets goe.
But sooner may a cheape whore, who hath beene
Worne by as many severall men in sinne,
As are black feathers, or musk-colour hose,   55
Name her childs right true father, 'mongst all those:
Sooner may one guesse, who shall beare away
The Infanta of London, Heire to an India;
And sooner may a gulling weather Spie
By drawing forth heavens Scheme tell certainly   60
What fashioned hats, or ruffes, or suits next yeare
Our subtile-witted antique youths will weare;
Then thou, when thou depart'st from mee, canst show
Whither, why, when, or with whom thou wouldst go.
But how shall I be pardon'd my offence   65
That thus have sinn'd against my conscience?
Now we are in the street; He first of all
Improvidently proud, creepes to the wall,
And so imprisoned, and hem'd in by mee
Sells for a little state his libertie;   70
Yet though he cannot skip forth now to greet
Every fine silken painted foole we meet,
He them to him with amorous smiles allures,

And grins, smacks, shrugs, and such an itch endures,
As prentises, or schoole-boyes which doe know   75
Of some gay sport abroad, yet dare not goe.
And as fidlers stop lowest, at highest sound,
So to the most brave, stoops hee nigh'st the ground.
But to a grave man, he doth move no more
Then the wise politique horse would heretofore,   80
Or thou O Elephant or Ape wilt doe,
When any names the King of Spaine to you.
Now leaps he upright, Joggs me, & cryes, Do you see
Yonder well favoured youth? Which? Oh, 'tis hee
That dances so divinely; Oh, said I,   85
Stand still, must you dance here for company?
Hee droopt, wee went, till one (which did excell
Th'Indians, in drinking his Tobacco well)
Met us; they talk'd; I whispered, let'us goe,
'T may be you smell him not, truely I doe;   90
He heares not mee, but, on the other side
A many-coloured Peacock having spide,
Leaves him and mee; I for my lost sheep stay;
He followes, overtakes, goes on the way,
Saying, him whom I last left, all repute   95
For his device, in hansoming a sute,
To judge of lace, pinke, panes, print, cut, and pleite,
Of all the Court, to have the best conceit;
Our dull Comedians want him, let him goe;
But Oh, God strengthen thee, why stoop'st thou so?   100
Why? he hath travayld; Long? No; but to me
(Which understand none,) he doth seeme to be
Perfect French, and Italian; I replyed,
So is the Poxe; He answered not, but spy'd
More men of sort, of parts, and qualities;   105
At last his Love, he in a windowe spies,
And like light dew exhal'd, he flings from mee
Violently ravish'd to his lechery.
Many were there, he could command no more;
Hee quarrell'd, fought, bled; and turn'd out of dore   110
    Directly came to mee hanging the head,
    And constantly a while must keepe his bed.

Satyre II

Sir; though (I thanke God for it) I do hate
Perfectly all this towne, yet there's one state
In all ill things so excellently best,
That hate, toward them, breeds pitty towards the rest.
Though Poëtry indeed be such a sinne   5
As I thinke That brings dearths, and Spaniards in,
Though like the Pestilence and old fashion'd love,
Ridlingly it catch men; and doth remove
Never, till it be sterv'd out; yet their state
Is poore, disarm'd, like Papists, not worth hate.   10
One, (like a wretch, which at Barre judg'd as dead,
Yet prompts him which stands next, and cannot reade,
And saves his life) gives ideot actors meanes
(Starving himselfe) to live by his labor'd sceanes;
As in some Organ, Puppits dance above   15
And bellows pant below, which them do move.
One would move Love by rithmes; but witchcrafts charms
Bring not now their old feares, nor their old harmes:
Rammes, and slings now are seely battery,
Pistolets are the best Artillerie.   20
And they who write to Lords, rewards to get,
Are they not like singers at doores for meat?
And they who write, because all write, have still
That excuse for writing, and for writing ill;
But hee is worst, who (beggarly) doth chaw   25
Others wits fruits, and in his ravenous maw
Rankly digested, doth those things out-spue,
As his owne things; and they are his owne, 'tis true,
For if one eate my meate, though it be knowne
The meate was mine, th'excrement is his owne: 30
But these do mee no harme, nor they which use
To out-doe Dildoes, and out-usure Jewes;
To out-drinke the sea, to out-sweare the Letanie;
Who with sinnes all kindes as familiar bee
As Confessors; and for whose sinfull sake,   35
Schoolemen new tenements in hell must make:
Whose strange sinnes, Canonists could hardly tell
In which Commandements large receit they dwell.

But these punish themselves; the insolence
Of Coscus onely breeds my just offence,   40
Whom time (which rots all, and makes botches poxe,
And plodding on, must make a calfe an oxe)
Hath made a Lawyer, which was (alas) of late
But a scarce Poët; jollier of this state,
Then are new benefic'd ministers, he throwes   45
Like nets, or lime-twigs, wheresoever he goes,
His title of Barrister, on every wench,
And wooes in language of the Pleas, and Bench:
A motion, Lady; Speake Coscus; I have beene
In love, ever since *tricesimo* of the Queene,   50
Continuall claimes I have made, injunctions got
To stay my rivals suit, that hee should not
Proceed; spare mee; In Hillary terme I went,
You said, If I return'd next size in Lent,
I should be in remitter of your grace;   55
In th'interim my letters should take place
Of affidavits: words, words, which would teare
The tender labyrinth of a soft maids eare,
More, more, then ten Sclavonians scolding, more
Then when winds in our ruin'd Abbeyes rore.   60
When sicke with Poëtrie, and possest with muse
Thou wast, and mad, I hop'd; but men which chuse
Law practise for meere gaine, bold soule, repute
Worse then imbrothel'd strumpets prostitute.
Now like an owlelike watchman, hee must walke   65
His hand still at a bill, now he must talke
Idly, like prisoners, which whole months will sweare
That onely suretiship hath brought them there,
And to every suitor lye in every thing,
Like a Kings favourite, yea like a King;   70
Like a wedge in a blocke, wring to the barre,
Bearing-like Asses; and more shamelesse farre
Then carted whores, lye, to the grave Judge; for
Bastardy abounds not in Kings titles, nor
Symonie and Sodomy in Churchmens lives,   75
As these things do in him; by these he thrives.
Shortly (as the sea) hee will compasse all our land;
From Scots, to Wight; from Mount, to Dover strand.

And spying heires melting with luxurie,
Satan will not joy at their sinnes, as hee.   80
For as a thrifty wench scrapes kitching-stuffe,
And barrelling the droppings, and the snuffe,
Of wasting candles, which in thirty yeare
(Relique-like kept) perchance buyes wedding geare;
Peecemeale he gets lands, and spends as much time   85
Wringing each Acre, as men pulling prime.
In parchments then, large as his fields, hee drawes
Assurances, bigge, as gloss'd civill lawes,
So huge, that men (in our times forwardnesse)
Are Fathers of the Church for writing lesse.   90
These hee writes not; nor for these written payes,
Therefore spares no length; as in those first dayes
When Luther was profest, He did desire
Short *Pater nosters,* saying as a Fryer
Each day his beads, but having left those lawes,   95
Addes to Christs prayer, the Power and glory clause.
But when he sells or changes land, he'impaires
His writings, and (unwatch'd) leaves out, *ses heires,*
As slily as any Commenter goes by
Hard words, or sense; or in Divinity   100
As controverters, in vouch'd Texts, leave out
Shrewd words, which might against them cleare the doubt.
Where are those spred woods which cloth'd hertofore
Those bought lands? not built, nor burnt within dore.
Where's th'old landlords troops, and almes? In great hals 105
Carthusian fasts, and fulsome Bachanalls
Equally I hate; meanes blesse; in rich mens homes
I bid kill some beasts, but no Hecatombs,
None starve, none surfet so; But (Oh) we allow,
Good workes as good, but out of fashion now,   110
Like old rich wardrops; but my words none drawes
Within the vast reach of th'huge statute lawes.

Satyre III

Kinde pitty chokes my spleene; brave scorn forbids
Those teares to issue which swell my eye-lids;
I must not laugh, nor weepe sinnes, and be wise,
Can railing then cure these worne maladies?
Is not our Mistresse faire Religion,   5
As worthy of all our Soules devotion,
As vertue was to the first blinded age?
Are not heavens joyes as valiant to asswage
Lusts, as earths honour was to them? Alas,
As wee do them in meanes, shall they surpasse   10
Us in the end, and shall thy fathers spirit
Meete blinde Philosophers in heaven, whose merit
Of strict life may be imputed faith, and heare
Thee, whom hee taught so easie wayes and neare
To follow, damn'd? O if thou dar'st, feare this;   15
This feare great courage, and high valour is.
Dar'st thou ayd mutinous Dutch, and dar'st thou lay
Thee in ships woodden Sepulchers, a prey
To leaders rage, to stormes, to shot, to dearth?
Dar'st thou dive seas, and dungeons of the earth?   20
Hast thou couragious fire to thaw the ice
Of frozen North discoveries? and thrise
Colder then Salamanders, like divine
Children in th'oven, fires of Spaine, and the line,
Whose countries limbecks to our bodies bee,   25
Canst thou for gaine beare? and must every hee
Which cryes not, Goddesse, to thy Mistresse, draw,
Or eate thy poysonous words? courage of straw!
O desperate coward, wilt thou seeme bold, and
To thy foes and his (who made thee to stand   30
Sentinell in his worlds garrison) thus yeeld,
And for forbidden warres, leave th'appointed field?
Know thy foes: The foule Devill (whom thou
Strivest to please,) for hate, not love, would allow
Thee faine, his whole Realme to be quit; and as   35
The worlds all parts wither away and passe,
So the worlds selfe, thy other lov'd foe, is
In her decrepit wayne, and thou loving this,

Dost love a withered and worne strumpet; last,
Flesh (it selfes death) and joyes which flesh can taste,   40
Thou lovest; and thy faire goodly soule, which doth
Give this flesh power to taste joy, thou dost loath.
Seeke true religion. O where? Mirreus
Thinking her unhous'd here, and fled from us,
Seekes her at Rome, there, because hee doth know   45
That shee was there a thousand yeares agoe,
He loves her ragges so, as wee here obey
The statecloth where the Prince sate yesterday.
Crantz to such brave Loves will not be inthrall'd,
But loves her onely, who at Geneva is call'd   50
Religion, plaine, simple, sullen, yong,
Contemptuous, yet unhansome; As among
Lecherous humors, there is one that judges
No wenches wholsome, but course country drudges.
Graius stayes still at home here, and because   55
Some Preachers, vile ambitious bauds, and lawes
Still new like fashions, bid him thinke that shee
Which dwels with us, is onely perfect, hee
Imbraceth her, whom his Godfathers will
Tender to him, being tender, as Wards still   60
Take such wives as their Guardians offer, or
Pay valewes. Carelesse Phrygius doth abhorre
All, because all cannot be good, as one
Knowing some women whores, dares marry none.
Graccus loves all as one, and thinkes that so   65
As women do in divers countries goe
In divers habits, yet are still one kinde,
So doth, so is Religion; and this blind-
nesse too much light breeds; but unmoved thou
Of force must one, and forc'd but one allow;   70
And the right; aske thy father which is shee,
Let him aske his; though truth and falshood bee
Neare twins, yet truth a little elder is;
Be busie to seeke her, beleeve mee this,
Hee's not of none, nor worst, that seekes the best.   75
To adore, or scorne an image, or protest,
May all be bad; doubt wisely; in strange way
To stand inquiring right, is not to stray;

To sleepe, or runne wrong, is. On a huge hill,
Cragged, and steep, Truth stands, and hee that will   80
Reach her, about must, and about must goe;
And what the hills suddennes resists, winne so;
Yet strive so, that before age, deaths twilight,
Thy Soule rest, for none can worke in that night.
To will, implyes delay, therefore now doe: 85
Hard deeds, the bodies paines; hard knowledge too
The mindes indeavours reach, and mysteries
Are like the Sunne, dazling, yet plaine to all eyes.
Keepe the truth which thou hast found; men do not stand
In so ill case here, that God hath with his hand   90
Sign'd Kings blanck-charters to kill whom they hate,
Nor are they Vicars, but hangmen to Fate.
Foole and wretch, wilt thou let thy Soule be tyed
To mans lawes, by which she shall not be tryed
At the last day? Oh, will it then boot thee   95
To say a Philip, or a Gregory,
A Harry, or a Martin taught thee this?
Is not this excuse for mere contraries,
Equally strong? cannot both sides say so?
That thou mayest rightly obey power, her bounds know;
Those past, her nature, and name is chang'd; to be
Then humble to her is idolatrie.
As streames are, Power is; those blest flowers that dwell
At the rough streames calme head, thrive and do well,
But having left their roots, and themselves given loss   105
To the streames tyrannous rage, alas, are driven
Through mills, and rockes, and woods, and at last, almost
Consum'd in going, in the sea are lost:
So perish Soules, which more chuse mens unjust
Power from God claym'd, then God himselfe to trust.   110

Satyre IIII

Well; I may now receive, and die; My sinne
Indeed is great, but I have beene in
A Purgatorie, such as fear'd hell is
A recreation to, and scarse map of this.
My minde, neither with prides itch nor yet hath been   5
Poyson'd with love to see, or to bee seene,
I had no suit there, nor new suite to shew,
Yet went to Court; But as Glaze which did goe
To'a Masse in jest, catch'd, was faine to disburse
The hundred markes, which is the Statutes curse;   10
Before he scapt, So'it pleas'd my destinie
(Guilty of my sin of going,) to thinke me
As prone to all ill, and of good as forget-
full, as proud, as lustfull, and as much in debt,
As vaine, as witlesse, and as false as they   15
Which dwell at Court, for once going that way.
Therefore I suffered this; Towards me did runne
A thing more strange, then on Niles slime, the Sunne
E'r bred; or all which into Noahs Arke came;
A thing, which would have pos'd Adam to name;   20
Stranger then seaven Antiquaries studies,
Then Africks Monsters, Guianaes rarities.
Stranger then strangers; One, who for a Dane,
In the Danes Massacre had sure beene slaine,
If he had liv'd then; And without helpe dies,   25
When next the Prentises, 'gainst Strangers rise.
One, whom the watch at noone lets scarce goe by,
One, to whom, the examining Justice sure would cry,
Sir, by your priesthood tell me what you are.
His cloths were strange, though coarse; and black,
           though bare;   30
Sleevelesse his jerkin was, and it had beene
Velvet, but 'twas now (so much ground was seene)
Become Tufftaffatie; and our children shall
See it plaine Rashe awhile, then nought at all.
This thing hath travail'd, and saith, speakes all tongues   35
And only knoweth what to all States belongs.
Made of th'Accents, and best phrase of all these,

He speakes no language; If strange meats displease,
Art can deceive, or hunger force my tast,
But Pedants motley tongue, souldiers bumbast,   40
Mountebankes drugtongue, nor the termes of law
Are strong enough preparatives, to draw
Me to beare this: yet I must be content
With his tongue, in his tongue call'd complement:
In which he can win widdowes, and pay scores,   45
Make men speake treason, cosen subtlest whores,
Out-flatter favorites, or outlie either
Jovius, or Surius, or both together.
He names mee, and comes to mee; I whisper, God!
How have I sinn'd, that thy wraths furious rod,   50
This fellow chuseth me? He saith, Sir,
I love your judgement; Whom doe you prefer,
For the best linguist? And I seelily
Said, that I thought Calepines Dictionarie;
Nay, but of men, most sweet Sir; Beza then,   55
Some other Jesuites, and two reverend men
Of our two Academies, I named; There
He stopt mee, and said; Nay, your Apostles were
Good pretty linguists, and so Panurge was;
Yet a poore gentleman, all these may passe   60
By travaile. Then, as if he would have sold
His tongue, he prais'd it, and such wonders told
That I was faine to say, If you'had liv'd, Sir,
Time enough to have beene Interpreter
To Babells bricklayers, sure the Tower had stood.   65
He adds, If of court life you knew the good,
You would leave lonenesse. I said, not alone
My lonenesse is, but Spartanes fashion,
To teach by painting drunkards, doth not last
Now; Aretines pictures have made few chast;   70
No more can Princes courts, though there be few
Better pictures of vice, teach me vertue;
He, like to a high stretcht lute string squeakt, O Sir,
'Tis sweet to talke of Kings. At Westminster,
Said I, The man that keepes the Abbey tombes,   75
And for his price doth with who ever comes,
Of all our Harries, and our Edwards talke,

From King to King and all their kin can walke:
Your eares shall heare nought, but Kings; your eyes meet
Kings only; The way to it, is Kingstreet.   80
He smack'd, and cry'd, He's base, Mechanique, coarse,
So are all your Englishmen in their discourse.
Are not your Frenchmen neate? Mine? as you see,
I have but one Frenchman, looke, hee followes mee.
Certes they are neatly cloth'd; I, of this minde am,   85
Your only wearing is your Grogaram.
Not so Sir, I have more. Under this pitch
He would not flie; I chaff'd him; But as Itch
Scratch'd into smart, and as blunt iron ground
Into an edge, hurts worse: So, I (foole) found,   90
Crossing hurt mee; To fit my sullennesse,
He to another key, his stile doth addresse,
And askes, what newes? I tell him of new playes.
He takes my hand, and as a Still, which staies
A Sembriefe, 'twixt each drop, he nigardly,   95
As loth to enrich mee, so tells many a lye.
More then ten Hollensheads, or Halls, or Stowes,
Of triviall houshold trash he knowes; He knowes
When the Queene frown'd, or smil'd, and he knowes what
A subtle States-man may gather of that;   100
He knowes who loves; whom; and who by poyson
Hasts to an Offices reversion;
He knowes who'hath sold his land, and now doth beg
A licence, old iron, bootes, shooes, and egge-
shels to transport; Shortly boyes shall not play   105
At span-counter, or blow-point, but they pay
Toll to some Courtier; And wiser then all us,
He knowes what Ladie is not painted; Thus
He with home-meats tries me; I belch, spue, spit,
Looke pale, and sickly, like a Patient; Yet   110
He thrusts on more; And as if he'd undertooke
To say Gallo-Belgicus without booke
Speakes of all States, and deeds, that have been since
The Spaniards came, to the losse of Amyens.
Like a bigge wife, at sight of loathed meat,   115
Readie to travaile: So I sigh, and sweat
To heare this Makeron talke: In vaine; for yet,

Either my humour, or his owne to fit,
He like a priviledg'd spie, whom nothing can
Discredit, Libells now 'gainst each great man.   120
He names a price for every office paid;
He saith, our warres thrive ill, because delai'd;
That offices are entail'd, and that there are
Perpetuities of them, lasting as farre
As the last day; And that great officers,   125
Doe with the Pirates share, and Dunkirkers.
Who wasts in meat, in clothes, in horse, he notes;
Who loves whores, who boyes, and who goats.
I more amas'd then Circes prisoners, when
They felt themselves turne beasts, felt my selfe then   130
Becomming Traytor, and mee thought I saw
One of our Giant Statutes ope his jaw
To sucke me in, for hearing him. I found
That as burnt venome Leachers do grow sound
By giving others their soares, I might growe   135
Guilty, and he free: Therefore I did shew
All signes of loathing; But since I am in,
I must pay mine, and my forefathers sinne
To the last farthing; Therefore to my power
Toughly and stubbornly I beare this crosse; But the'houre
Of mercy now was come; He tries to bring
Me to pay a fine to scape his torturing,
And saies, Sir, can you spare me; I said, willingly;
Nay, Sir, can you spare me a crowne? Thankfully I
Gave it, as Ransome; But as fidlers, still,   145
Though they be paid to be gone, yet needs will
Thrust one more jigge upon you; so did hee
With his long complementall thankes vexe me.
But he is gone, thankes to his needy want,
And the prerogative of my Crowne: Scant   150
His thankes were ended, when I, (which did see
All the court fill'd with more strange things then hee
Ran from thence with such or more hast, then one
Who feares more actions, doth make from prison.
At home in wholesome solitarinesse   155
My precious soule began, the wretchednesse
Of suiters at court to mourne, and a trance

Like his, who dreamt he saw hell, did advance
It selfe on mee; Such men as he saw there,
I saw at court, and worse, and more; Low feare   160
Becomes the guiltie, not the accuser; Then,
Shall I, nones slave, of high borne, or rais'd men
Feare frownes? And, my Mistresse Truth, betray thee
To th'huffing braggart, puft Nobility?
No, no, Thou which since yesterday hast beene   165
Almost about the whole world, hast thou seene,
O Sunne, in all thy journey, Vanitie,
Such as swells the bladder of our court? I
Thinke he which made your waxen garden, and
Transported it from Italy to stand   170
With us, at London, flouts our Presence, for
Just such gay painted things, which no sappe, nor
Tast have in them, ours are; And naturall
Some of the stocks are, their fruits, bastard all.
'Tis ten a clock and past; All whom the Mues,   175
Baloune, Tennis, Dyet, or the stewes,
Had all the morning held, now the second
Time made ready, that day, in flocks, are found
In the Presence, and I, (God pardon mee.)
As fresh, and sweet their Apparrells be, as bee   180
The fields they sold to buy them; For a King
Those hose are, cry the flatterers; And bring
Them next weeke to the Theatre to sell;
Wants reach all states; Me seemes they doe as well
At stage, as court; All are players; who e'r lookes   185
(For themselves dare not goe) o'r Cheapside books,
Shall finde their wardrops Inventory. Now,
The Ladies come; As Pirats, which doe know
That there came weak ships fraught with Cutchannel,
The men board them; and praise, as they thinke, well, 190
Their beauties; they the mens wits; Both are bought.
Why good wits ne'r weare scarlet gownes, I thought
This cause, These men, mens wits for speeches buy,
And women buy all reds which scarlets die.
He call'd her beauty limetwigs, her haire net;   195
She feares her drugs ill laid, her haire loose set.
Would not Heraclitus laugh to see Macrine,

From hat to shooe, himselfe at doore refine,
As if the Presence were a Moschite, and lift
His skirts and hose, and call his clothes to shrift,   200
Making them confesse not only mortall
Great staines and holes in them; but veniall
Feathers and dust, wherewith they fornicate:
And then by *Durers* rules survay the state
Of his each limbe, and with strings the odds trye   205
Of his neck to his legge, and wast to thighe.
So in immaculate clothes, and Symetrie
Perfect as circles, with such nicetie
As a young Preacher at his first time goes
To preach, he enters, and a Lady which owes   210
Him not so much as good will, he arrests,
And unto her protests protests protests,
So much as at Rome would serve to have throwne
Ten Cardinalls into the Inquisition;
And whisperd by Jesu, so often, that A   215
Pursevant would have ravish'd him away
For saying of our Ladies psalter; But'tis fit
That they each other plague, they merit it.
But here comes Glorius that will plague them both,
Who, in the other extreme, only doth   220
Call a rough carelessenesse, good fashion;
Whose cloak his spurres teare; whom he spits on
He cares not, His ill words doe no harme
To him; he rusheth in, as if arme, arme,
He meant to crie; And though his face be as ill   225
As theirs which in old hangings whip Christ, still
He strives to looke worse, he keepes all in awe;
Jeasts like a licenc'd foole, commands like law.
Tyr'd, now I leave this place, and but pleas'd so
As men which from gaoles to'execution goe,   230
Goe through the great chamber (why is it hung
With the seaven deadly sinnes?). Being among
Those Askaparts, men big enough to throw
Charing Crosse for a barre, men that doe know
No token of worth, but Queenes man, and fine   235
Living, barrells of beefe, flaggons of wine;
I shooke like a spyed Spie. Preachers which are

Seas of Wit and Arts, you can, then dare,
Drowne the sinnes of this place, for, for mee
Which am but a scarce brooke, it enough shall bee   240
To wash the staines away; Although I yet
With *Macchabees* modestie, the knowne merit
Of my worke lessen: yet some wise man shall,
I hope, esteeme my writs Canonicall.

Satyre V

Thou shalt not laugh in this leafe, Muse, nor they
Whom any pitty warmes; He which did lay
Rules to make Courtiers, (hee being understood
May make good Courtiers, but who Courtiers good?)
Frees from the sting of jests all who in extreme   5
Are wreched or wicked: of these two a theame
Charity and liberty give me. What is hee
Who Officers rage, and Suiters misery
Can write, and jest? If all things be in all,
As I thinke, since all, which were, are, and shall   10
Bee, be made of the same elements:
Each thing, each thing implyes or represents.
Then man is a world; in which, Officers
Are the vast ravishing seas; and Suiters,
Springs; now full, now shallow, now drye; which, to   15
That which drownes them, run: These selfe reasons do
Prove the world a man, in which, officers
Are the devouring stomacke, and Suiters
The excrements, which they voyd. All men are dust;
How much worse are Suiters, who to mens lust   20
Are made preyes? O worse then dust, or wormes meat,
For they do eate you now, whose selves wormes shall eate.
They are the mills which grinde you, yet you are
The winde which drives them; and a wastfull warre
Is fought against you, and you fight it; they   25
Adulterate lawe, and you prepare their way
Like wittals; th'issue your owne ruine is.
Greatest and fairest Empresse, know you this?
Alas, no more then Thames calme head doth know

Whose meades her armes drowne, or whose corne o'rflow:
You Sir, whose righteousnes she loves, whom I
By having leave to serve, am most richly
For service paid, authoriz'd, now beginne
To know and weed out this enormous sinne.
O Age of rusty iron! Some better wit   35
Call it some worse name, if ought equall it;
The iron Age *that* was, when justice was sold; now
Injustice is sold dearer farre. Allow
All demands, fees, and duties, gamsters, anon
The mony which you sweat, and sweare for, is gon   40
Into other hands: So controverted lands
Scape, like Angelica, the strivers hands.
If Law be in the Judges heart, and hee
Have no heart to resist letter, or fee,
Where wilt thou appeale? powre of the Courts below   45
Flow from the first maine head, and these can throw
Thee, if they sucke thee in, to misery,
To fetters, halters; But if the injury
Steele thee to dare complaine, Alas, thou go'st
Against the stream, when upwards: when thou art most   50
Heavy and most faint; and in these labours they,
'Gainst whom thou should'st complaine, will in the way
Become great seas, o'r which, when thou shalt bee
Forc'd to make golden bridges, thou shalt see
That all thy gold was drown'd in them before;   55
All things follow their like, only who have may have more.
Judges are Gods; he who made and said them so,
Meant not that men should be forc'd to them to goe,
By meanes of Angels; When supplications
We send to God, to Dominations,   60
Powers, Cherubins, and all heavens Courts, if wee
Should pay fees as here, Daily bread would be
Scarce to Kings; so 'tis. Would it not anger
A Stoicke, a coward, yea a Martyr,
To see a Pursivant come in, and call   65
All his cloathes, Copes; Bookes, Primers; and all
His Plate, Challices; and mistake them away,
And aske a fee for comming? Oh, ne'r may
Faire lawes white reverend name be strumpeted,

To warrant thefts: she is established   70
Recorder to Destiny, on earth, and shee
Speakes Fates words, and but tells us who must bee
Rich, who poore, who in chaires, who in jayles:
Shee is all faire, but yet hath foule long nailes,
With which she scracheth Suiters; In bodies   75
Of men, so in law, nailes are th'extremities,
So Officers stretch to more then Law can doe,
As our nailes reach what no else part comes to.
Why barest thou to yon Officer? Foole, Hath hee
Got those goods, for which erst men bar'd to thee?   80
Foole, twice, thrice, thou hast bought wrong, and now
          hungerly
Beg'st right; But that dole comes not till these dye.
Thou had'st much, and lawes Urim and Thummim trie
Thou wouldst for more; and for all hast paper
Enough to cloath all the great Carricks Pepper.   85
Sell that, and by that thou much more shalt leese,
Then Haman, when he sold his Antiquities.
 O wretch that thy fortunes should moralize
Esops fables, and make tales, prophesies.
Thou'art the swimming dog whom shadows cosened,   90
And div'st, neare drowning, for what's vanished.

Upon Mr. Thomas Coryats Crudities

Oh to what height will love of greatnesse drive
Thy leavened spirit, *Sesqui-superlative?*
Venice vast lake thou hadst seen, and would seek than
Some vaster thing, and found'st a Curtizan.
That inland Sea having discovered well,   5
A Cellar gulfe, where one might saile to hell
From Heydelberg, thou longdst to see: And thou
This Booke, greater then all, producest now.
Infinite worke, which doth so far extend,
That none can study it to any end.   10
'Tis no one thing, it is not fruit nor roote;
Nor poorely limited with head or foot.
If man be therefore man, because he can

Reason, and laugh, thy booke doth halfe make man.
One halfe being made, thy modestie was such,   15
That thou on th'other half wouldst never touch.
When wilt thou be at full, great Lunatique?
Not till thou exceed the world? Canst thou be like
A prosperous nose-borne wenne, which sometimes growes
To be farre greater then the Mother-nose?   20
Goe then; and as to thee, when thou didst go,
Munster did Townes, and *Gesner* Authors show,
Mount now to *Gallo-belgicus;* appear
As deepe a States-man, as a Gazettier.
Homely and familiarly, when thou com'st back,   25
Talke of *Will. Conquerour,* and *Prester Jack.*
Go bashfull man, lest here thou blush to looke
Upon the progresse of thy glorious booke,
To which both Indies sacrifices send;
The West sent gold, which thou didst freely spend,   30
(Meaning to see't no more) upon the presse.
The East sends hither her deliciousnesse;
And thy leaves must imbrace what comes from thence,
The Myrrhe, the Pepper, and the Frankincense.
This magnifies thy leaves; but if they stoope   35
To neighbour wares, when Merchants do unhoope
Voluminous barrels; if thy leaves do then
Convey these wares in parcels unto men;
If for vast Tons of Currans, and of Figs,
Of Medicinall and Aromatique twigs,   40
Thy leaves a better method do provide,
Divide to pounds, and ounces sub-divide;
If they stoope lower yet, and vent our wares,
Home-*manufactures,* to thick popular Faires,
If *omni-praegnant* there, upon warme stalls,   45
They hatch all wares for which the buyer calls;
Then thus thy leaves we justly may commend,
That they all kinde of matter comprehend.
Thus thou, by means which th'Ancients never took,
A Pandect makest, and Universall Booke.   50
The bravest Heroes, for publike good,
Scattered in divers Lands their limbs and blood.
Worst malefactors, to whom men are prize,

Do publike good, cut in Anatomies;
So will thy booke in peeces; for a Lord   55
Which casts at Portescues, and all the board,
Provide whole books; each leafe enough will be
For friends to passe time, and keep company.
Can all carouse up thee? no, thou must fit
Measures; and fill out for the half-pint wit: 60
Some shall wrap pils, and save a friends life so,
Some shall stop muskets, and so kill a foe.
Thou shalt not ease the Criticks of next age
So much, at once their hunger to asswage:
Nor shall wit-pirats hope to finde thee lye   65
All in one bottome, in one Librarie.
Some Leaves may paste strings there in other books,
And so one may, which on another looks,
Pilfer, alas, a little wit from you;
But hardly* much; and yet I think this true;   70
As Sibyls was, your booke is mysticall,
For every peece is as much worth as all.
Therefore mine impotency I confesse,
The healths which my braine bears must be far lesse:
Thy Gyant-wit'orethrowes me, I am gone;   75
And rather then read all, I would reade none.

                                                          J. D.

In eundem Macaronicon

Quot, dos haec, **Linguists** perfetti, *Disticha* fairont,
Tot cuerdos **States-men** , *hic* livre fara *tuus.*
Es sat a my l'honneur estre *hic* inteso; Car **J leabe**
L'honra, de personne nestre creduto, *tibi.*

                                    Explicit Joannes Donne.

* I meane from one page which shall paste strings in a booke.
  [*Donne's sidenote, 1611*]

LETTERS TO SEVERALL PERSONAGES

THE STORME
To Mr Christopher Brooke

Thou which art I, ('tis nothing to be soe)
Thou which art still thy selfe, by these shalt know
Part of our passage; And, a hand, or eye
By *Hilliard* drawne, is worth an history,
By a worse painter made; and (without pride)   5
When by thy judgment they are dignifi'd,
My lines are such: 'Tis the preheminence
Of friendship onely to'impute excellence.
England to whom we'owe, what we be, and have,
Sad that her sonnes did seeke a forraine grave   10
(For, Fates, or Fortunes drifts none can soothsay,
Honour and misery have one face and way.)
From out her pregnant intrailes sigh'd a winde
Which at th'ayres middle marble roome did finde
Such strong resistance, that it selfe it threw   15
Downeward againe; and so when it did view
How in the port, our fleet deare time did leese,
Withering like prisoners, which lye but for fees,
Mildly it kist our sailes and, fresh and sweet,
As to a stomack sterv'd, whose insides meete,   20
Meate comes, it came; and swole our sailes, when wee
So joyd, as *Sara*'her swelling joy'd to see.
But 'twas but so kinde, as our countrimen,
Which bring friends one dayes way, and leave them then.
Then like two mighty Kings, which dwelling farre   25
Asunder, meet against a third to warre,
The South and West winds joyn'd, and, as they blew,
Waves like a rowling trench before them threw.
Sooner then you read this line, did the gale,
Like shot, not fear'd till felt, our sailes assaile;   30
And what at first was call'd a gust, the same
Hath now a stormes, anon a tempests name.
Jonas, I pitty thee, and curse those men,
Who when the storm rag'd most, did wake thee then;

Sleepe is paines easiest salve, and doth fullfill   35
All offices of death, except to kill.
But when I wakt, I saw, that I saw not;
I, and the Sunne, which should teach mee'had forgot
East, West, Day, Night, and I could onely say,
If the world had lasted, now it had beene day.   40
Thousands our noyses were, yet wee'mongst all
Could none by his right name, but thunder call:
Lightning was all our light, and it rain'd more
Then if the Sunne had drunke the sea before.
Some coffin'd in their cabbins lye,'equally   45
Griev'd that they are not dead, and yet must dye;
And as sin-burd'ned soules from graves will creepe,
At the last day, some forth their cabbins peepe:
And tremblingly'aske what newes, and doe heare so,
Like jealous husbands, what they would not know.   50
Some sitting on the hatches, would seeme there,
With hideous gazing to feare away feare.
Then note they the ships sicknesses, the Mast
Shak'd with this ague, and the Hold and Wast
With a salt dropsie clog'd, and all our tacklings   55
Snapping, like too-high-stretched treble strings.
And from our totterd sailes, ragges drop downe so,
As from one hang'd in chaines, a yeare agoe.
Even our Ordinance plac'd for our defence,
Strive to breake loose, and scape away from thence.   60
Pumping hath tir'd our men, and what's the gaine?
Seas into seas throwne, we suck in againe;
Hearing hath deaf'd our saylers; and if they
Knew how to heare, there's none knowes what to say.
Compar'd to these stormes, death is but a qualme,   65
Hell somewhat lightsome, and the'Bermuda calme.
Darknesse, lights elder brother, his birth-right
Claims o'r this world, and to heaven hath chas'd light.
All things are one, and that one none can be,
Since all formes, uniforme deformity   70
Doth cover, so that wee, except God say
Another *Fiat*, shall have no more day.
So violent, yet long these furies bee,
That though thine absence sterve me,'I wish not thee.

THE CALME

Our storme is past, and that storms tyrannous rage,
A stupid calme, but nothing it, doth swage.
The fable is inverted, and farre more
A blocke afflicts, now, then a storke before.
Stormes chafe, and soone weare out themselves, or us;   5
In calmes, Heaven laughs to see us languish thus.
As steady'as I can wish, that my thoughts were,
Smooth as thy mistresse glasse, or what shines there,
The sea is now. And, as the Iles which wee
Seeke, when wee can move, our ships rooted bee.   10
As water did in stormes, now pitch runs out:
As lead, when a fir'd Church becomes one spout.
And all our beauty, and our trimme, decayes,
Like courts removing, or like ended playes.
The fighting place now seamens ragges supply;   15
And all the tackling is a frippery.
No use of lanthornes; and in one place lay
Feathers and dust, to day and yesterday.
Earths hollownesses, which the worlds lungs are,
Have no more winde then the upper valt of aire.   20
We can nor lost friends, nor sought foes recover,
But meteorlike, save that wee move not, hover.
Onely the Calenture together drawes
Deare friends, which meet dead in great fishes jawes:
And on the hatches as on Altars lyes   25
Each one, his owne Priest, and owne Sacrifice.
Who live, that miracle do multiply
Where walkers in hot Ovens, doe not dye.
If in despite of these, wee swimme, that hath
No more refreshing, then our brimstone Bath,   30
But from the sea, into the ship we turne,
Like parboyl'd wretches, on the coales to burne.
Like *Bajazet* encag'd, the shepheards scoffe,
Or like slacke sinew'd *Sampson,* his haire off,
Languish our ships. Now, as a Miriade   35
Of Ants, durst th'Emperours lov'd snake invade,
The crawling Gallies, Sea-goales, finny chips,
Might brave our Pinnaces, now bed-ridde ships.

Whether a rotten state, and hope of gaine,
Or to disuse mee from the queasie paine   40
Of being belov'd, and loving, or the thirst
Of honour, or faire death, out pusht mee first,
I lose my end: for here as well as I
A desperate may live, and a coward die.
Stagge, dogge, and all which from, or towards flies,   45
Is paid with life, or pray, or doing dyes.
Fate grudges us all, and doth subtly lay
A scourge,'gainst which wee all forget to pray,
He that at sea prayes for more winde, as well
Under the poles may begge cold, heat in hell.   50
What are wee then? How little more alas
Is man now, then before he was? he was
Nothing; for us, wee are for nothing fit;
Chance, or our selves still disproportion it.
Wee have no power, no will, no sense; I lye,   55
I should not then thus feele this miserie.

To Sir Henry Wotton

Sir, more then kisses, letters mingle Soules;
For, thus friends absent speake. This ease controules
The tediousnesse of my life: But for these
I could ideate nothing, which could please,
But I should wither in one day, and passe   5
To'a bottle'of Hay, that am a locke of Grasse.
Life is a voyage, and in our lifes wayes
Countries, Courts, Towns are Rockes, or Remoraes;
They breake or stop all ships, yet our state's such,
That though then pitch they staine worse,wee must touch.
If in the furnace of the even line,   10
Or under th'adverse icy poles thou pine,
Thou know'st two temperate Regions girded in,
Dwell there: But Oh, what refuge canst thou winne
Parch'd in the Court, and in the country frozen?   15
Shall cities, built of both extremes, be chosen?
Can dung and garlike be'a perfume? or can
A Scorpion and Torpedo cure a man?

Cities are worst of all three; of all three
(O knottie riddle) each is worst equally.   20
Cities are Sepulchers; they who dwell there
Are carcases, as if no such there were.
And Courts are Theaters, where some men play
Princes, some slaves, all to one end, and of one clay.
The Country is a desert, where no good,   25
Gain'd (as habits, not borne,) is understood.
There men become beasts, and prone to more evils;
In cities blockes, and in a lewd court, devills.
As in the first Chaos confusedly
Each elements qualities were in the'other three;   30
So pride, lust, covetize, being severall
To these three places, yet all are in all,
And mingled thus, their issue incestuous.
Falshood is denizon'd. Virtue is barbarous.
Let no man say there, Virtues flintie wall   35
Shall locke vice in mee, I'll do none, but know all.
Men are spunges, which to poure out, receive.
Who know false play, rather then lose, deceive.
For in best understandings, sinne beganne,
Angels sinn'd first, then Devills, and then man.   40
Onely perchance beasts sinne not; wretched wee
Are beasts in all, but white integritie.
I thinke if men, which in these places live
Durst looke for themselves, and themselves retrive,
They would like strangers greet themselves, seeing than   45
Utopian youth, growne old Italian.
　　　Be thou thine owne home, and in thy selfe dwell;
Inne any where, continuance maketh hell.
And seeing the snaile, which every where doth rome,
Carrying his owne house still, still is at home,   50
Follow (for he is easie pac'd) this snaile,
Bee thine owne Palace, or the world's thy gaile.
And in the worlds sea, do not like corke sleepe
Upon the waters face; nor in the deepe
Sinke like a lead without a line: but as   55
Fishes glide, leaving no print where they passe,
Nor making sound; so closely thy course goe,
Let men dispute, whether thou breathe, or no.

Onely'in this one thing, be no Galenist: To make
Courts hot ambitions wholesome, do not take   60
A dramme of Countries dulnesse; do not adde
Correctives, but as chymiques, purge the bad.
But, Sir, I advise not you, I rather doe
Say o'er those lessons, which I learn'd of yous
Whom, free from German schismes, and lightnesse   65
Of France, and faire Italies faithlesnesse,
Having from these suck'd all they had of worth,
And brought home that faith, which you carried forth,
I throughly love. But if my selfe, I'have wonne
To know my rules, I have, and you have   70
                                        DONNE:

To Sir Henry Goodyere

Who makes the Past, a patterne for next yeare,
    Turnes no new leafe, but still the same things reads,
Seene things, he sees againe, heard things doth heare,
    And makes his life, but like a paire of beads.

A Palace, when 'tis that, which it should be,   5
    Leaves growing, and stands such, or else decayes:
But hee which dwels there, is not so; for hee
    Strives to urge upward, and his fortune raise;

So had your body'her morning, hath her noone,
    And shall not better; her next change is night: 10
But her faire larger guest, to'whom Sun and Moone
    Are sparkes, and short liv'd, claimes another right.

The noble Soule by age growes lustier,
    Her appetite, and her digestion mend,
Wee must not sterve, nor hope to pamper her   15
    With womens milke, and pappe unto the end.

Provide you manlyer dyet; you have seene
    All libraries, which are Schools, Camps, and Courts;
But aske your Garners if you have not beene
    In harvests, too indulgent to your sports.   20

Would you redeeme it? then your selfe transplant
   A while from hence. Perchance outlandish ground
Beares no more wit, then ours, but yet more scant
   Are those diversions there, which here abound.

To be a stranger hath that benefit,   25
   Wee can beginnings, but not habits choke.
Goe; whither? Hence; you get, if you forget;
   New faults, till they prescribe in us, are smoake.

Our soule, whose country'is heaven, and God her father,
   Into this world, corruptions sinke, is sent,   30
Yet, so much in her travaile she doth gather,
   That she returnes home, wiser then she went;

It payes you well, if it teach you to spare,
   And make you,'asham'd, to make your hawks praise, yours,
Which when herselfe she lessens in the aire,   35
   You then first say, that high enough she toures.

However, keepe the lively tast you hold
   Of God, love him as now, but feare him more,
And in your afternoones thinke what you told
   And promis'd him, at morning prayer before.   40

Let falshood like a discord anger you,
   Else be not froward. But why doe I touch
Things, of which none is in your practise new,
   And Tables, or fruit-trenchers teach as much;

But thus I make you keepe your promise Sir,   45
   Riding I had you, though you still staid there,
And in these thoughts, although you never stirre,
   You came with mee to Micham, and are here.

To Mr Rowland Woodward

Like one who'in her third widdowhood doth professe
Her selfe a Nunne, tyed to retirednesse,
So'affects my muse now, a chast fallownesse;

Since shee to few, yet to too many'hath showne
How love-song weeds, and Satyrique thornes are growne   5
Where seeds of better Arts, were early sown.

Though to use, and love Poëtrie, to mee,
Betroth'd to no'one Art, be no'adulterie;
Omissions of good, ill, as ill deeds bee.

For though to us it seeme,'and be light and thinne,   10
Yet in those faithfull scales, where God throwes in
Mens workes, vanity weighs as much as sinne.

If our Soules have stain'd their first white, yet wee
May cloth them with faith, and deare honestie,
Which God imputes, as native puritie.   15

There is no Vertue, but Religion:
Wise, valiant, sober, just, are names, which none
Want, which want not Vice-covering discretion.

Seeke wee then our selves in our selves; for as
Men force the Sunne with much more force to passe,   20
By gathering his beames with a christall glasse;

So wee, If wee into our selves will turne,
Blowing our sparkes of vertue, may outburne
The straw, which doth about our hearts sojourne.

You know, Physitians, when they would infuse   25
Into any'oyle, the Soules of Simples, use
Places, where they may lie still warme, to chuse.

So workes retirednesse in us; To rome
Giddily, and be every where, but at home,
Such freedome doth a banishment become.   30

Wee are but farmers of our selves, yet may,
If we can stocke our selves, and thrive, uplay
Much, much deare treasure for the great rent day.

Manure thy selfe then, to thy selfe be'approv'd,
And with vaine outward things be no more mov'd, 35
But to know, that I love thee'and would be lov'd.

To Sir Henry Wootton

Here's no more newes, then vertue,'I may as well
Tell you *Cales,* or St *Michaels* tale for newes, as tell
That vice doth here habitually dwell.

Yet, as to'get stomachs, we walke up and downe,
And toyle to sweeten rest, so, may God frowne, 5
If, but to loth both, I haunt Court, or Towne.

For here no one is from the'extremitie
Of vice, by any other reason free,
But that the next to'him, still, is worse then hee.

In this worlds warfare, they whom rugged Fate, 10
(Gods Commissary,) doth so throughly hate,
As in'the Courts Squadron to marshall their state:

If they stand arm'd with seely honesty,
With wishing prayers, and neat integritie,
Like Indians 'gainst Spanish hosts they bee. 15

Suspitious boldnesse to this place belongs,
And to'have as many eares as all have tongues;
Tender to know, tough to acknowledge wrongs.

Beleeve mee Sir, in my youths giddiest dayes,
When to be like the Court, was a playes praise, 20
Playes were not so like Courts, as Courts'are like playes.

Then let us at these mimicke antiques jeast,
Whose deepest projects, and egregious gests
Are but dull Moralls of a game at Chests.

But now 'tis incongruity to smile,   25
Therefore I end; and bid farewell a while,
At Court; though *From Court*, were the better stile.

H: W: in Hiber: belligeranti

Went you to conquer? and have so much lost
Yourself, that what in you was best and most,
Respective friendship, should so quickly dye?
In publique gaine my share'is not such that I
Would lose your love for Ireland: better cheap   5
I pardon death (who though he do not reap
Yet gleanes hee many of our frends away)
Then that your waking mind should bee a prey
To lethargies. Lett shott, and boggs, and skeines
With bodies deale, as fate bids and restreynes;   10
Ere sicknesses attack, yong death is best,
Who payes before his death doth scape arrest.
Lett not your soule (at first with graces fill'd,
And since, and thorough crooked lymbecks, still'd
In many schools and courts, which quicken it,)   15
It self unto the Irish negligence submit.
I aske not labored letters which should weare
Long papers out: nor letters which should frare
Dishonest carriage: or a seers art:
Nor such as from the brayne come, but the hart.   20

To the Countesse of Bedford

MADAME,
Reason is our Soules left hand, Faith her right,
By these wee reach divinity, that's you;
Their loves, who have the blessings of your light,
Grew from their reason, mine from faire faith grew.

But as, although a squint lefthandednesse   5
Be'ungracious, yet we cannot want that hand,
So would I, not to encrease, but to expresse
My faith, as I beleeve, so understand.

Therefore I study you first in your Saints,
Those friends, whom your election glorifies,   10
Then in your deeds, accesses, and restraints,
And what you reade, and what your selfe devize.

But soone, the reasons why you'are lov'd by all,
Grow infinite, and so passe reasons reach,
Then backe againe to'implicite faith I fall,   15
And rest on what the Catholique voice doth teach;

That you are good: and not one Heretique
Denies it: if he did, yet you are so.
For, rockes, which high top'd and deep rooted sticke,
Waves wash, not undermine, nor overthrow.   20

In every thing there naturally growes
A *Balsamum* to keepe it fresh, and new,
If 'twere not injur'd by extrinsique blowes;
Your birth and beauty are this Balme in you.

But you of learning and religion,   25
And vertue,'and such ingredients, have made
A methridate, whose operation
Keepes off, or cures what can be done or said.

Yet, this is not your physicke, but your food,
A dyet fit for you; for you are here   30
The first good Angell, since the worlds frame stood,
That ever did in womans shape appeare.

Since you are then Gods masterpeece, and so
His Factor for our loves; do as you doe,
Make your returne home gracious; and bestow   35
This life on that; so make one life of two.
    For so God helpe mee,'I would not misse you there
    For all the good which you can do me here.

To the Countesse of Bedford

MADAME,
You have refin'd mee, and to worthyest things
(Vertue, Art, Beauty, Fortune,) now I see
Rarenesse, or use, not nature value brings;
And such, as they are circumstanc'd, they bee.
    Two ills can ne're perplexe us, sinne to'excuse;   5
    But of two good things, we may leave and chuse.

Therefore at Court, which is not vertues clime,
(Where a transcendent height, (as, lownesse mee)
Makes her not be, or not show) all my rime
Your vertues challenge, which there rarest bee;   10
    For, as darke texts need notes: there some must bee
    To usher vertue, and say, *This is shee.*

So in the country'is beauty; to this place
You are the season (Madame) you the day,
'Tis but a grave of spices, till your face   15
Exhale them, and a thick close bud display.
    Widow'd and reclus'd else, her sweets she'enshrines;
    As China, when the Sunne at Brasill dines.

Out from your chariot, morning breaks at night,
And falsifies both computations so;   20

Since a new world doth rise here from your light,
We your new creatures, by new recknings goe.
 This showes that you from nature lothly stray,
 That suffer not an artificiall day.

In this you'have made the Court the Antipodes,   25
And will'd your Delegate, the vulgar Sunne,
To doe profane autumnall offices,
Whilst here to you, wee sacrificers runne;
 And whether Priests, or Organs, you wee'obey,
 We sound your influence, and your Dictates say.   30

Yet to that Deity which dwels in you,
Your vertuous Soule, I now not sacrifice;
These are *Petitions,* and not *Hymnes;* they sue
But that I may survay the edifice.
 In all Religions as much care hath bin   35
 Of Temples frames, and beauty,'as Rites within.

As all which goe to Rome, doe not thereby
Esteeme religions, and hold fast the best,
But serve discourse, and curiosity,
With that which doth religion but invest,   40
 And shunne th'entangling laborinths of Schooles,
 And make it wit, to thinke the wiser fooles:

So in this pilgrimage I would behold
You as you'are vertues temple, not as shee,
What walls of tender christall her enfold,   45
What eyes, hands, bosome, her pure Altars bee;
 And after this survay, oppose to all
 Bablers of Chappels, you th'Escuriall.

Yet not as consecrate, but merely'as faire,
On these I cast a lay and country eye.   50
Of past and future stories, which are rare,
I finde you all record, and prophecie.
 Purge but the booke of Fate, that it admit
 No sad nor guilty legends, you are it.

If good and lovely were not one, of both   55
You were the transcript, and originall,
The Elements, the Parent, and the Growth,
And every peece of you, is both their All:
    So'intire are all your deeds, and you, that you
    Must do the same thinge still; you cannot two.   60

But these (as nice thinne Schoole divinity
Serves heresie to furder or represse)
Tast of Poëtique rage, or flattery,
And need not, where all hearts one truth professe;
    Oft from new proofes,and new phrase, new doubts grow,
    As strange attire aliens the men wee know.

Leaving then busie praise, and all appeale
To higher Courts, senses decree is true,
The Mine, the Magazine, the Commonweale,
The story of beauty,'in Twicknam is, and you.   70
    Who hath seene one, would both; As, who had bin
    In Paradise, would seeke the Cherubin.

To Sir Edward Herbert at Julyers

Man is a lumpe, where all beasts kneaded bee,
    Wisdome makes him an Arke where all agree;
The foole, in whom these beasts do live at jarre,
    Is sport to others, and a Theater,
Nor scapes hee so, but is himselfe their prey;   5
    All which was man in him, is eate away,
And now his beasts on one another feed,
    Yet couple'in anger, and new monsters breed.
How happy'is hee, which hath due place assign'd
    To'his beasts, and disaforested his minde!   10
Empail'd himselfe to keepe them out, not in;
    Can sow, and dares trust corne, where they have bin;
Can use his horse, goate, wolfe, and every beast,
    And is not Asse himselfe to all the rest.
Else, man not onely is the heard of swine,   15
    But he's those devills too, which did incline

Them to a headlong rage, and made them worse:
    For man can adde weight to heavens heaviest curse.
As Soules (they say) by our first touch, take in
    The poysonous tincture of Originall sinne,   20
So, to the punishments which God doth fling,
    Our apprehension contributes the sting.
To us, as to his chickins, he doth cast
    Hemlocke, and wee as men, his hemlocke taste;
We do infuse to what he meant for meat,   25
    Corrosivenesse, or intense cold or heat.
For, God no such specifique poyson hath
    As kills we know not how; his fiercest wrath
Hath no antipathy, but may be good
    At least for physicke, if not for our food.   30
Thus man, that might be'his pleasure, is his rod,
    And is his devill, that might be his God.
Since then our businesse is, to rectifie
    Nature, to what she was, wee'are led awry
By them, who man to us in little show;   35
    Greater then due, no forme we can bestow
On him; for Man into himselfe can draw
    All; All his faith can swallow,'or reason chaw.
All that is fill'd, and all that which doth fill,
    All the round world, to man is but a pill,   40
In all it workes not, but it is in all
    Poysonous, or purgative, or cordiall
For, knowledge kindles Calentures in some,
    And is to others icy *Opium*.
As brave as true, is that profession than   45
    Which you doe use to make; that you know man.
This makes it credible; you have dwelt upon
    All worthy bookes, and now are such an one.
Actions are authors, and of those in you
    Your friends finde every day a mart of new.   50

To the Countesse of Bedford

T'have written then, when you writ, seem'd to mee
    Worst of spirituall vices, Simony,
And not t'have written then, seemes little lesse
    Then worst of civill vices, thanklessenesse.
In this, my debt I seem'd loath to confesse,   5
    In that, I seem'd to shunne beholdingnesse.
But 'tis not soe; *nothings,* as I am, may
    Pay all they have, and yet have all to pay.
Such borrow in their payments, and owe more
    By having leave to write so, then before.   10
Yet since rich mines in barren grounds are showne,
    May not I yeeld (not gold) but coale or stone?
Temples were not demolish'd, though prophane:
    Here *Peter Joves,* there *Paul* hath *Dian's* Fane.
So whether my hymnes you admit or chuse,   15
    In me you'have hallowed a Pagan Muse,
And denizend a stranger, who mistaught
    By blamers of the times they mard, hath sought
Vertues in corners, which now bravely doe
    Shine in the worlds best part, or all It; You.   20
I have beene told, that vertue in Courtiers hearts
    Suffers an Ostracisme, and departs.
Profit, ease, fitnesse, plenty, bid it goe,
    But whither, only knowing you, I know;
Your (or you) vertue two vast uses serves,   25
    It ransomes one sex, and one Court preserves.
There's nothing but your worth, which being true,
    Is knowne to any other, not to you:
And you can never know it; To admit
    No knowledge of your worth, is some of it.   30
But since to you, your praises discords bee,
    Stoop, others ills to meditate with mee.
Oh ! to confesse wee know not what we should,
    Is halfe excuse; wee know not what we would:
Lightnesse depresseth us, emptinesse fills,   35
    We sweat and faint, yet still goe downe the hills.
As new Philosophy arrests the Sunne,
    And bids the passive earth about it runne,

So wee have dull'd our minde, it hath no ends;
   Onely the bodie's busie, and pretends;   40
As dead low earth ecclipses and controules
   The quick high Moone: so doth the body, Soules.
In none but us, are such mixt engines found,
   As hands of double office: For, the ground
We till with them; and them to heav'n wee raise;   45
   Who prayer-lesse labours, or, without this, prayes,
Doth but one halfe, that's none; He which said, *Plough*
   And looke not back, to looke up doth allow.
Good seed degenerates, and oft obeyes
   The soyles disease, and into cockle strayes;   50
Let the minds thoughts be but transplanted so,
   Into the body,'and bastardly they grow.
What hate could hurt our bodies like our love?
   Wee (but no forraine tyrants could) remove
These not ingrav'd, but inborne dignities,   55
   Caskets of soules; Temples, and Palaces:
For, bodies shall from death redeemed bee,
   Soules but preserv'd, not naturally free.
As men to'our prisons, new soules to us are sent,
   Which learne vice there, and come in innocent.   60
First seeds of every creature are in us,
   What ere the world hath bad, or pretious,
Mans body can produce, hence hath it beene
   That stones, wormes, frogges, and snakes in man are seene:
But who ere saw, though nature can worke soe,   65
   That pearle, or gold, or corne in man did grow?
We'have added to the world Virginia,'and sent
   Two new starres lately to the firmament;
Why grudge wee us (not heaven) the dignity
   T'increase with ours, those faire soules company.   70
But I must end this letter, though it doe
   Stand on two truths, neither is true to you.
Vertue hath some perversenesse; For she will
   Neither beleeve her good, nor others ill.
Even in you, vertues best paradise,   75
   Vertue hath some, but wise degrees of vice.
Too many vertues, or too much of one

Begets in you unjust suspition;
And ignorance of vice, makes vertue lesse,
   Quenching compassion of our wrechednesse.   80
But these are riddles; Some aspersion
   Of vice becomes well some complexion.
Statesmen purge vice with vice, and may corrode
   The bad with bad, a spider with a toad:
For so, ill thralls not them, but they tame ill   85
   And make her do much good against her will,
But in your Commonwealth, or world in you,
   Vice hath no office, or good worke to doe.
Take then no vitious purge, but be content
   With cordiall vertue, your knowne nourishment.   90

To the Countesse of Bedford

On New-yeares day

This twilight of two yeares, not past nor next,
   Some embleme is of mee, or I of this;
Who Meteor-like, of stuffe and forme perplext,
   Whose *what,* and *where,* in disputation is,
   If I should call mee *any thing,* should misse.   5

I summe the yeares, and mee, and finde mee not
   Debtor to th'old, nor Creditor to th'new,
That cannot say, My thankes I have forgot,
   Nor trust I this with hopes, and yet scarce true
   This bravery is, since these times shew'd mee you.   10

In recompence I would show future times
   What you were, and teach them to'urge towards such.
Verse embalmes vertue;'and Tombs, or Thrones of rimes,
   Preserve fraile transitory fame, as much
   As spice doth bodies from corrupt aires touch.   15

Mine are short-liv'd; the tincture of your name
  Creates in them, but dissipates as fast,
New spirits: for, strong agents with the same
  Force that doth warme and cherish, us doe wast;
  Kept hot with strong extracts, no bodies last: 20

So, my verse built of your just praise, might want
  Reason and likelihood, the firmest Base,
And made of miracle, now faith is scant,
  Will vanish soone, and so possesse no place,
  And you, and it, too much grace might disgrace.   25

When all (as truth commands assent) confesse
  All truth of you, yet they will doubt how I,
One corne of one low anthills dust, and lesse,
  Should name, know, or expresse a thing so high,
  And not an inch, measure infinity.   30

I cannot tell them, nor my selfe, nor you,
  But leave, lest truth b'endanger'd by my praise,
And turne to God, who knowes I thinke this true,
  And useth oft, when such a heart mis-sayes,
  To make it good, for, such a praiser prayes.   35

Hee will best teach you, how you should lay out
  His stock of *beauty, learning, favour, blood;*
He will perplex security with doubt,
  And cleare those doubts; hide from you,'and shew you good,
  And so increase your appetite and food;   40

Hee will teach you, that good and bad have not
  One latitude in cloysters, and in Court;
Indifferent there the greatest space hath got;
  Some pitty'is not good there, some vaine disport,
  On this side sinne, with that place may comport.   45

Yet he, as hee bounds seas, will fixe your houres,
   Which pleasure, and delight may not ingresse,
And though what none else lost, be truliest yours,
   Hee will make you, what you did not, possesse,
    By using others, not vice, but weakenesse.   50

He will make you speake truths, and credibly,
   And make you doubt, that others doe not so:
Hee will provide you keyes, and locks, to spie,
   And scape spies, to good ends, and hee will show
    What you may not acknowledge, what not know.   55

For your owne conscience, he gives innocence,
   But for your fame, a discreet warinesse,
And though to scape, then to revenge offence
   Be better, he showes both, and to represse
    Joy, when your state swells, *sadnesse* when'tis lesse.   60

From need of teares he will defend your soule,
   Or make a rebaptizing of one teare;
Hee cannot, (that's, he will not) dis-inroule
   Your name; and when with active joy we heare
    This private Ghospell, then'tis our New Yeare.   65

To the Countesse of Huntingdon

MADAME,
Man to Gods image; *Eve,* to mans was made,
   Nor finde wee that God breath'd a soule in her.
Canons will not Church functions you invade,
   Nor lawes to civill office you preferre.

Who vagrant transitory Comets sees,   5
   Wonders, because they'are rare; But a new starre
Whose motion with the firmament agrees,
   Is miracle; for, there no new things are;

In woman so perchance milde innocence
   A seldome comet is, but active good   10
A miracle, which reason scapes, and sense;
   For, Art and Nature this in them withstood.

As such a starre, the *Magi* led to view
   The manger-cradled infant, God below:
By vertues beames by fame deriv'd from you,   15
   May apt soules, and the worst may, vertue know.

If the worlds age, and death be argued well
   By the Sunnes fall, which now towards earth doth bend,
Then we might feare that vertue, since she fell
   So low as woman, should be neare her end.   20

But she's not stoop'd, but rais'd; exil'd by men
   She fled to heaven, that's heavenly things, that's you;
She was in all men, thinly scatter'd then,
   But now amass'd, contracted in a few.

She guilded us: But you are gold, and Shee;   25
   Us she inform'd, but transubstantiates you;
Soft dispositions which ductile bee,
   Elixarlike, she makes not cleane, but new.

Though you a wifes and mothers name retaine,
   'Tis not as woman, for all are not soe,   30
But vertue having made you vertue,'is faine
   T'adhere in these names, her and you to show,

Else, being alike pure, wee should neither see;
   As, water being into ayre rarify'd,
Neither appeare, till in one cloud they bee,   35
   So, for our sakes you do low names abide;

Taught by great constellations, which being fram'd,
   Of the most starres, take low names, *Crab,* and *Bull,*
When single planets by the *Gods* are nam'd,
   You covet not great names, of great things full.   40

So you, as woman, one doth comprehend,
    And in the vaile of kindred others see;
To some ye are reveal'd, as in a friend,
    And as a vertuous Prince farre off, to mee.

To whom, because from you all vertues flow,   45
    And 'tis not none, to dare contemplate you,
I, which doe so, as your true subject owe
    Some tribute for that, so these lines are due.

If you can thinke these flatteries, they are,
    For then your judgement is below my praise,   50
If they were so, oft, flatteries worke as farre,
    As Counsels, and as farre th'endeavour raise.

So my ill reaching you might there grow good,
    But I remaine a poyson'd fountaine still;
But not your beauty, vertue, knowledge, blood   55
    Are more above all flattery, then my will.

And if I flatter any, 'tis not you
    But my owne judgement, who did long agoe
Pronounce, that all these praises should be true,
    And vertue should your beauty, 'and birth outgrow.   60

Now that my prophesies are all fulfill'd,
    Rather then God should not be honour'd too,
And all these gifts confess'd, which hee instill'd,
    Your selfe were bound to say that which I doe.

So I, but your Recorder am in this,   65
    Or mouth, or Speaker of the universe,
A ministeriall Notary, for 'tis
    Not I, but you and fame, that make this verse;

I was your Prophet in your yonger dayes,
And now your Chaplaine, God in you to praise.   70

To Mr T. W.

All haile sweet Poët, more full of more strong fire,
  Then hath or shall enkindle any spirit,
  I lov'd what nature gave thee, but this merit
Of wit and Art I love not but admire;
Who have before or shall write after thee,   5
Their workes, though toughly laboured, will bee
  Like infancie or age to mans firme stay,
  Or earely and late twilights to mid-day.

Men say, and truly, that they better be
  Which be envyed then pittied: therefore I,   10
  Because I wish thee best, doe thee envie:
O wouldst thou, by like reason, pitty mee !
But care not for mee: I, that ever was
In Natures, and in Fortunes gifts, (alas,
  Before thy grace got in the Muses Schoole)   15
  A monster and a begger, am now a foole.

Oh how I grieve, that late borne modesty
  Hath got such root in easie waxen hearts,
  That men may not themselves, their owne good parts
Extoll, without suspect of surquedrie,   20
For, but thy selfe, no subject can be found
Worthy thy quill, nor any quill resound
  Thy worth but thine: how good it were to see
  A Poëm in thy praise, and writ by thee.

Now if this song be too'harsh for rime, yet, as   25
  The Painters bad god made a good devill,
  'Twill be good prose, although the verse be evill,
If thou forget the rime as thou dost passe.
Then write, that I may follow, and so bee
Thy debter, thy'eccho, thy foyle, thy zanee.   30
  I shall be thought, if mine like thine I shape,
  All the worlds Lyon, though I be thy Ape.

To Mr T. W.

Hast thee harsh verse, as fast as thy lame measure
    Will give thee leave, to him, my pain and pleasure.
I have given thee, and yet thou art too weake,
    Feete, and a reasoning soule and tongue to speake.
Plead for me, and so by thine and my labour   5
    I am thy Creator, thou my Saviour.
Tell him, all questions, which men have defended
    Both of the place and paines of hell, are ended;
And 'tis decreed our hell is but privation
    Of him, at least in this earths habitation: 10
And 'tis where I am, where in every street
    Infections follow, overtake, and meete:
Live I or die, by you my love is sent,
    And you'are my pawnes, or else my Testament.

To Mr T. W.

Pregnant again with th'old twins Hope, and Feare,
Oft have I askt for thee, both how and where
Thou wert, and what my hopes of letters were;

As in our streets sly beggers narrowly
Watch motions of the givers hand and eye,   5
And evermore conceive some hope thereby.

And now thy Almes is given, thy letter'is read,
The body risen againe, the which was dead,
And thy poore starveling bountifully fed.

After this banquet my Soule doth say grace,   10
And praise thee for'it, and zealously imbrace
Thy love; though I thinke thy love in this case
    To be as gluttons, which say 'midst their meat,
    They love that best of which they most do eat.

To Mr T. W.

At once, from hence, my lines and I depart,
I to my soft still walks, they to my Heart;
I to the Nurse, they to the child of Art;

Yet as a firme house, though the Carpenter
Perish, doth stand: As an Embassadour   5
Lyes safe, how e'r his king be in danger:

So, though I languish, prest with Melancholy,
My verse, the strict Map of my misery,
Shall live to see that, for whose want I dye.

Therefore I envie them, and doe repent,   10
That from unhappy mee, things happy'are sent;
Yet as a Picture, or bare Sacrament,
   Accept these lines, and if in them there be
   Merit of love, bestow that love on mee.

To Mr R. W

Zealously my Muse doth salute all thee,
Enquiring of that mistique trinitee
Whereof thou,'and all to whom heavens do infuse
Like fyer, are made; thy body, mind, and Muse.
Dost thou recover sicknes, or prevent?   5
Or is thy Mind travail'd with discontent?
Or art thou parted from the world and mee,
In a good skorn of the worlds vanitee?
Or is thy devout Muse retyr'd to sing
Upon her tender Elegiaque string?   10
Our Minds part not, joyne then thy Muse with myne,
For myne is barren thus devore'd from thyne.

To Mr R. W.

Muse not that by thy mind thy body is led:
For by thy mind, my mind's distempered.
So thy Care lives long, for I bearing part
It eates not only thyne, but my swolne heart.
And when it gives us intermission   5
We take new harts for it to feede upon.
But as a Lay Mans Genius doth controule
Body and mind; the Muse beeing the Soules Soule
Of Poets, that methinks should ease our anguish,
Although our bodyes wither and minds languish.   10
Write then, that my griefes which thine got may bee
Cur'd by thy charming soveraigne melodee.

To Mr C. B.

Thy friend, whom thy deserts to thee enchaine,
Urg'd by this unexcusable occasion,
    Thee and the Saint of his affection
Leaving behinde, doth of both wants complaine;
And let the love I beare to both sustaine   5
    No blott nor maime by this division,
    Strong is this love which ties our hearts in one,
And strong that love pursu'd with amorous paine;
But though besides thy selfe I leave behind
    Heavens liberall, and earths thrice-fairer Sunne,   10
    Going to where sterne winter aye doth wonne,
Yet, loves hot fires, which martyr my sad minde,
    Doe send forth scalding sighes, which have the Art
    To melt all Ice, but that which walls her heart.

To Mr E. G.

Even as lame things thirst their perfection, so
The slimy rimes bred in our vale below,
Bearing with them much of my love and hart,
Fly unto that Parnassus, where thou art.
There thou oreseest London: Here I have beene,   5
By staying in London, too much overseene.
Now pleasures dearth our City doth posses,
Our Theaters are fill'd with emptines;
As lancke and thin is every street and way
As a woman deliver'd yesterday.   10
Nothing whereat to laugh my spleen espyes
But bearbaitings or Law exercise.
Therefore I'le leave it, and in the Country strive
Pleasure, now fled from London, to retrive.
Do thou so too: and fill not like a Bee   15
Thy thighs with hony, but as plenteously
As Russian Marchants, thy selfes whole vessell load,
And then at Winter retaile it here abroad.
Blesse us with Suffolks sweets; and as it is
Thy garden, make thy hive and warehouse this.   20

To Mr R. W.

If, as mine is, thy life a slumber be,
    Seeme, when thou read'st these lines, to dreame of me,
Never did Morpheus nor his brother weare
    Shapes soe like those Shapes, whom they would appeare,
As this my letter is like me, for it
    Hath my name, words, hand, feet, heart, minde and wit;
It is my deed of gift of mee to thee,
    It is my Will, my selfe the Legacie.
So thy retyrings I love, yea envie,
    Bred in thee by a wise melancholy,   10
That I rejoyce, that unto where thou art,
    Though I stay here, I can thus send my heart,
As kindly'as any enamored Patient
    His Picture to his absent Love hath sent.

All newes I thinke sooner reach thee then mee;   15
   Havens are Heavens, and Ships wing'd Angels be,
The which both Gospell, and sterne threatnings bring;
   Guyanaes harvest is nip'd in the spring,
I feare; And with us (me thinkes) Fate deales so
   As with the Jewes guide God did; he did show   20
Him the rich land, but bar'd his entry in:
   Oh, slownes is our punishment and sinne.
Perchance, these Spanish businesse being done,
   Which as the Earth betweene the Moone and Sun
Eclipse the light which Guyana would give,   25
   Our discontinued hopes we shall retrive:
But if (as all th'All must) hopes smoake away,
   Is not Almightie Vertue'an India?

If men be worlds, there is in every one
   Some thing to answere in some proportion   30
All the worlds riches: And in good men, this,
   Vertue, our formes forme and our soules soule, is.

To Mr R. W.

Kindly I envy thy songs perfection
   Built of all th'elements as our bodyes are:
   That Litle of earth that is in it, is a faire
Delicious garden where all sweetes are sowne.
In it is cherishing fyer which dryes in mee   5
   Griefe which did drowne me: and halfe quench'd by it
   Are satirique fyres which urg'd me to have writt
In skorne of all: for now I admyre thee.
   And as Ayre doth fullfill the hollownes
   Of rotten walls; so it myne emptines,   10
Where tost and mov'd it did beget this sound
Which as a lame Eccho of thyne doth rebound.
   Oh, I was dead; but since thy song new Life did give,
   I recreated, even by thy creature, live.

To Mr S. B.

O Thou which to search out the secret parts
    Of the India, or rather Paradise
    Of knowledge, hast with courage and advise
Lately launch'd into the vast Sea of Arts,
Disdaine not in thy constant travailing   5
    To doe as other Voyagers, and make
    Some turnes into lesse Creekes, and wisely take
Fresh water at the Heliconian spring;
I sing not, Siren like, to tempt; for I
    Am harsh; nor as those Scismatiques with you,   10
    Which draw all wits of good hope to their crew;
But seeing in you bright sparkes of Poetry,
    I, though I brought no fuell, had desire
    With these Articulate blasts to blow the fire.

To Mr I. L.

Of that short Roll of friends writ in my heart
    Which with thy name begins, since their depart,
Whether in the English Provinces they be,
    Or drinke of Po, Sequan, or Danubie,
There's none that sometimes greets us not, and yet   5
    Your Trent is Lethe; that past, us you forget.
You doe not duties of Societies,
    If from the'embrace of a lov'd wife you rise,
View your fat Beasts, stretch'd Barnes, and labour'd fields,
    Eate, play, ryde, take all joyes which all day yeelds,   10
And then againe to your embracements goe:
    Some houres on us your frends, and some bestow
Upon your Muse, else both wee shall repent,
    I that my love, she that her guifts on you are spent.

To Mr B. B.

Is not thy sacred hunger of science
   Yet satisfy'd? Is not thy braines rich hive
   Fulfil'd with hony which thou dost derive
From the Arts spirits and their Quintessence?
Then weane thy selfe at last, and thee withdraw   5
   From Cambridge thy old nurse, and, as the rest,
   Here toughly chew, and sturdily digest
Th'immense vast volumes of our common law;
And begin soone, lest my griefe grieve thee too,
   Which is, that that which I should have begun   10
   In my youthes morning, now late must be done;
And I as Giddy Travellers must doe,
   Which stray or sleepe all day, and having lost
   Light and strength, darke and tir'd must then ride post.

If thou unto thy Muse be marryed,   15
   Embrace her ever, ever multiply,
   Be far from me that strange Adulterie
To tempt thee and procure her widowhed.
My Muse, (for I had one,) because I'am cold,
   Divorc'd her selfe: the cause being in me,   20
   That I can take no new in Bigamye,
Not my will only but power doth withhold.
Hence comes it, that these Rymes which never had
   Mother, want matter, and they only have
   A little forme, the which their Father gave;   25
They are prophane, imperfect, oh, too bad
   To be counted Children of Poetry
   Except confirm'd and Bishoped by thee.

To Mr I. L.

Blest are your North parts, for all this long time
　My Sun is with you, cold and darke'is our Clime;
Heavens Sun, which staid so long from us this yeare,
　Staid in your North (I thinke) for she was there,
And hether by kinde nature drawne from thence,　　5
　Here rages, chafes, and threatens pestilence;
Yet I, as long as shee from hence doth staie,
　Thinke this no South, no Sommer, nor no day.
With thee my kinde and unkinde heart is run,
　There sacrifice it to that beauteous Sun:　　10
And since thou art in Paradise and need'st crave
　No joyes addition, helpe thy friend to save.
So may thy pastures with their flowery feasts,
　As suddenly as Lard, fat thy leane beasts;
So may thy woods oft poll'd, yet ever weare　　15
　A greene, and when thee list, a golden haire;
So may all thy sheepe bring forth Twins; and so
　In chace and race may thy horse all out goe;
So may thy love and courage ne'r be cold;
　Thy Sonne ne'r Ward; Thy lov'd wife ne'r seem old;
But maist thou wish great things, and them attaine,
　As thou telst her, and none but her, my paine.

To Sir H. W. at his going Ambassador to Venice

After those reverend papers, whose soule is
　Our good and great Kings lov'd hand and fear'd name,
By which to you he derives much of his,
　And (how he may) makes you almost the same,

A Taper of his Torch, a copie writ　　5
　From his Originall, and a faire beame
Of the same warme, and dazeling Sun, though it
　Must in another Sphere his vertue streame:

After those learned papers which your hand
    Hath stor'd with notes of use and pleasure too,   10
From which rich treasury you may command
    Fit matter whether you will write or doe:

After those loving papers, where friends send
    With glad griefe, to your Sea-ward steps, farewel,
Which thicken on you now, as prayers ascend   15
    To heaven in troupes at'a good mans passing bell:

Admit this honest paper, and allow
    It such an audience as your selfe would aske;
What you must say at Venice this meanes now,
    And hath for nature, what you have for taske: 20

To sweare much love, not to be chang'd before
    Honour alone will to your fortune fit;
Nor shall I then honour your fortune, more
    Then I have done your honour wanting it.

But 'tis an easier load (though both oppresse)   25
    To want, then governe greatnesse, for wee are
In that, our owne and onely businesse,
    In this, wee must for others vices care;

'Tis therefore well your spirits now are plac'd
    In their last Furnace, in activity;   30
Which fits them (Schooles and Courts and Warres o'rpast)
    To touch and test in any best degree.

For mee, (if there be such a thing as I)
    Fortune (if there be such a thing as shee)
Spies that I beare so well her tyranny,   35
    That she thinks nothing else so fit for mee;

But though she part us, to heare my oft prayers
    For your increase, God is as neere mee here;
And to send you what I shall begge, his staires
    In length and ease are alike every where.   40

To Mrs M. H.

Mad paper stay, and grudge not here to burne
   With all those sonnes whom my braine did create,
At lest lye hid with mee, till thou returne
   To rags againe, which is thy native state.

What though thou have enough unworthinesse   5
   To come unto great place as others doe,
That's much; emboldens, pulls, thrusts I confesse,
   But 'tis not all; Thou should'st be wicked too.

And, that thou canst not learne, or not of mee;
   Yet thou wilt goe? Goe, since thou goest to her   10
Who lacks but faults to be a Prince, for shee,
   Truth, whom they dare not pardon, dares preferre.

But when thou com'st to that perplexing eye
   Which equally claimes *love* and *reverence,*
Thou wilt not long dispute it, thou wilt die;   15
   And, having little now, have then no sense.

Yet when her warme redeeming hand, which is
   A miracle; and made such to worke more,
Doth touch thee (saples leafe) thou grow'st by this
   Her creature; glorify'd more then before.   20

Then as a mother which delights to heare
   Her early child mis-speake halfe uttered words,
Or, because majesty doth never feare
   Ill or bold speech, she Audience affords.

And then, cold speechlesse wretch, thou diest againe, 25
   And wisely; what discourse is left for thee?
For, speech of ill, and her, thou must abstaine,
   And is there any good which is not shee?

Yet maist thou praise her servants, though not her,
   And wit, and vertue,'and honour her attend,   30
And since they'are but her cloathes, thou shalt not erre,
   If thou her shape and beauty'and grace commend.

Who knowes thy destiny? when thou hast done,
   Perchance her Cabinet may harbour thee,
Whither all noble ambitious wits doe runne,   35
   A nest almost as full of Good as shee.

When thou art there, if any, whom wee know,
   Were sav'd before, and did that heaven partake,
When she revolves his papers, marke what show
   -Of favour, she alone, to them doth make.   40

Marke, if to get them, she o'r skip the rest,
   Marke, if shee read them twice, or kisse the name;
Marke, if she doe the same that they protest,
   Marke, if she marke whether her woman came.

Marke, if slight things be'objected, and o'r blowne,   45
   Marke, if her oathes against him be not still
Reserv'd, and that shee grieves she's not her owne,
   And chides the doctrine that denies Freewill.

I bid thee not doe this to be my spie;
   Nor to make my selfe her familiar;   50
But so much I doe love her choyce, that I
   Would faine love him that shall be lov'd of her.

To the Countesse of Bedford

Honour is so sublime perfection,
And so refinde; that when God was alone
And creaturelesse at first, himselfe had none;

But as of the elements, these which wee tread,
Produce all things with which wee'are joy'd or fed,   5
And, those are barren both above our head:

So from low persons doth all honour flow;
Kings, whom they would have honoured, to us show,
And but *direct* our honour, not *bestow*.

For when from herbs the pure part must be wonne   10
From grosse, by Stilling, this is better done
By despis'd dung, then by the fire or Sunne.

Care not then, Madame,'how low your praysers lye;
In labourers balads oft more piety
God findes, then in *Te Deums* melodie.   15

And, ordinance rais'd on Towers, so many mile
Send not their voice, nor last so long a while
As fires from th'earths low vaults in *Sicil* Isle.

Should I say I liv'd darker then were true,
Your radiation can all clouds subdue;   20
But one,'tis best light to contemplate you.

You, for whose body God made better clay,
Or tooke Soules stuffe such as shall late decay,
Or such as needs small change at the last day.

This, as an Amber drop enwraps a Bee,   25
Covering discovers your quicke Soule; that we
May in your through-shine front your hearts thoughts see.

You teach (though wee learne not) a thing unknowne
To our late times, the use of specular stone,
Through which all things within without were shown. 30

Of such were Temples; so and of such you are;
Beeing and *seeming* is your equall care,
And *vertues* whole *summe* is but *know* and *dare*.

But as our Soules of growth and Soules of sense
Have birthright of our reasons Soule, yet hence   35
They fly not from that, nor seeke presidence:

Natures first lesson, so, discretion,
Must not grudge zeale a place, nor yet keepe none,
Not banish it selfe, nor religion.

Discretion is a wisemans Soule, and so   40
Religion is a Christians, and you know
How these are one; her *yea*, is not her *no*.

Nor may we hope to sodder still and knit
These two, and dare to breake them; nor must wit
Be colleague to religion, but be it.   45

In those poor types of God (round circles) so
Religions tipes, the peecelesse centers flow,
And are in all the lines which all wayes goe.

If either ever wrought in you alone
Or principally, then religion   50
Wrought your ends, and your wayes discretion.

Goe thither still, goe the same way you went,
Who so would change, do covet or repent;
Neither can reach you, great and innocent.

To the Countesse of Huntington

That unripe side of earth, that heavy clime
That gives us man up now; like *Adams* time
Before he ate; mans shape, that would yet bee
(Knew they not it, and fear'd beasts companie)
So naked at this day, as though man there   5
From Paradise so great a distance were,
As yet the newes could not arrived bee
Of *Adams* tasting the forbidden tree;
Depriv'd of that free state which they were in,
And wanting the reward, yet beare the sinne.   10
        But, as from extreme hights who downward looks,
Sees men at childrens shapes, Rivers at brookes,
And loseth younger formes; so, to your eye,
These (Madame) that without your distance lie,
Must either mist, or nothing seeme to be,   15
Who are at home but wits mere *Atomi*.
But, I who can behold them move, and stay,

Have found my selfe to you, just their midway;
And now must pitty them; for, as they doe
Seeme sick to me, just so must I to you.   20
Yet neither will I vexe your eyes to see
A sighing Ode, nor crosse-arm'd Elegie.
I come not to call pitty from your heart,
Like some white-liver'd dotard that would part
Else from his slipperie soule with a faint groane,   25
And faithfully, (without you smil'd) were gone.
I cannot feele the tempest of a frowne,
I may be rais'd by love, but not throwne down.
Though I can pittie those sigh twice a day,
I hate that thing whispers it selfe away.   30
Yet since all love is fever, who to trees
Doth talke, doth yet in loves cold ague freeze.
'Tis love, but, with such fatall weaknesse made,
That it destroyes it selfe with its owne shade.
Who first look'd sad, griev'd, pin'd, and shew'd his paine,
Was he that first taught women, to disdaine.
          As all things were one nothing, dull and weake,
Untill this raw disordered heape did breake,
And severall desires led parts away,
Water declin'd with earth, the ayre did stay,   40
Fire rose, and each from other but unty'd,
Themselves unprison'd were and purify'd:
So was love, first in vast confusion hid,
An unripe willingnesse which nothing did,
A thirst, an Appetite which had no ease,   45
That found a want, but knew not what would please.
What pretty innocence in those dayes mov'd?
Man ignorantly walk'd by her he lov'd;
Both sigh'd and enterchang'd a speaking eye,
Both trembled and were sick, both knew not why.   50
That naturall fearefulnesse that struck man dumbe,
Might well (those times consider'd) man become.
As all discoverers whose first assay
Findes but the place, after, the nearest way:
So passion is to womans love, about,   55
Nay, farther off, than when we first set out.
It is not love that sueth, or doth contend;

Love either conquers, or but meets a friend.
Man's better part consists of purer fire,
And findes it selfe allow'd, ere it desire.   60
Love is wise here, keepes home, gives reason sway,
And Journeys not till it finde summer-way.
A weather-beaten Lover but once knowne,
Is sport for every girle to practise on.
Who strives through womans scornes, women to know,   65
Is lost, and seekes his shadow to outgoe;
It must bee sicknesse, after one disdaine,
Though he be call'd aloud, to looke againe.
Let others sigh, and grieve; one cunning sleight
Shall freeze my Love to Christall in a night.   70
I can love first, and (if I winne) love still;
And cannot be remov'd, unlesse she will.
It is her fault if I unsure remaine,
Shee onely can untie, and binde againe.
The honesties of love with ease I doe,   75
But am no porter for a tedious woo.
    But (madame) I now thinke on you; and here
Where we are at our hights, you but appeare,
We are but clouds you rise from, our noone-ray
But a foule shadow, not your breake of day.   80
You are at first hand all that's faire and right,
And others good reflects but backe your light.
You are a perfectnesse, so curious hit,
That youngest flatteries doe scandall it.
For, what is more doth what you are restraine,   85
And though beyond, is downe the hill againe.
We'have no next way to you, we crosse to it:
You are the straight line, thing prais'd, attribute;
Each good in you's a light; so many a shade
You make, and in them are your motions made.   90
These are your pictures to the life. From farre
We see you move, and here your *Zani's* are:
So that no fountaine good there is, doth grow
In you, but our dimme actions faintly shew.
    Then finde I, if mans noblest part be love,   95
Your purest luster must that shadow move.
The soule with body, is a heaven combin'd

With earth, and for mans ease, but nearer joyn'd.
Where thoughts the starres of soule we understand,
We guesse not their large natures, but command.   100
And love in you, that bountie is of light,
That gives to all, and yet hath infinite.
Whose heat doth force us thither to intend,
But soule we finde too earthly to ascend,
'Till slow accesse hath made it wholy pure,   105
Able immortall clearnesse to endure.
Who dare aspire this journey with a staine,
Hath waight will force him headlong backe againe.
No more can impure man retaine and move
In that pure region of a worthy love: 110
Then earthly substance can unforc'd aspire,
And leave his nature to converse with fire:
Such may have eye, and hand; may sigh, may speak;
But like swoln bubles, when they are high'st they break.

      Though far removed Northerne fleets scarce finde   115
The Sunnes comfort; others thinke him too kinde.
There is an equall distance from her eye,
Men perish too farre off, and burne too nigh.
But as ayre takes the Sunne-beames equall bright
From the first Rayes, to his last opposite: 120
So able men, blest with a vertuous Love,
Remote or neare, or howsoe'r they move;
Their vertue breakes all clouds that might annoy,
There is no Emptinesse, but all is Ioy.
He much profanes whom violent heats do move   125
To stile his wandring rage of passion, *Love*:
Love that imparts in every thing delight,
Is fain'd, which only tempts mans appetite.
Why love among the vertues is not knowne
Is, that love is them all contract in one.   130

To the Countesse of Bedford

Begun in France but never perfected

Though I be *dead,* and buried, yet I have
   (Living in you,) Court enough in my grave,
As oft as there I thinke my selfe to bee,
   So many resurrections waken mee.
That thankfullnesse your favours have begot   5
   In mee, embalmes mee, that I doe not rot.
This season as 'tis Easter, as 'tis spring,
   Must both to growth and to confession bring
My thoughts dispos'd unto your influence; so,
   These verses bud, so these confessions grow.   10
First I confesse I have to others lent
   Your stock, and over prodigally spent
Your treasure, for since I had never knowne
   Vertue or beautie, but as they are growne
In you, I should not thinke or say they shine,   15
   (So as I have) in any other Mine.
Next I confesse this my confession,
   For, 'tis some fault thus much to touch upon
Your praise to you, where half rights seeme too much,
   And make your minds sincere complexion blush.   20
Next I confesse my'impenitence, for I
   Can scarce repent my first fault, since thereby
Remote low Spirits, which shall ne'r read you,
   May in lesse lessons finde enough to doe,
By studying copies, not Originals,   25
               Desunt cætera

Letter to the Lady Carey, and Mrs Essex Riche, From Amyens

MADAME,
Here where by All All Saints invoked are,
'Twere too much schisme to be singular,
And 'gainst a practise generall to warre.

Yet turning to Saincts, should my'humility
To other Sainct then you directed bee,   5
That were to make my schisme, heresie.

Nor would I be a Convertite so cold,
As not to tell it; If this be too bold,
Pardons are in this market cheaply sold.

Where, because Faith is in too low degree,   10
I thought it some Apostleship in mee
To speake things which by faith alone I see.

That is, of you, who are a firmament
Of virtues, where no one is growne, or spent,
They'are your materials, not your ornament.   15

Others whom wee call vertuous, are not so
In their whole substance, but, their vertues grow
But in their humours, and at seasons show.

For when through tastlesse flat humilitie
In dow bak'd men some harmelessenes we see,   20
'Tis but his *flegme* that's *Virtuous,* and not Hee:

Soe is the Blood sometimes; who ever ran
To danger unimportun'd, he was than
No better then a *sanguine* Vertuous man.

So cloysterall men, who, in pretence of feare   25
All contributions to this life forbeare,
Have Vertue in *Melancholy,* and only there.

Spirituall *Cholerique* Crytiques, which in all
Religions find faults, and forgive no fall,
Have, through this zeale, Vertue but in their Gall.   30

We'are thus but parcel guilt; to Gold we'are growne
When Vertue is our Soules complexion;
Who knowes his Vertues name or place, hath none.

Vertue'is but aguish, when 'tis severall,
By occasion wak'd, and circumstantiall.   35
True vertue is *Soule,* Alwaies in all deeds *All.*

This Vertue thinking to give dignitie
To your soule, found there no infirmitie,
For, your soule was as good Vertue, as shee;

Shee therefore wrought upon that part of you   40
Which is scarce lesse then soule, as she could do,
And so hath made your beauty, Vertue too.

Hence comes it, that your Beauty wounds not hearts,
As Others, with prophane and sensuall Darts,
But as an influence, vertuous thoughts imparts.   45

But if such friends by the honor of your sight
Grow capable of this so great a light,
As to partake your vertues, and their might,

What must I thinke that influence must doe,
Where it findes sympathie and matter too,   50
Vertue, and beauty of the same stuffe, as you?

Which is, your noble worthie sister, shee
Of whom, if what in this my Extasie
And revelation of you both I see,

I should write here, as in short Galleries   55
The Master at the end large glasses ties,
So to present the roome twice to our eyes,

So I should give this letter length, and say
That which I said of you; there is no way
From either, but by the other, not to stray.   60

May therefore this be enough to testifie
My true devotion, free from flattery;
He that beleeves himselfe, doth never lie.

To the Countesse of Salisbury. August. 1614

Faire, great, and good, since seeing you, wee see
What Heaven can doe, and what any Earth can be:
Since now your beauty shines, now when the Sunne
Growne stale, is to so low a value runne,
That his disshevel'd beames and scattered fires   5
Serve but for Ladies Periwigs and Tyres
In lovers Sonnets: you come to repaire
Gods booke of creatures, teaching what is faire.
Since now, when all is withered, shrunke, and dri'd,
All Vertues ebb'd out to a dead low tyde,   10
All the worlds frame being crumbled into sand,
Where every man thinks by himselfe to stand,
Integritie, friendship, and confidence,
(Ciments of greatnes) being vapor'd hence,
And narrow man being fill'd with little shares,   15
Court, Citie, Church, are all shops of small-wares,
All having blowne to sparkes their noble fire,
And drawne their sound gold-ingot into wyre;
All trying by a love of littlenesse
To make abridgments, and to draw to lesse,   20
Even that nothing, which at first we were;
Since in these times, your greatnesse doth appeare,
And that we learne by it, that man to get
Towards him that's infinite, must first be great.
Since in an age so ill, as none is fit   25
So much as to accuse, must lesse mend it,
(For who can judge, or witnesse of those times
Where all alike are guiltie of the crimes?)

Where he that would be good, is thought by all
A monster, or at best fantasticall;   30
Since now you durst be good, and that I doe
Discerne, by daring to contemplate you,
That there may be degrees of faire, great, good,
Through your light, largenesse, vertue understood:
If in this sacrifice of mine, be showne   35
Any small sparke of these, call it your owne.
And if things like these, have been said by mee
Of others; call not that Idolatrie.
For had God made man first, and man had seene
The third daies fruits, and flowers, and various greene,   40
He might have said the best that he could say
Of those faire creatures, which were made that day;
And when next day he had admir'd the birth
Of Sun, Moone, Stars, fairer then late-prais'd earth,
Hee might have said the best that he could say,   45
And not be chid for praising yesterday;
So though some things are not together true,
As, that another is worthiest, and, that you:
Yet, to say so, doth not condemne a man,
If when he spoke them, they were both true than.   50
How faire a proofe of this, in our soule growes?
Wee first have soules of growth, and sense, and those,
When our last soule, our soule immortall came,
Were swallowed into it, and have no name.
Nor doth he injure those soules, which doth cast   55
The power and praise of both them, on the last;
No more doe I wrong any; I adore
The same things now, which I ador'd before,
The subject chang'd, and measure; the same thing
In a low constable, and in the King   60
I reverence; His power to work on mee:
So did I humbly reverence each degree
Of faire, great, good; but more, now I am come
From having found their *walkes,* to find their *home.*
And as I owe my first soules thankes, that they   65
For my last soule did fit and mould my clay,
So am I debtor unto them, whose worth,
Enabled me to profit, and take forth

This new great lesson, thus to study you;
Which none, not reading others, first, could doe.   70
Nor lacke I light to read this booke, though I
In a darke Cave, yea in a Grave doe lie;
For as your fellow Angells, so you doe
Illustrate them who come to study you.
The first whom we in Histories doe finde   75
To have profest all Arts, was one borne blinde:
He lackt those eyes beasts have as well as wee,
Not those, by which Angels are seene and see;
So, though I'am borne without those eyes to live,
Which fortune, who hath none her selfe, doth give,   80
Which are, fit meanes to see bright courts and you,
Yet may I see you thus, as now I doe;
I shall by that, all goodnesse have discern'd,
And though I burne my librarie, be learn'd.

To the Lady Bedford

You that are she and you, that's double shee,
    In her dead face, halfe of your selfe shall see;
Shee was the other part, for so they doe
    Which build them friendships, become one of two;
So two, that but themselves no third can fit,   5
    Which were to be so, when they were not yet;
Twinnes, though their birth *Cusco,* and *Musco* take,
    As divers starres one Constellation make;
Pair'd like two eyes, have equall motion, so
    Both but one meanes to see, one way to goe.   10
Had you dy'd first, a carcasse shee had beene;
    And wee your rich Tombe in her face had seene;
She like the Soule is gone, and you here stay,
    Not a live friend; but th'other halfe of clay.
And since you act that part, As men say, here   15
    Lies such a Prince, when but one part is there,
And do all honour and devotion due
    Unto the whole, so wee all reverence you;
For, such a friendship who would not adore
    In you, who are all what both were before,   20

Not all, as if some perished by this,
    But so, as all in you contracted is.
As of this all, though many parts decay,
    The pure which elemented them shall stay;
And though diffus'd, and spread in infinite,   25
    Shall recollect, and in one All unite:
So madame, as her Soule to heaven is fled,
    Her flesh rests in the earth, as in the bed;
Her vertues do, as to their proper spheare,
    Returne to dwell with you, of whom they were: 30
As perfect motions are all circular,
    So they to you, their sea, whence lesse streames are.
Shee was all spices, you all metalls; so
    In you two wee did both rich Indies know.
And as no fire, nor rust can spend or waste   35
    One dramme of gold, but what was first shall last,
Though it bee forc'd in water, earth, salt, aire,
    Expans'd in infinite, none will impaire;
So, to your selfe you may additions take,
    But nothing can you lesse, or changed make.   40
Seeke not in seeking new, to seeme to doubt,
    That you can match her, or not be without;
But let some faithfull booke in her roome be,
    Yet but of *Judith* no such booke as shee.

AN ANATOMIE OF THE WORLD

*Wherein, By occasion of the untimely death of
Mistris ELIZABETH DRURY, the frailty and the decay of this
whole World is represented.*

THE FIRST ANNIVERSARY

To the Praise of the Dead, and the Anatomie

Well dy'd the World, that we might live to see
This world of wit, in his Anatomie
No evill wants his good; so wilder heires
Bedew their Fathers Tombes, with forced teares,
Whose state requites their losse: whiles thus we gain,   5
Well may wee walke in blacks, but not complaine.
Yet how can I consent the world is dead
While this Muse lives? which in his spirits stead
Seemes to informe a World; and bids it bee,
In spight of losse or fraile mortalitie?   10
And thou the subject of this welborne thought,
Thrice noble maid, couldst not have found nor sought
A fitter time to yeeld to thy sad Fate,
Then whiles this spirit lives, that can relate
Thy worth so well to our last Nephews eyne,   15
That they shall wonder both at his and thine:
Admired match! where strives in mutuall grace
The cunning pencill, and the comely face:
A taske which thy faire goodnesse made too much
For the bold pride of vulgar pens to touch;   20
Enough is us to praise them that praise thee,
And say, that but enough those prayses bee,
Which hadst thou liv'd, had hid their fearfull head
From th'angry checkings of thy modest red:
Death barres reward and shame: when envy's gone,   25
And gaine, 'tis safe to give the dead their owne
As then the wise Egyptians wont to lay
More on their Tombes, then houses: these of clay,
But those of brasse, or marble were: so wee
Give more unto thy Ghost, then unto thee.   30

Yet what wee give to thee, thou gav'st to us,
And may'st but thanke thy selfe, for being thus:
Yet what thou gav'st, and wert, O happy maid,
Thy grace profest all due, where 'tis repayd.
So these high songs that to thee suited bin   35
Serve but to sound thy Makers praise, in thine,
Which thy deare soule as sweetly sings to him
Amid the Quire of Saints, and Seraphim,
As any Angels tongue can sing of thee;
The subjects differ, though the skill agree: 40
For as by infant-yeares men judge of age,
Thy early love, thy vertues, did presage
What an high part thou bear'st in those best songs,
Whereto no burden, nor no end belongs.
Sing on thou virgin Soule, whose lossfull gaine   45
Thy lovesick parents have bewail'd in vaine;
Never may thy Name be in our songs forgot,
Till wee shall sing thy ditty and thy note.

AN ANATOMY OF THE WORLD

The First Anniversary

The entrie When that rich Soule which to her heaven is gone,
into the Whom all do celebrate, who know they have one,
worke. (For who is sure he hath a Soule, unlesse
It see, and judge, and follow worthinesse,
And by Deedes praise it? hee who doth not this,   5
May lodge an In-mate soule, but 'tis not his.)
When that Queene ended here her progresse time,
And, as t'her standing house to heaven did climbe,
Where loath to make the Saints attend her long,
She's now a part both of the Quire, and Song,   10
This World, in that great earthquake languished;
For in a common bath of teares it bled,
Which drew the strongest vitall spirits out:
But succour'd then with a perplexed doubt,
Whether the world did lose, or gaine in this,   15
(Because since now no other way there is,
But goodnesse, to see her, whom all would see,
All must endeavour to be good as shee,)

This great consumption to a fever turn'd,
And so the world had fits; it joy'd, it mourn'd;   20
And, as men thinke, that Agues physick are,
And th'Ague being spent, give over care,
So thou sicke World, mistak'st thy selfe to bee
Well, when alas, thou'rt in a Lethargie.
Her death did wound and tame thee than, and than   25
Thou might'st have better spar'd the Sunne, or Man.
That wound was deep, but 'tis more misery,
That thou hast lost thy sense and memory.
'Twas heavy then to heare thy voyce of mone,
But this is worse, that thou art speechlesse growne.   30
Thou hast forgot thy name, thou hadst; thou wast
Nothing but shee, and her thou hast o'rpast.
For as a child kept from the Font, untill
A prince, expected long, come to fulfill
The ceremonies, thou unnam'd had'st laid,   35
Had not her comming, thee her Palace made:
Her name defin'd thee, gave thee forme, and frame,
And thou forgett'st to celebrate thy name.
Some moneths she hath beene dead (but being dead,
Measures of times are all determined)   40
But long she'ath beene away, long, long, yet none
Offers to tell us who it is that's gone.
But as in states doubtfull of future heires,
When sicknesse without remedie empaires
The present Prince, they're loth it should be said,   45
The Prince doth languish, or the Prince is dead:
So mankinde feeling now a generall thaw,
A strong example gone, equall to law,
The Cyment which did faithfully compact,
And glue all vertues, now resolv'd, and slack'd,   50
Thought it some blasphemy to say sh'was dead,
Or that our weaknesse was discovered
In that confession; therefore spoke no more
Then tongues, the Soule being gone, the losse deplore.
But though it be too late to succour thee,   55
Sicke World, yea, dead, yea putrified, since shee
Thy'intrinsique balme, and thy preservative,
Can never be renew'd, thou never live,

I (since no man can make thee live) will try,
What wee may gaine by thy Anatomy.   60
Her death hath taught us dearely, that thou art
Corrupt and mortall in thy purest part.
Let no man say, the world it selfe being dead,
'Tis labour lost to have discovered
The worlds infirmities, since there is none   65
Alive to study this dissection;

*What life
the world
hath stil.*

For there's a kinde of World remaining still,
Though shee which did inanimate and fill
The world, be gone, yet in this last long night,
Her Ghost doth walke; that is, a glimmering light,   70
A faint weake love of vertue, and of good,
Reflects from her, on them which understood
Her worth; and though she have shut in all day,
The twilight of her memory doth stay;
Which, from the carcasse of the old world, free,   75
Creates a new world, and new creatures bee
Produc'd: the matter and the stuffe of this,
Her vertue, and the forme our practice is:
And though to be thus elemented, arme
These creatures, from home-borne intrinsique harme,   80
(For all assum'd unto this dignitie,
So many weedlesse Paradises bee,
Which of themselves produce no venemous sinne,
Except some forraine Serpent bring it in)
Yet, because outward stormes the strongest breake,   85
And strength it selfe by confidence growes weake,
This new world may be safer, being told

*The
sicknesses
of the
World.
Impossi-
bility of
health.*

The dangers and diseases of the old:
For with due temper men doe then forgoe,
Or covet things, when they their true worth know.   90
There is no health; Physitians say that wee,
At best, enjoy but a neutralitie.
And can there bee worse sicknesse, then to know
That we are never well, nor can be so?
Wee are borne ruinous: poore mothers cry,   95
That children come not right, nor orderly;
Except they headlong come and fall upon
An ominous precipitation.

How witty's ruine! how importunate
Upon mankinde! it labour'd to frustrate   100
Even Gods purpose; and made woman, sent
For mans reliefe, cause of his languishment.
They were to good ends, and they are so still,
But accessory, and principall in ill;
For that first marriage was our funerall: 105
One woman at one blow, then kill'd us all,
And singly, one by one, they kill us now.
We doe delightfully our selves allow
To that consumption; and profusely blinde,
Wee kill our selves to propagate our kinde.   110
And yet we do not that; we are not men:
There is not now that mankinde, which was then,
When as the Sunne and man did seeme to strive,
(Joynt tenants of the world) who should survive;   *Shortnesse*
When, Stagge, and Raven, and the long-liv'd tree,   *of life.*
Compar'd with man, dy'd in minoritie;
When, if a slow pac'd starre had stolne away
From the observers marking, he might stay
Two or three hundred yeares to see't againe,
And then make up his observation plaine;   120
When, as the age was long, the sise was great;
Mans growth confess'd, and recompenc'd the meat;
So spacious and large, that every Soule
Did a faire Kingdome, and large Realme controule:
And when the very stature, thus erect,   125
Did that soule a good way towards heaven direct.
Where is this mankinde now? who lives to age,
Fit to be made *Methusalem* his page?
Alas, we scarce live long enough to try
Whether a true made clocke run right, or lie.   130
Old Grandsires talke of yesterday with sorrow,
And for our children wee reserve to morrow.
So short is life, that every peasant strives,
In a torne house, or field, to have three lives.
And as in lasting, so in length is man   *Smalnesse*
Contracted to an inch, who was a spanne;   *of stature.*
For had a man at first in forrests stray'd,
Or shipwrack'd in the Sea, one would have laid

A wager, that an Elephant, or Whale,
That met him, would not hastily assaile   140
A thing so equall to him: now alas,
The Fairies, and the Pigmies well may passe
As credible; mankinde decayes so soone,
We'are scarce our Fathers shadowes cast at noone:
Onely death addes t'our length: nor are wee growne   145
In stature to be men, till we are none.
But this were light, did our lesse volume hold
All the old Text; or had wee chang'd to gold
Their silver; or dispos'd into lesse glasse
Spirits of vertue, which then scatter'd was.   150
But 'tis not so: w'are not retir'd, but dampt;
And as our bodies, so our mindes are crampt:
'Tis shrinking, not close weaving that hath thus,
In minde, and body both bedwarfed us.
Wee seeme ambitious, Gods whole worke t'undoe;   155
Of nothing hee made us, and we strive too,
To bring our selves to nothing backe; and wee
Doe what wee can, to do't so soone as hee.
With new diseases on our selves we warre,
And with new Physicke, a worse Engin farre.   160
Thus man, this worlds Vice-Emperour, in whom
All faculties, all graces are at home;
And if in other creatures they appeare,
They're but mans Ministers, and Legats there,
To worke on their rebellions, and reduce   165
Them to Civility, and to mans use:
This man, whom God did wooe, and loth t'attend
Till man came up, did downe to man descend,
This man, so great, that all that is, is his,
Oh what a trifle, and poore thing he is!   170
If man were any thing, he's nothing now:
Helpe, or at least some time to wast, allow
T'his other wants, yet when he did depart
With her whom we lament, hee lost his heart.
She, of whom th'Ancients seem'd to prophesie,   175
When they call'd vertues by the name of *shee*;
Shee in whom vertue was so much refin'd,
That for Allay unto so pure a minde

Shee tooke the weaker Sex; shee that could drive
The poysonous tincture, and the staine of *Eve*,   180
Out of her thoughts, and deeds; and purifie
All, by a true religious Alchymie;
Shee, shee is dead; shee's dead: when thou knowest this,
Thou knowest how poore a trifling thing man is.
And learn'st thus much by our Anatomie,   185
The heart being perish'd, no part can be free.
And that except thou feed (not banquet) on
The supernaturall food, Religion,
Thy better Growth growes withered, and scant;
Be more then man, or thou'rt lesse then an Ant.   190
Then, as mankinde, so is the worlds whole frame
Quite out of joynt, almost created lame:
For, before God had made up all the rest,
Corruption entred, and deprav'd the best:
It seis'd the Angels, and then first of all   195
The world did in her cradle take a fall,
And turn'd her braines, and tooke a generall maime,
Wronging each joynt of th'universall frame.
The noblest part, man, felt it first; and than
Both beasts and plants, curst in the curse of man.

Decay of nature in other parts.

So did the world from the first houre decay,
That evening was beginning of the day,
And now the Springs and Sommers which we see,
Like sonnes of women after fiftie bee.
And new Philosophy calls all in doubt,   205
The Element of fire is quite put out;
The Sun is lost, and th'earth, and no mans wit
Can well direct him where to looke for it.
And freely men confesse that this world's spent,
When in the Planets, and the Firmament   210
They seeke so many new; they see that this
Is crumbled out againe to his Atomies.
'Tis all in peeces, all cohaerence gone;
All just supply, and all Relation:
Prince, Subject, Father, Sonne, are things forgot,   215
For every man alone thinkes he hath got
To be a Phœnix, and that then can bee
None of that kinde, of which he is, but hee

This is the worlds condition now, and now
She that should all parts to reunion bow,   220
She that had all Magnetique force alone,
To draw, and fasten sundred parts in one;
She whom wise nature had invented then
When she observ'd that every sort of men
Did in their voyage in this worlds Sea stray,   225
And needed a new compasse for their way;
She that was best, and first originall
Of all faire copies, and the generall
Steward to Fate; she whose rich eyes, and brest
Guilt the West Indies, and perfum'd the East;   230
Whose having breath'd in this world, did bestow
Spice on those Iles, and bad them still smell so,
And that rich Indie which doth gold interre,
Is but as single money, coyn'd from her:
She to whom this world must it selfe refer,   235
As Suburbs, or the Microcosme of her,
Shee, shee is dead; shee's dead: when thou knowst this,
Thou knowst how lame a cripple this world is.
And learn'st thus much by our Anatomy,
That this worlds generall sickenesse doth not lie   240
In any humour, or one certaine part;
But as thou sawest it rotten at the heart,
Thou seest a Hectique feaver hath got hold
Of the whole substance, not to be contrould,
And that thou hast but one way, not t'admit   245
The worlds infection, to be none of it.
For the worlds subtilst immateriall parts
Feele this consuming wound, and ages darts.
Disformity   For the worlds beauty is decai'd, or gone,
of parts.   Beauty, that's colour, and proportion.   250
We thinke the heavens enjoy their Sphericall,
Their round proportion embracing all.
But yet their various and perplexed course,
Observ'd in divers ages, doth enforce
Men to finde out so many Eccentrique parts,   255
Such divers downe-right lines, such overthwarts,
As disproportion that pure forme: It teares
The Firmament in eight and forty sheires,

And in these Constellations then arise
New starres, and old doe vanish from our eyes: 260
As though heav'n suffered earthquakes, peace or war,
When new Towers rise, and old demolish't are.
They have impal'd within a Zodiake
The free-borne Sun, and keepe twelve Signes awake
To watch his steps; the Goat and Crab controule,   265
And fright him backe, who else to either Pole
(Did not these Tropiques fetter him) might runne:
For his course is not round; nor can the Sunne
Perfit a Circle, or maintaine his way
One inch direct; but where he rose to-day   270
He comes no more, but with a couzening line,
Steales by that point, and so is Serpentine:
And seeming weary with his reeling thus,
He meanes to sleepe, being now falne nearer us.
So, of the Starres which boast that they doe runne   275
In Circle still, none ends where he begun.
All their proportion's lame, it sinkes, it swels.
For of Meridians, and Parallels,
Man hath weav'd out a net, and this net throwne
Upon the Heavens, and now they are his owne.   280
Loth to goe up the hill, or labour thus
To goe to heaven, we make heaven come to us.
We spur, we reine the starres, and in their race
They're diversly content t'obey our pace.
But keepes the earth her round proportion still?   285
Doth not a Tenarif, or higher Hill
Rise so high like a Rocke, that one might thinke
The floating Moone would shipwracke there, and sinke?
Seas are so deepe, that Whales being strooke to day,
Perchance to morrow, scarce at middle way   290
Of their wish'd journies end, the bottome, die.
And men, to sound depths, so much line untie,
As one might justly thinke, that there would rise
At end thereof, one of th'Antipodies:
If under all, a Vault infernall bee,   295
(Which sure is spacious, except that we
Invent another torment, that there must
Millions into a strait hot roome be thrust)

Then solidnesse, and roundnesse have no place.
Are these but warts, and pock-holes in the face   300
Of th'earth? Thinke so: but yet confesse, in this

Disorder The worlds proportion disfigured is;
in the   That those two legges whereon it doth rely,
world.   Reward and punishment are bent awry.
And, Oh, it can no more be questioned,   305
That beauties best, proportion, is dead,
Since even griefe it selfe, which now alone
Is left us, is without proportion.
Shee by whose lines proportion should bee
Examin'd, measure of all Symmetree,   310
Whom had that Ancient seen, who thought soules made
Of Harmony, he would at next have said
That Harmony was shee, and thence infer,
That soules were but Resultances from her,
And did from her into our bodies goe,   315
As to our eyes, the formes from objects flow:
Shee, who if those great Doctors truly said
That the Arke to mans proportions was made,
Had been a type for that, as that might be
A type of her in this, that contrary   320
Both Elements, and Passions liv'd at peace
In her, who caus'd all Civill war to cease.
Shee, after whom, what forme so'er we see,
Is discord, and rude incongruitie;
Shee, shee is dead, shee's dead; when thou knowst this   325
Thou knowst how ugly a monster this world is:
And learn'st thus much by our Anatomie,
That here is nothing to enamour thee:
And that, not only faults in inward parts,
Corruptions in our braines, or in our hearts,   330
Poysoning the fountaines, whence our actions spring,
Endanger us: but that if every thing
Be not done fitly'and in proportion,
To satisfie wise, and good lookers on,
(Since most men be such as most thinke they bee)   335
They're lothsome too, by this Deformitee.
For good, and well, must in our actions meete;
Wicked is not much worse than indiscreet.

But beauties other second Element,
Colour, and lustre now, is as neere spent.   340
And had the world his just proportion,
Were it a ring still, yet the stone is gone.
As a compassionate Turcoyse which doth tell
By looking pale, the wearer is not well,
As gold falls sicke being stung with Mercury,   345
All the worlds parts of such complexion bee.
When nature was most busie, the first weeke,
Swadling the new borne earth, God seem'd to like
That she should sport her selfe sometimes, and play,
To mingle, and vary colours every day: 350
And then, as though shee could not make inow,
Himselfe his various Rainbow did allow.
Sight is the noblest sense of any one,
Yet sight hath only colour to feed on,
And colour is decai'd: summers robe growes   355
Duskie, and like an oft dyed garment showes.
Our blushing red, which us'd in cheekes to spred,
Is inward sunke, and only our soules are red.
Perchance the world might have recovered,
If she whom we lament had not beene dead: 360
But shee, in whom all white, and red, and blew
(Beauties ingredients) voluntary grew,
As in an unvext Paradise; from whom
Did all things verdure, and their lustre come,
Whose composition was miraculous,   365
Being all colour, all Diaphanous,
(For Ayre, and Fire but thick grosse bodies were,
And liveliest stones but drowsie, and pale to her,)
Shee, shee, is dead: shee's dead: when thou know'st this,
Thou knowst how wan a Ghost this our world is: 370
And learn'st thus much by our Anatomie,
That it should more affright, then pleasure thee.
And that, since all faire colour then did sinke,
'Tis now but wicked vanitie, to thinke
To colour vicious deeds with good pretence,   *Weaknesse in*
Or with bought colors to illude mens sense.   *the want of*
Nor in ought more this worlds decay appeares,   *correspondence*
Then that her influence the heav'n forbeares,   *of heaven*
                                                       and earth.

Or that the Elements doe not feele this,
The father, or the mother barren is.   380
The cloudes conceive not raine, or doe not powre,
In the due birth time, downe the balmy showre;
Th'Ayre doth not motherly sit on the earth,
To hatch her seasons, and give all things birth;
Spring-times were common cradles, but are tombes;   385
And false-conceptions fill the generall wombes;
Th'Ayre showes such Meteors, as none can see,
Not only what they meane, but what they bee;
Earth such new wormes, as would have troubled much
Th'Ægyptian *Mages* to have made more such.   390
What Artist now dares boast that he can bring
Heaven hither, or constellate any thing,
So as the influence of those starres may bee
Imprison'd in an Hearbe, or Charme, or Tree,
And doe by touch, all which those stars could doe?   395
The art is lost, and correspondence too.
For heaven gives little, and the earth takes lesse,
And man least knowes their trade and purposes.
If this commerce twixt heaven and earth were not
Embarr'd, and all this traffique quite forgot,   400
She, for whose losse we have lamented thus,
Would worke more fully, and pow'rfully on us:
Since herbes, and roots, by dying lose not all,
But they, yea Ashes too, are medicinall,
Death could not quench her vertue so, but that   405
It would be (if not follow'd) wondred at:
And all the world would be one dying Swan,
To sing her funerall praise, and vanish than.
But as some Serpents poyson hurteth not,
Except it be from the live Serpent shot,   410
So doth her vertue need her here, to fit
That unto us; shee working more then it.
But shee, in whom to such maturity
Vertue was growne, past growth, that it must die;
Shc, from whose influence all Impressions came,   415
But, by Receivers impotencies, lame,
Who, though she could not transubstantiate

All states to gold, yet guilded every state,
So that some Princes have some temperance;
Some Counsellers some purpose to advance   420
The common profit; and some people have
Some stay, no more then Kings should give, to crave;
Some women have some taciturnity,
Some nunneries some graines of chastitie.
She that did thus much, and much more could doe,   425
But that our age was Iron, and rustie too,
Shee, shee is dead; shee's dead; when thou knowst this,
Thou knowst how drie a Cinder this world is.
And learn'st thus much by our Anatomy,
That 'tis in vaine to dew, or mollifie   430
It with thy teares, or sweat, or blood: nothing
Is worth our travaile, griefe, or perishing,
But those rich joyes, which did possesse her heart,
Of which she's now partaker, and a part.
But as in cutting up a man that's dead,   *Conclusion.*
The body will not last out, to have read
On every part, and therefore men direct
Their speech to parts, that are of most effect;
So the worlds carcasse would not last, if I
Were punctuall in this Anatomy;   440
Nor smels it well to hearers, if one tell
Them their disease, who faine would think they're well.
Here therefore be the end: And, blessed maid,
Of whom is meant what ever hath been said,
Or shall be spoken well by any tongue,   445
Whose name refines course lines, and makes prose song,
Accept this tribute, and his first yeares rent,
Who till his darke short tapers end be spent,
As oft as thy feast sees this widowed earth,
Will yearely celebrate thy second birth,   450
That is, thy death; for though the soule of man
Be got when man is made, 'tis borne but than
When man doth die; our body's as the wombe,
And, as a Mid-wife, death directs it home.
And you her creatures, whom she workes upon,   455
And have your last, and best concoction
From her example, and her vertue, if you

In reverence to her, do thinke it due,
That no one should her praises thus rehearse,
As matter fit for Chronicle, not verse;   460
Vouchsafe to call to minde that God did make
A last, and lasting'st peece, a song. He spake
To *Moses* to deliver unto all,
That song, because hee knew they would let fall
The Law, the Prophets, and the History,   465
But keepe the song still in their memory:
Such an opinion (in due measure) made
Me this great Office boldly to invade:
Nor could incomprehensiblenesse deterre
Mee, from thus trying to emprison her,   470
Which when I saw that a strict grave could doe,
I saw not why verse might not do so too.
Verse hath a middle nature: heaven keepes Soules,
The Grave keepes bodies, Verse the Fame enroules.

A Funerall Elegie

'Tis lost, to trust a Tombe with such a guest,
Or to confine her in a marble chest.
Alas, what's Marble, Jeat, or Porphyrie,
Priz'd with the Chrysolite of either eye,
Or with those Pearles, and Rubies, which she was?   5
Joyne the two Indies in one Tombe, 'tis glasse;
And so is all to her materials,
Though every inch were ten Escurials,
Yet she's demolish'd: can wee keepe her then
In works of hands, or of the wits of men?   10
Can these memorials, ragges of paper, give
Life to that name, by which name they must live?
Sickly, alas, short-liv'd, aborted bee
Those carcasse verses, whose soule is not shee.
And can shee, who no longer would be shee,   15
Being such a Tabernacle, stoop to be
In paper wrapt; or, when shee would not lie
In such a house, dwell in an Elegie?
But 'tis no matter; wee may well allow

Verse to live so long as the world will now,   20
For her death wounded it. The world containes
Princes for armes, and Counsellors for braines,
Lawyers for tongues, Divines for hearts, and more,
The Rich for stomackes, and for backes, the Poore;
The Officers for hands, Merchants for feet,   25
By which, remote and distant Countries meet.
But those fine spirits which do tune, and set
This Organ, are those peeces which beget
Wonder and love; and these were shee; and shee
Being spent, the world must needs decrepit bee;   30
For since death will proceed to triumph still,
He can finde nothing, after her, to kill,
Except the world it selfe, so great as shee.
Thus brave and confident may Nature bee,
Death cannot give her such another blow,   35
Because shee cannot such another show.
But must wee say she's dead? may't not be said
That as a sundred clocke is peecemeale laid,
Not to be lost, but by the makers hand
Repollish'd, without errour then to stand,   40
Or as the Affrique Niger streame enwombs
It selfe into the earth, and after comes
(Having first made a naturall bridge, to passe
For many leagues) farre greater then it was,
May't not be said, that her grave shall restore   45
Her, greater, purer, firmer, then before?
Heaven may say this, and joy in't, but can wee
Who live, and lacke her, here this vantage see?
What is't to us, alas, if there have beene
An Angell made a Throne, or Cherubin?   50
Wee lose by't: and as aged men are glad
Being tastlesse growne, to joy in joyes they had,
So now the sick starv'd world must feed upon
This joy, that we had her, who now is gone.
Rejoyce then Nature, and this World, that you,   55
Fearing the last fires hastning to subdue
Your force and vigour, ere it were neere gone,
Wisely bestow'd and laid it all on one.
One, whose cleare body was so pure and thinne,

Because it need disguise no thought within.   60
'Twas but a through-light scarfe, her minde t'inroule;
Or exhalation breath'd out from her Soule.
One, whom all men who durst no more, admir'd:
And whom, who ere had worth enough, desir'd;
As when a Temple's built, Saints emulate   65
To which of them, it shall be consecrate.
But, as when heaven lookes on us with new eyes,
Those new starres every Artist exercise,
What place they should assigne to them they doubt,
Argue,'and agree not, till those starres goe out: 70
So the world studied whose this peece should be,
Till shee can be no bodies else, nor shee:
But like a Lampe of Balsamum, desir'd
Rather t'adorne, then last, she soone expir'd,
Cloath'd in her virgin white integritie,   75
For marriage, though it doe not staine, doth dye.
To scape th'infirmities which wait upon
Woman, she went away, before sh'was one;
And the worlds busie noyse to overcome,
Tooke so much death, as serv'd for *opium;*   80
For though she could not, nor could chuse to dye,
She'ath yeelded to too long an extasie:
Hee which not knowing her said History,
Should come to reade the booke of destiny,
How faire, and chast, humble, and high she'ad been,   85
Much promis'd, much perform'd, at not fifteene,
And measuring future things, by things before,
Should turne the leafe to reade, and reade no more,
Would thinke that either destiny mistooke,
Or that some leaves were torne out of the booke.   90
But 'tis not so; Fate did but usher her
To yeares of reasons use, and then inferre
Her destiny to her selfe, which liberty
She tooke but for thus much, thus much to die.
Her modestie not suffering her to bee   95
Fellow-Commissioner with Destinie,
She did no more but die; if after her
Any shall live, which dare true good prefer,
Every such person is her deligate,

T'accomplish that which should have beene her Fate.   100
They shall make up that Booke and shall have thanks
Of Fate, and her, for filling up their blankes.
For future vertuous deeds are Legacies,
Which from the gift of her example rise;
And 'tis in heav'n part of spirituall mirth,   105
To see how well the good play her, on earth.

OF THE PROGRESSE OF THE SOULE

*Wherein, By occasion of the Religious death of
Mistris ELIZABETH DRURY, the incommodities of the Soule in this life,
and her exaltation in the next, are contemplated.*

THE SECOND ANNIVERSARY

The Harbinger to the Progresse

Two soules move here, and mine (a third) must move
Paces of admiration, and of love;
Thy Soule (deare virgin) whose this tribute is,
Mov'd from this mortall Spheare to lively blisse;
And yet moves still, and still aspires to see   5
The worlds last day, thy glories full degree:
Like as those starres which thou o'r-lookest farre,
Are in their place, and yet still moved are:
No soule (whiles with the luggage of this clay
It clogged is) can follow thee halfe way;   10
Or see thy flight, which doth our thoughts outgoe
So fast, that now the lightning moves but slow:
But now thou art as high in heaven flowne
As heaven's from us; what soule besides thine owne
Can tell thy joyes, or say he can relate   15
Thy glorious Journals in that blessed state?
I envie thee (Rich soule) I envy thee,
Although I cannot yet thy glory see:
And thou (great spirit) which hers follow'd hast
So fast, as none can follow thine so fast;   20
So far, as none can follow thine so farr,
(And if this flesh did not the passage barre
Hadst caught her) let me wonder at thy flight
Which long agone hadst lost the vulgar sight,
And now mak'st proud the better eyes, that they   25
Can see thee less'ned in thine ayery way;
So while thou mak'st her soule by progresse knowne
Thou mak'st a noble progresse of thine owne,
From this worlds carkasse having mounted high
To that pure life of immortalitie.   30

Since thine aspiring thoughts themselves so raise
That more may not beseeme a creatures praise,
Yet still thou vow'st her more; and every yeare
Mak'st a new progresse, while thou wandrest here;
Still upward mount; and let thy Makers praise   35
Honor thy Laura, and adorne thy laies.
And since thy Muse her head in heaven shrouds,
Oh let her never stoope below the clouds:
And if those glorious sainted soules may know
Or what wee doe, or what wee sing below,   40
Those acts, those songs shall still content them best
Which praise those awfull Powers that make them blest.

OF THE PROGRESSE OF THE SOULE

The Second Anniversarie

The   Nothing could make me sooner to confesse
entrance.   That this world had an everlastingnesse,
              Then to consider, that a yeare is runne,
              Since both this lower world's, and the Sunnes Sunne,
              The Lustre and the vigor of this All,   5
              Did set; 'twere blasphemie to say, did fall.
              But as a ship which hath strooke saile, doth runne
              By force of that force which before, it wonne:
              Or as sometimes in a beheaded man,
              Though at those two Red seas, which freely ranne,   10
              One from the Trunke, another from the Head,
              His soule be sail'd, to her eternall bed,
              His eyes will twinckle, and his tongue will roll,
              As though he beckned, and cal'd backe his soule,
              He graspes his hands, and he pulls up his feet,   15
              And seemes to reach, and to step forth to meet
              His soule; when all these motions which we saw,
              Are but as Ice, which crackles at a thaw:
              Or as a Lute, which in moist weather, rings
              Her knell alone, by cracking of her strings: 20
              So struggles this dead world, now shee is gone;

For there is motion in corruption.
As some daies are at the Creation nam'd,
Before the Sunne, the which fram'd daies, was fram'd,
So after this Sunne's set, some shew appeares,   25
And orderly vicissitude of yeares.
Yet a new Deluge, and of *Lethe* flood,
Hath drown'd us all, All have forgot all good,
Forgetting her, the maine reserve of all.
Yet in this deluge, grosse and generall,   30
Thou seest me strive for life; my life shall bee,
To be hereafter prais'd, for praysing thee;
Immortall Maid, who though thou would'st refuse
The name of Mother, be unto my Muse
A Father, since her chast Ambition is,   35
Yearely to bring forth such a child as this.
These Hymnes may worke on future wits, and so
May great Grand children of thy prayses grow.
And so, though not revive, embalme and spice
The world, which else would putrifie with vice.   40
For thus, Man may extend thy progeny,
Untill man doe but vanish, and not die.
These Hymnes thy issue, may encrease so long,
As till Gods great *Venite* change the song.
Thirst for that time, O my insatiate soule,
And serve thy thirst, with Gods safe-sealing Bowle.   *A just*
Be thirstie still, and drinke still till thou goe   *disestimation*
To th'only Health, to be Hydroptique so.   *of this world.*
Forget this rotten world; And unto thee
Let thine owne times as an old storie bee.   50
Be not concern'd; studie not why, nor when;
Doe not so much as not beleeve a man.
For though to erre, be worst, to try truths forth,
Is far more businesse, then this world is worth.
The world is but a carkasse; thou art fed   55
By it, but as a worme, that carkasse bred;
And why should'st thou, poore worme, consider more,
When this world will grow better then before,
Then those thy fellow wormes doe thinke upon
That carkasses last resurrection.   60
Forget this world, and scarce thinke of it so,

As of old clothes, cast off a yeare agoe.
To be thus stupid is Alacritie;
Men thus Lethargique have best Memory.
Look upward; that's towards her, whose happy state   65
We now lament not, but congratulate.
Shee, to whom all this world was but a stage,
Where all sat harkning how her youthfull age
Should be emploi'd, because in all shee did,
Some Figure of the Golden times was hid.   70
Who could not lacke, what e'r this world could give,
Because shee was the forme, that made it live;
Nor could complaine, that this world was unfit
To be staid in, then when shee was in it;
Shee that first tried indifferent desires   75
By vertue, and vertue by religious fires,
Shee to whose person Paradise adher'd,
As Courts to Princes, shee whose eyes ensphear'd
Star-light enough, t'have made the South controule,
(Had shee beene there) the Star-full Northerne Pole,   80
Shee, shee is gone; she is gone; when thou knowest this,
What fragmentary rubbidge this world is
Thou knowest, and that it is not worth a thought;
He honors it too much that thinkes it nought.

Contem- Thinke then, my soule, that death is but a Groome,   85
plation of Which brings a Taper to the outward roome,
our state Whence thou spiest first a little glimmering light,
in our And after brings it nearer to thy sight:
death-bed. For such approaches doth heaven make in death.
Thinke thy selfe labouring now with broken breath,   90
And thinke those broken and soft Notes to bee
Division, and thy happyest Harmonie.
Thinke thee laid on thy death-bed, loose and slacke;
And thinke that, but unbinding of a packe,
To take one precious thing, thy soule from thence.   95
Thinke thy selfe parch'd with fevers violence,
Anger thine ague more, by calling it
Thy Physicke; chide the slacknesse of the fit.
Thinke that thou hear'st thy knell, and think no more,
But that, as Bels cal'd thee to Church before,   100
So this, to the Triumphant Church, calls thee.

Thinke Satans Sergeants round about thee bee,
And thinke that but for Legacies they thrust;
Give one thy Pride, to'another give thy Lust:
Give them those sinnes which they gave thee before,   105
And trust th'immaculate blood to wash thy score.
Thinke thy friends weeping round, and thinke that they
Weepe but because they goe not yet thy way.
Thinke that they close thine eyes, and thinke in this,
That they confesse much in the world, amisse,   110
Who dare not trust a dead mans eye with that,
Which they from God, and Angels cover not.
Thinke that they shroud thee up, and think from thence
They reinvest thee in white innocence.
Thinke that thy body rots, and (if so low,   115
Thy soule exalted so, thy thoughts can goe,)
Think thee a Prince, who of themselves create
Wormes which insensibly devoure their State.
Thinke that they bury thee, and thinke that right
Laies thee to sleepe but a Saint Lucies night.   120
Thinke these things cheerefully: and if thou bee
Drowsie or slacke, remember then that shee,
Shee whose Complexion was so even made,
That which of her Ingredients should invade
The other three, no Feare, no Art could guesse: 125
So far were all remov'd from more or lesse.
But as in Mithridate, or just perfumes,
Where all good things being met, no one presumes
To governe, or to triumph on the rest,
Only because all were, no part was best.   130
And as, though all doe know, that quantities
Are made of lines, and lines from Points arise,
None can these lines or quantities unjoynt,
And say this is a line, or this a point,
So though the Elements and Humors were   135
In her, one could not say, this governes there.
Whose even constitution might have wonne
Any disease to venter on the Sunne,
Rather then her: and make a spirit feare,
That hee to disuniting subject were.   140
To whose proportions if we would compare

Cubes, th'are unstable; Circles, Angular;
She who was such a chaine as Fate employes
To bring mankinde all Fortunes it enjoyes;
So fast, so even wrought, as one would thinke,   145
No Accident could threaten any linke;
Shee, shee embrac'd a sicknesse, gave it meat
The purest blood, and breath, that e'r it eate,
And hath taught us, that though a good man hath
Title to heaven, and plead it by his Faith,   150
And though he may pretend a conquest, since
Heaven was content to suffer violence,
Yea though hee plead a long possession too,
(For they're in heaven on earth who heavens workes do)
Though hee had right and power and place, before,   155
Yet Death must usher, and unlocke the doore.

Incommo-
dities of
the Soule
in the
Body.

Thinke further on thy selfe, my Soule, and thinke
How thou at first wast made but in a sinke;
Thinke that it argued some infirmitie,
That those two soules, which then thou foundst in me,   160
Thou fedst upon, and drewst into thee, both
My second soule of sense, and first of growth.
Thinke but how poore thou wast, how obnoxious;
Whom a small lumpe of flesh could poyson thus.
This curded milke, this poore unlittered whelpe   165
My body, could, beyond escape or helpe,
Infect thee with Originall sinne, and thou
Couldst neither then refuse, nor leave it now.
Thinke that no stubborne sullen Anchorit,
Which fixt to a pillar, or a grave, doth sit   170
Bedded, and bath'd in all his ordures, dwels
So fowly as our Soules in their first-built Cels.
Thinke in how poore a prison thou didst lie
After, enabled but to suck, and crie.
Thinke, when'twas growne to most,'twas a poore Inne,   175
A Province pack'd up in two yards of skinne,
And that usurp'd or threatned with the rage
Of sicknesses, or their true mother, Age.

Her
liberty
by death.

But thinke that Death hath now enfranchis'd thee,
Thou hast thy'expansion now, and libertie;   180
Thinke that a rustie Peece, discharg'd, is flowne

In peeces, and the bullet is his owne,
And freely flies: This to thy Soule allow,
Thinke thy shell broke, thinke thy Soule hatch'd but now.
And think this slow-pac'd soule, which late did cleave   185
To'a body, and went but by the bodies leave,
Twenty, perchance, or thirty mile a day,
Dispatches in a minute all the way
Twixt heaven, and earth; she stayes not in the ayre,
To looke what Meteors there themselves prepare;   190
She carries no desire to know, nor sense,
Whether th'ayres middle region be intense;
For th'Element of fire, she doth not know,
Whether she past by such a place or no;
She baits not at the Moone, nor cares to trie   195
Whether in that new world, men live, and die.
Venus retards her not, to'enquire, how shee
Can, (being one starre) Hesper, and Vesper bee;
Hee that charm'd Argus eyes, sweet Mercury,
Workes not on her, who now is growne all eye;   200
Who, if she meet the body of the Sunne,
Goes through, not staying till his course be runne;
Who findes in Mars his Campe no corps of Guard;
Nor is by Jove, nor by his father barr'd;
But ere she can consider how she went,   205
At once is at, and through the Firmament.
And as these starres were but so many beads
Strung on one string, speed undistinguish'd leads
Her through those Spheares, as through the beads, a string,
Whose quick succession makes it still one thing:
As doth the pith, which, lest our bodies slacke,
Strings fast the little bones of necke, and backe;
So by the Soule doth death string Heaven and Earth;
For when our Soule enjoyes this her third birth,
(Creation gave her one, a second, grace,)   215
Heaven is as neare, and present to her face,
As colours are, and objects, in a roome
Where darknesse was before, when Tapers come.
This must, my Soule, thy long-short Progresse bee;
To'advance these thoughts, remember then, that shee,   220
Shee, whose faire body no such prison was,

But that a Soule might well be pleas'd to passe
An age in her; she whose rich beauty lent
Mintage to other beauties, for they went
But for so much as they were like to her;   225
Shee, in whose body (if we dare preferre
This low world, to so high a marke as shee,)
The Westerne treasure, Easterne spicerie,
Europe, and Afrique, and the unknowne rest
Were easily found, or what in them was best;   230
And when w'have made this large discoverie
Of all, in her some one part then will bee
Twenty such parts, whose plenty and riches is
Enough to make twenty such worlds as this;
Shee, whom had they knowne who did first betroth   235
The Tutelar Angels, and assign'd one, both
To Nations, Cities, and to Companies,
To Functions, Offices, and Dignities,
And to each severall man, to him, and him,
They would have given her one for every limbe;   240
She, of whose soule, if wee may say, 'twas Gold,
Her body was th'Electrum, and did hold
Many degrees of that; wee understood
Her by her sight; her pure, and eloquent blood
Spoke in her cheekes, and so distinctly wrought,   245
That one might almost say, her body thought;
Shee, shee, thus richly and largely hous'd, is gone:
And chides us slow-pac'd snailes who crawle upon
Our prisons prison, earth, nor thinke us well,
Longer, then whil'st wee beare our brittle shell.   250

Her But 'twere but little to have chang'd our roome,
ignorance If, as we were in this our living Tombe
in this life Oppress'd with ignorance, wee still were so.
and Poore soule, in this thy flesh what dost thou know?
knowledge Thou know'st thy selfe so little, as thou know'st not,   255
in the How thou didst die, nor how thou wast begot.
next. Thou neither know'st, how thou at first cam'st in,
Nor how thou took'st the poyson of mans sinne.
Nor dost thou, (though thou know'st, that thou art so)
By what way thou art made immortall, know.   260
Thou art too narrow, wretch, to comprehend

Even thy selfe: yea though thou wouldst but bend
To know thy body. Have not all soules thought
For many ages, that our body'is wrought
Of Ayre, and Fire, and other Elements?   265
And now they thinke of new ingredients,
And one Soule thinkes one, and another way
Another thinkes, and 'tis an even lay.
Knowst thou but how the stone doth enter in
The bladders cave, and never breake the skinne?   270
Know'st thou how blood, which to the heart doth flow,
Doth from one ventricle to th'other goe?
And for the putrid stuffe, which thou dost spit,
Know'st thou how thy lungs have attracted it?
There are no passages, so that there is   275
(For ought thou know'st) piercing of substances.
And of those many opinions which men raise
Of Nailes and Haires, dost thou know which to praise?
What hope have wee to know our selves, when wee
Know not the least things, which for our use be?   280
Wee see in Authors, too stiffe to recant,
A hundred controversies of an Ant;
And yet one watches, starves, freeses, and sweats,
To know but Catechismes and Alphabets
Of unconcerning things, matters of fact;   285
How others on our stage their parts did Act;
What *Cæsar* did, yea, and what *Cicero* said.
Why grasse is greene, or why our blood is red,
Are mysteries which none have reach'd unto.
In this low forme, poore soule, what wilt thou doe?   290
When wilt thou shake off this Pedantery,
Of being taught by sense, and Fantasie?
Thou look'st through spectacles; small things seeme great
Below; But up unto the watch-towre get,
And see all things despoyl'd of fallacies: 295
Thou shalt not peepe through lattices of eyes,
Nor heare through Labyrinths of eares, nor learne
By circuit, or collections to discerne.
In heaven thou straight know'st all, concerning it,
And what concernes it not, shalt straight forget.   300
There thou (but in no other schoole) maist bee

Perchance, as learned, and as full, as shee,
Shee who all libraries had throughly read
At home in her owne thoughts, and practised
So much good as would make as many more: 305
Shee whose example they must all implore,
Who would or doe, or thinke well, and confesse
That all the vertuous Actions they expresse,
Are but a new, and worse edition
Of her some one thought, or one action: 310
She who in th'art of knowing Heaven, was growne
Here upon earth, to such perfection,
That she hath, ever since to Heaven she came,
(In a far fairer print,) but read the same:
Shee, shee not satisfied with all this waight,   315
(For so much knowledge, as would over-fraight
Another, did but ballast her) is gone
As well t'enjoy, as get perfection.
And cals us after her, in that shee tooke,
(Taking her selfe) our best, and worthiest booke.   320

Of our
company
in this
life, and
in the
next.

Returne not, my Soule, from this extasie,
And meditation of what thou shalt bee,
To earthly thoughts, till it to thee appeare,
With whom thy conversation must be there.
With whom wilt thou converse? what station   325
Canst thou choose out, free from infection,
That will not give thee theirs, nor drinke in thine?
Shalt thou not finde a spungie slacke Divine
Drinke and sucke in th'instructions of Great men,
And for the word of God, vent them agen?   330
Are there not some Courts (and then, no things bee
So like as Courts) which, in this let us see,
That wits and tongues of Libellers are weake,
Because they do more ill, then these can speake?
The poyson's gone through all, poysons affect   335
Chiefly the chiefest parts, but some effect
In nailes, and haires, yea excrements, will show;
So lyes the poyson of sinne in the most low.
Up, up, my drowsie Soule, where thy new eare
Shall in the Angels songs no discord heare;   340
Where thou shalt see the blessed Mother-maid

Joy in not being that, which men have said.
Where she is exalted more for being good,
Then for her interest of Mother-hood.
Up to those Patriarchs, which did longer sit   345
Expecting Christ, then they'have enjoy'd him yet.
Up to those Prophets, which now gladly see
Their Prophesies growne to be Historie.
Up to th'Apostles, who did bravely runne
All the Suns course, with more light then the Sunne. 350
Up to those Martyrs, who did calmly bleed
Oyle to th'Apostles Lamps, dew to their seed.
Up to those Virgins, who thought, that almost
They made joyntenants with the Holy Ghost,
If they to any should his Temple give.   355
Up, up, for in that squadron there doth live
She, who hath carried thither new degrees
(As to their number) to their dignities.
Shee, who being to her selfe a State, injoy'd
All royalties which any State employ'd;   360
For shee made warres, and triumph'd; reason still
Did not o'rthrow, but rectifie her will:
And she made peace, for no peace is like this,
That beauty, and chastity together kisse:
She did high justice, for she crucified   365
Every first motion of rebellious pride:
And she gave pardons, and was liberall,
For, onely her selfe except, she pardon'd all:
Shee coy'nd, in this, that her impressions gave
To all our actions all the worth they have: 370
She gave protections; the thoughts of her brest
Satans rude Officers could ne'r arrest.
As these prerogatives being met in one,
Made her a soveraigne State; religion
Made her a Church; and these two made her all.   375
She who was all this All, and could not fall
To worse, by company, (for she was still
More Antidote, then all the world was ill,)
Shee, shee doth leave it, and by Death, survive
All this, in Heaven; whither who doth not strive   380
The more, because shees there, he doth not know

Of
essentiall
joy in this
life and in
the next.

That accidentall joyes in Heaven doe grow.
But pause, my soule; And study, ere thou fall
On accidentall joyes, th'essentiall.
Still before Accessories doe abide   385
A triall, must the principall be tride.
And what essentiall joy can'st thou expect
Here upon earth? what permanent effect
Of transitory causes? Dost thou love
Beauty? (And beauty worthy'st is to move)   390
Poore cousened cousenor, *that* she, and *that* thou,
Which did begin to love, are neither now;
You are both fluid, chang'd since yesterday;
Next day repaires, (but ill) last dayes decay.
Nor are, (although the river keepe the name)   395
Yesterdaies waters, and to daies the same.
So flowes her face, and thine eyes, neither now
That Saint, nor Pilgrime, which your loving vow
Concern'd, remaines; but whilst you thinke you bee
Constant, you'are hourely in inconstancie.   400
Honour may have pretence unto our love,
Because that God did live so long above
Without this Honour, and then lov'd it so,
That he at last made Creatures to bestow
Honour on him; not that he needed it,   405
But that, to his hands, man might grow more fit.
But since all Honours from inferiours flow,
(For they doe give it; Princes doe but shew
Whom they would have so honor'd) and that this
On such opinions, and capacities   410
Is built, as rise and fall, to more and lesse:
Alas, 'tis but a casuall happinesse.
Hath ever any man to'himselfe assign'd
This or that happinesse to'arrest his minde,
But that another man which takes a worse,   415
Thinks him a foole for having tane that course?
They who did labour Babels tower to'erect,
Might have considered, that for that effect,
All this whole solid Earth could not allow
Nor furnish forth materialls enow;   420
And that this Center, to raise such a place,

Was farre too little, to have beene the Base;
No more affords this world, foundation
To erect true joy, were all the meanes in one.
But as the Heathen made them severall gods,   425
Of all Gods Benefits, and all his Rods,
(For as the Wine, and Corne, and Onions are
Gods unto them, so Agues bee, and Warre)
And as by changing that whole precious Gold
To such small Copper coynes, they lost the old,   430
And lost their only God, who ever must
Be sought alone, and not in such a thrust:
So much mankinde true happinesse mistakes;
No Joy enjoyes that man, that many makes.
Then, Soule, to thy first pitch worke up againe;   435
Know that all lines which circles doe containe,
For once that they the Center touch, doe touch
Twice the circumference; and be thou such;
Double on heaven thy thoughts on earth emploid;
All will not serve; Only who have enjoy'd   440
The sight of God, in fulnesse, can thinke it;
For it is both the object, and the wit.
This is essentiall joy, where neither hee
Can suffer diminution, nor wee;
'Tis such a full, and such a filling good,   445
Had th'Angels once look'd on him, they had stood.
To fill the place of one of them, or more,
Shee whom wee celebrate, is gone before.
She, who had Here so much essentiall joy,
As no chance could distract, much lesse destroy;   450
Who with Gods presence was acquainted so,
(Hearing, and speaking to him) as to know
His face in any naturall Stone, or Tree,
Better then when in Images they bee:
Who kept by diligent devotion,   455
Gods Image, in such reparation,
Within her heart, that what decay was growne,
Was her first Parents fault, and not her owne:
Who being solicited to any act,
Still heard God pleading his safe precontract;   460
Who by a faithfull confidence, was here

Betroth'd to God, and now is married there;
Whose twilights were more cleare, then our mid-day;
Who dreamt devoutlier, then most use to pray;
Who being here fil'd with grace, yet strove to bee,   465
Both where more grace, and more capacitie
At once is given: she to Heaven is gone,
Who made this world in some proportion
A heaven, and here, became unto us all,
Joy, (as our joyes admit) essentiall.   470

Of
accidentall
joys in
both
places.

But could this low world joyes essentiall touch,
Heavens accidentall joyes would passe them much.
How poore and lame, must then our casuall bee?
If thy Prince will his subjects to call thee
My Lord, and this doe swell thee, thou art than,   475
By being greater, growne to bee lesse Man.
When no Physitian of redresse can speake,
A joyfull casuall violence may breake
A dangerous Apostem in thy breast;
And whil'st thou joyest in this, the dangerous rest,   480
The bag may rise up, and so strangle thee.
What e'r was casuall, may ever bee.
What should the nature change? Or make the same
Certaine, which was but casuall, when it came?
All casuall joy doth loud and plainly say,   485
Only by comming, that it can away.
Only in Heaven joyes strength is never spent;
And accidentall things are permanent.
Joy of a soules arrivall ne'r decaies;
For that soule ever joyes and ever staies.   490
Joy that their last great Consummation
Approaches in the resurrection;
When earthly bodies more celestiall
Shall be, then Angels were, for they could fall;
This kinde of joy doth every day admit   495
Degrees of growth, but none of losing it.
In this fresh joy, 'tis no small part, that shee,
Shee, in whose goodnesse, he that names degree,
Doth injure her; ('Tis losse to be cal'd best,
There where the stuffe is not such as the rest)   500
Shee, who left such a bodie, as even shee

Only in Heaven could learne, how it can bee
Made better; for shee rather was two soules,
Or like to full on both sides written Rols,
Where eyes might reade upon the outward skin,   505
As strong Records for God, as mindes within;
Shee, who by making full perfection grow,
Peeces a Circle, and still keepes it so,
Long'd for, and longing for it, to heaven is gone,
Where shee receives, and gives addition.
Here in a place, where mis-devotion frames   *Conclusion.*
A thousand Prayers to Saints, whose very names
The ancient Church knew not, Heaven knows not yet:
And where, what lawes of Poetry admit,
Lawes of Religion have at least the same,   515
Immortall Maide, I might invoke thy name.
Could any Saint provoke that appetite,
Thou here should'st make me a French convertite.
But thou would'st not; nor would'st thou be content,
To take this, for my second yeares true Rent,   520
Did this Coine beare any other stampe, then his,
That gave thee power to doe, me, to say this.
Since his will is, that to posteritie,
Thou should'st for life, and death, a patterne bee,
And that the world should notice have of this,   525
The purpose, and th'Authoritie is his;
Thou art the proclamation; and I am
The Trumpet, at whose voyce the people came.

EPICEDES AND OBSEQUIES
upon the deaths of sundry Personages

Elegie upon the untimely death of the incomparable Prince Henry

Looke to mee faith, and looke to my faith, God;
For both my centers feele this period.
Of waight one center, one of greatnesse is;
And Reason is that center, Faith is this;
For into'our reason flow, and there do end   5
All, that this naturall world doth comprehend:
Quotidian things, and equidistant hence,
Shut in, for man, in one circumference.
But for th'enormous greatnesses, which are
So disproportion'd, and so angulare,   10
As is Gods essence, place and providence,
Where, how, when, what soules do, departed hence,
These things (eccentrique else) on faith do strike;
Yet neither all, nor upon all, alike.
For reason, put to'her best extension,   15
Almost meetes faith, and makes both centers one.
And nothing ever came so neare to this,
As contemplation of that Prince, wee misse.
For all that faith might credit mankinde could,
Reason still seconded, that this prince would.   20
If then least moving of the center, make
More, then if whole hell belch'd, the world to shake,
What must this do, centers distracted so,
That wee see not what to beleeve or know?
Was it not well beleev'd till now, that hee,   25
Whose reputation was an extasie
On neighbour States, which knew not why to wake,
Till hee discover'd what wayes he would take;
For whom, what Princes angled, when they tryed,
Met a *Torpedo,* and were stupified;   30
And others studies, how he would be bent;
Was his great fathers greatest instrument,
And activ'st spirit, to convey and tie
This soule of peace, through Christianity?

Was it not well beleev'd, that hee would make   35
This generall peace, th'Eternall overtake,
And that his times might have stretch'd out so farre,
As to touch those, of which they emblems are?
For to confirme this just beleefe, that now
The last dayes came, wee saw heav'n did allow,   40
That, but from his aspect and exercise,
In peacefull times, Rumors of war did rise.
But now this faith is heresie: we must
Still stay, and vexe our great-grand-mother, Dust.
Oh, is God prodigall? hath he spent his store   45
Of plagues, on us; and onely now, when more
Would ease us much, doth he grudge misery;
And will not let's enjoy our curse; to dy?
As, for the earth throwne lowest downe of all,
T'were an ambition to desire to fall,   50
So God, in our desire to dye, doth know
Our plot for ease, in being wretched so.
Therefore we live; though such a life wee have,
As but so many mandrakes on his grave.
What had his growth, and generation done,   55
When, what we are, his putrefaction
Sustaines in us; Earth, which griefes animate?
Nor hath our world now, other Soule then that.
And could griefe get so high as heav'n, that Quire,
Forgetting this their new joy, would desire   60
(With griefe to see him) hee had staid below,
To rectifie our errours, They foreknow.
Is th'other center, Reason, faster then?
Where should we looke for that, now we'are not men?
For if our Reason be'our connexion   65
Of causes, now to us there can be none.
For, as, if all the substances were spent,
'Twere madnesse, to enquire of accident,
So is't to looke for reason, hee being gone,
The onely subject reason wrought upon.   70
If Fate have such a chaine, whose divers links
Industrious man discerneth, as hee thinks;
When miracle doth come, and so steale in
A new linke, man knowes not, where to begin:

At a much deader fault must reason bee,   75
Death having broke off such a linke as hee.
But now, for us, with busie proofe to come,
That we'have no reason, would prove wee had some.
So would just lamentations: Therefore wee
May safelyer say, that we are dead, then hee.   80
So, if our griefs wee do not well declare,
We'have double excuse; he'is not dead; and we are.
Yet I would not dy yet; for though I bee
Too narrow, to thinke him, as hee is hee,
(Our Soules best baiting, and midd-period,   85
In her long journey, of considering God)
Yet, (no dishonour) I can reach him thus,
As he embrac'd the fires of love, with us.
Oh may I, (since I live) but see, or heare,
That she-Intelligence which mov'd this spheare,   90
I pardon Fate, my life: Who ere thou bee,
Which hast the noble conscience, thou art shee,
I conjure thee by all the charmes he spoke,
By th'oathes, which onely you two never broke,
By all the soules yee sigh'd, that if you see   95
These lines, you wish, I knew your history.
So much, as you two mutuall heav'ns were here,
I were an Angell, singing what you were.

To the Countesse of Bedford

MADAME,

have learn'd by those lawes wherein I am a little conversant, that hee which
bestowes any cost upon the dead, obliges him which is dead, but not the heire; I
do not therefore send this paper to your Ladyship, that you should thanke mee
or it, or thinke that I thanke you in it; your favours and benefits to mee are so
much above my merits, that they are even above my gratitude, if that were to be
judged by words which must expresse it: But, Madame, since your noble
brothers fortune being yours, the evidences also concerning it are yours, so his
vertue being yours, the evidences concerning it, belong also to you, of which by
our acceptance this may be one peece, in which quality I humbly present it, and
is a testimony how intirely your familie possesseth

Your Ladiships most humble
and thankfull servant
JOHN DONNE.

Obsequies to the Lord Harrington, Brother to the Lady Lucy, Countesse of Bedford

Faire soule, which wast, not onely, as all soules bee,
Then when thou wast infused, harmony,
But did'st continue so; and now dost beare
A part in Gods great organ, this whole Spheare:
If looking up to God; or downe to us,   5
Thou finde that any way is pervious,
Twixt heav'n and earth, and that mans actions doe
Come to your knowledge, and affections too,
See, and with joy, mee to that good degree
Of goodnesse growne, that I can studie thee,   10
And, by these meditations refin'd,
Can unapparell and enlarge my minde,
And so can make by this soft extasie,
This place a map of heav'n, my selfe of thee.
Thou seest mee here at midnight, now all rest;   15
Times dead-low water; when all mindes devest
To morrows businesse, when the labourers have
Such rest in bed, that their last Church-yard grave,
Subject to change, will scarce be'a type of this,
Now when the clyent, whose last hearing is   20
To morrow, sleeps, when the condemned man,
(Who when hee opes his eyes, must shut them than
Againe by death,) although sad watch hee keepe,
Doth practice dying by a little sleepe,
Thou at this midnight seest mee, and as soone   25
As that Sunne rises to mee, midnight's noone,
All the world growes transparent, and I see
Through all, both Church and State, in seeing thee;
And I discerne by favour of this light,
My selfe, the hardest object of the sight.   30
God is the glasse; as thou when thou dost see
Him who sees all, seest all concerning thee,
So, yet unglorified, I comprehend
All, in these mirrors of thy wayes, and end.
Though God be our true glasse, through which we see   35
All, since the beeing of all things is hee,
Yet are the trunkes which doe to us derive

Things, in proportion fit, by perspective,
Deeds of good men; for by their living here,
Vertues, indeed remote, seeme to be neare.   40
But where can I affirme, or where arrest
My thoughts on his deeds? which shall I call best?
For fluid vertue cannot be look'd on,
Nor can endure a contemplation.
As bodies change, and as I do not weare   45
Those Spirits, humors, blood I did last yeare,
And, as if on a streame I fixe mine eye,
That drop, which I looked on, is presently
Pusht with more waters from my sight, and gone,
So in this sea of vertues, can no one   50
Bee'insisted on; vertues, as rivers, passe,
Yet still remaines that vertuous man there was.
And as if man feed on mans flesh, and so
Part of his body to another owe,
Yet at the last two perfect bodies rise,   55
Because God knowes where every Atome lyes;
So, if one knowledge were made of all those,
Who knew his minutes well, hee might dispose
His vertues into names, and ranks; but I
Should injure Nature, Vertue, and Destinie,   60
Should I divide and discontinue so,
Vertue, which did in one intirenesse grow.
For as, hee that would say, spirits are fram'd
Of all the purest parts that can be nam'd,
Honours not spirits halfe so much, as hee   65
Which sayes, they have no parts, but simple bee;
So is't of vertue; for a point and one
Are much entirer then a million.
And had Fate meant to have his vertues told,
It would have let him live to have beene old;   70
So, then that vertue in season, and then this,
We might have seene, and said, that now he is
Witty, now wise, now temperate, now just:
In good short lives, vertues are faine to thrust,
And to be sure betimes to get a place,   75
When they would exercise, lacke time, and space.
So was it in this person, forc'd to bee

For lack of time, his owne epitome:
So to exhibit in few yeares as much,
As all the long breath'd Chronicles can touch.   80
As when an Angell down from heav'n doth flye,
Our quick thought cannot keepe him company,
Wee cannot thinke, now hee is at the Sunne,
Now through the Moon, now he through th'aire doth run,
Yet when he's come, we know he did repaire   85
To all twixt Heav'n and Earth, Sunne, Moon, and Aire;
And as this Angell in an instant knowes,
And yet wee know, this sodaine knowledge growes
By quick amassing severall formes of things,
Which he successively to order brings;   90
When they, whose slow-pac'd lame thoughts cannot goe
So fast as hee, thinke that he doth not so;
Just as a perfect reader doth not dwell,
On every syllable, nor stay to spell,
Yet without doubt, hee doth distinctly see   95
And lay together every A, and B;
So, in short liv'd good men, is'not understood
Each severall vertue, but the compound good;
For, they all vertues paths in that pace tread,
As Angells goe, and know, and as men read.   100
O why should then these men, these lumps of Balme
Sent hither, this worlds tempests to becalme,
Before by deeds they are diffus'd and spred,
And so make us alive, themselves be dead?
O Soule, O circle, why so quickly bee   105
Thy ends, thy birth and death, clos'd up in thee?
Since one foot of thy compasse still was plac'd
In heav'n, the other might securely'have pac'd
In the most large extent, through every path,
Which the whole world, or man the abridgment hath.   110
Thou knowst, that though the tropique circles have
(Yea and those small ones which the Poles engrave,)
All the same roundnesse, evennesse, and all
The endlesnesse of the equinoctiall;
Yet, when we come to measure distances,   115
How here, how there, the Sunne affected is,
When he doth faintly worke, and when prevaile,

Onely great circles, then can be our scale:
So, though thy circle to thy selfe expresse
All, tending to thy endlesse happinesse,   120
And wee, by our good use of it may trye,
Both how to live well young, and how to die,
Yet, since we must be old, and age endures
His Torrid Zone at Court, and calentures
Of hot ambitions, irreligions ice,   125
Zeales agues, and hydroptique avarice,
Infirmities which need the scale of truth,
As well as lust, and ignorance of youth;
Why did'st thou not for these give medicines too,
And by thy doing tell us what to doe?   130
Though as small pocket-clocks, whose every wheele
Doth each mismotion and distemper feele,
Whose *hand* gets shaking palsies, and whose *string*
(His sinewes) slackens, and whose *Soule,* the spring,
Expires, or languishes, whose pulse, the *flye,*   135
Either beates not, or beates unevenly,
Whose voice, the *Bell,* doth rattle, or grow dumbe,
Or idle,'as men, which to their last houres come,
If these clockes be not wound, or be wound still,
Or be not set, or set at every will;   140
So, youth is easiest to destruction,
If then wee follow all, or follow none.
Yet, as in great clocks, which in steeples chime,
Plac'd to informe whole towns, to'imploy their time,
An error doth more harme, being generall,   145
When, small clocks faults, only'on the wearer fall;
So worke the faults of age, on which the eye
Of children, servants, or the State relie.
Why wouldst not thou then, which hadst such a soule,
A clock so true, as might the Sunne controule,   150
And daily hadst from him, who gave it thee,
Instructions, such as it could never be
Disordered, stay here, as a generall
And great Sun-dyall, to have set us All?
O why wouldst thou be any instrument   155
To this unnaturall course, or why consent
To this, not miracle, but Prodigie,

That when the ebbs, longer then flowings be,
Vertue, whose flood did with thy youth begin,
Should so much faster ebb out, then flow in?   160
Though her flood was blowne in, by thy first breath,
All is at once sunke in the whirle-poole death.
Which word I would not name, but that I see
Death, else a desert, growne a Court by thee.
Now I grow sure, that if a man would have   165
Good companie, his entry is a grave.
Mee thinkes all Cities, now, but Anthills bee,
Where, when the severall labourers I see,
For children, house, Provision, taking paine,
They'are all but Ants, carrying eggs, straw, and grain;   170
And Church-yards are our cities, unto which
The most repaire, that are in goodnesse rich.
There is the best concourse, and confluence,
There are the holy suburbs, and from thence
Begins Gods City, New Jerusalem,   175
Which doth extend her utmost gates to them.
At that gate then Triumphant soule, dost thou
Begin thy Triumph; But since lawes allow
That at the Triumph day, the people may,
All that they will, 'gainst the Triumpher say,   180
Let me here use that freedome, and expresse
My griefe, though not to make thy Triumph lesse.
By law, to Triumphs none admitted bee,
Till they as Magistrates get victorie;
Though then to thy force, all youthes foes did yield,   185
Yet till fit time had brought thee to that field,
To which thy ranke in this state destin'd thee,
That there thy counsailes might get victorie,
And so in that capacitie remove
All jealousies 'twixt Prince and subjects love,   190
Thou could'st no title, to this triumph have,
Thou didst intrude on death, usurp'dst a grave.
Then (though victoriously) thou hadst fought as yet
But with thine owne affections, with the heate
Of youths desires, and colds of ignorance,   195
But till thou should'st successefully advance
Thine armes 'gainst forraine enemies, which are

Both Envy, and acclamations popular,
(For, both these engines equally defeate,
Though by-a divers Mine, those which are great,)   200
Till then thy War was but a civill War,
For which to Triumph, none admitted are.
No more are they, who though with good successe,
In a defensive war, their power expresse;
Before men triumph, the dominion   205
Must be *enlarg'd,* and not *preserv'd* alone;
Why should'st thou then, whose battailes were to win
Thy selfe, from those straits nature put thee in,
And to deliver up to God that state,
Of which he gave thee the vicariate,   210
(Which is thy soule and body) as intire
As he, who takes endeavours, doth require,
But didst not stay, t'enlarge his kingdome too,
By making others, what thou didst, to doe;
Why shouldst thou Triumph now, when Heav'n no more
Hath got, by getting thee, then't had before?
For, Heav'n and thou, even when thou livedst here,
Of one another in possession were.
But this from Triumph most disables thee,
That, that place which is conquered, must bee   220
Left safe from present warre, and likely doubt
Of imminent commotions to breake out:
And hath he left us so? or can it bee
His territory was no more then Hee?
No, we were all his charge, the Diocis   225
Of ev'ry exemplar man, the whole world is,
And he was joyned in commission
With Tutelar Angels, sent to every one.
But though this freedome to upbraid, and chide
Him who Triumph'd, were lawfull, it was ty'd   230
With this, that it might never reference have
Unto the Senate, who this triumph gave;
Men might at Pompey jeast, but they might not
At that authoritie, by which he got
Leave to Triumph, before, by age, he might;   235
So, though, triumphant soule, I dare to write,
Mov'd with a reverentiall anger, thus,

That thou so earely wouldst abandon us;
Yet I am farre from daring to dispute
With that great soveraigntie, whose absolute   240
Prerogative hath thus dispens'd with thee,
'Gainst natures lawes, which just impugners bee
Of early triumphs; And I (though with paine)
Lessen our losse, to magnifie thy gaine
Of triumph, when I say, It was more fit,   245
That all men should lacke thee, then thou lack it.
Though then in our time, be not suffered
That testimonie of love, unto the dead,
To die with them, and in their graves be hid,
As Saxon wives, and French soldurii did;   250
And though in no degree I can expresse
Griefe in great Alexanders great excesse,
Who at his friends death, made whole townes devest
Their walls and bullwarks which became them best:
Doe not, faire soule, this sacrifice refuse,   255
That in thy grave I doe interre my Muse,
Who, by my griefe, great as thy worth, being cast
Behind hand, yet hath spoke, and spoke her last.

Elegie on the Lady Marckham

Man is the World, and death th'Ocean,
   To which God gives the lower parts of man.
This Sea invirons all, and though as yet
   God hath set markes, and bounds, twixt us and it,
Yet doth it rore, and gnaw, and still pretend,   5
   And breaks our bankes, when ere it takes a friend.
Then our land waters (teares of passion) vent;
   Our waters, then, above our firmament,
(Teares which our Soule doth for her sins let fall)
   Take all a brackish tast, and Funerall,   10
And even these teares, which should wash sin, are sin.
   We, after Gods *Noe*, drowne our world againe.
Nothing but man of all invenom'd things
   Doth worke upon itselfe, with inborne stings.

Teares are false Spectacles, we cannot see 15
  Through passions mist, what wee are, or what shee.
In her this sea of death hath made no breach,
  But as the tide doth wash the slimie beach,
And leaves embroder'd workes upon the sand,
  So is her flesh refin'd by deaths cold hand. 20
As men of China,'after an ages stay,
  Do take up Porcelane, where they buried Clay;
So at this grave, her limbecke, which refines
  The Diamonds, Rubies, Saphires, Pearles, and Mines,
Of which this flesh was, her soule shall inspire 25
  Flesh of such stuffe, as God, when his last fire
Annuls this world, to recompence it, shall,
  Make and name then, th'Elixar of this All.
They say, the sea, when it gaines, loseth too;
  If carnall Death (the younger brother) doe 30
Usurpe the body,'our soule, which subject is
  To th'elder death, by sinne, is freed by this;
They perish both, when they attempt the just;
  For, graves our trophies are, and both deaths dust.
So, unobnoxious now, she'hath buried both; 35
  For, none to death sinnes, that to sinne is loth,
Nor doe they die, which are not loth to die;
  So hath she this, and that virginity.
Grace was in her extremely diligent,
  That kept her from sinne, yet made her repent. 40
Of what small spots pure white complaines! Alas,
  How little poyson cracks a christall glasse!
She sinn'd, but just enough to let us see
  That God's word must be true, All, sinners be.
Soe much did zeale her conscience rarefie, 45
  That, extreme truth lack'd little of a lye,
Making omissions, acts; laying the touch
  Of sinne, on things that sometimes may be such.
As *Moses* Cherubines, whose natures doe
  Surpasse all speed, by him are winged too: 50
So would her soule, already'in heaven, seeme then,
  To clyme by teares, the common staires of men.
How fit she was for God, I am content
  To speake, that Death his vaine hast may repent.

How fit for us, how even and how sweet,   55
   How good in all her titles, and how meet,
To have reform'd this forward heresie,
   That women can no parts of friendship bee;
How Morall, how Divine shall not be told,
   Lest they that heare her vertues, thinke her old: 60
And lest we take Deaths part, and make him glad
   Of such a prey, and to his tryumph adde.

Elegie on Mistress Boulstred

Death I recant, and say, unsaid by mee
   What ere hath slip'd, that might diminish thee.
Spirituall treason, atheisme 'tis, to say,
   That any can thy Summons disobey.
Th'earths face is but thy Table; there are set   5
   Plants, cattell, men, dishes for Death to eate.
In a rude hunger now hee millions drawes
   Into his bloody, or plaguy, or sterv'd jawes.
Now hee will seeme to spare, and doth more wast,
   Eating the best first, well preserv'd to last.   10
Now wantonly he spoiles, and eates us not,
   But breakes off friends, and lets us peecemeale rot.
Nor will this earth serve him; he sinkes the deepe
   Where harmelesse fish monastique silence keepe,
Who (were Death dead) by Roes of living sand,   15
   Might spunge that element, and make it land.
He rounds the aire, and breakes the hymnique notes
   In birds (Heavens choristers,) organique throats,
Which (if they did not dye) might seeme to bee
   A tenth ranke in the heavenly hierarchie.   20
O strong and long-liv'd death, how cam'st thou in?
   And how without Creation didst begin?
Thou hast, and shalt see dead, before thou dyest,
   All the foure Monarchies, and Antichrist.
How could I thinke thee nothing, that see now   25
   In all this All, nothing else is, but thou.
Our births and lives, vices, and vertues, bee
   Wastfull consumptions, and degrees of thee.

For, wee to live, our bellowes weare, and breath,
   Nor are wee mortall, dying, dead, but death.   30
And though thou beest, O mighty bird of prey,
   So much reclaim'd by God, that thou must lay
All that thou kill'st at his feet, yet doth hee
   Reserve but few, and leaves the most to thee.
And of those few, now thou hast overthrowne   35
   One whom thy blow makes, not ours, nor thine own.
She was more stories high: hopelesse to come
   To her Soule, thou'hast offer'd at her lower roome.
Her Soule and body was a King and Court:
   But thou hast both of Captaine mist and fort.   40
As houses fall not, though the King remove,
   Bodies of Saints rest for their soules above.
Death gets 'twixt soules and bodies such a place
   As sinne insinuates 'twixt just men and grace,
Both worke a separation, no divorce.   45
   Her Soule is gone to usher up her corse,
Which shall be'almost another soule, for there
   Bodies are purer, then best Soules are here.
Because in her, her virtues did outgoe
   Her yeares, would'st thou, O emulous death, do so?   50
And kill her young to thy losse? must the cost
   Of beauty,'and wit, apt to doe harme, be lost?
What though thou found'st her proofe 'gainst sins of youth?
   Oh, every age a diverse sinne pursueth.
Thou should'st have stay'd, and taken better hold,   55
   Shortly, ambitious; covetous, when old,
She might have prov'd: and such devotion
   Might once have stray'd to superstition.
If all her vertues must have growne, yet might
   Abundant virtue'have bred a proud delight.   60
Had she persever'd just, there would have bin
   Some that would sinne, mis-thinking she did sinne.
Such as would call her friendship, love, and faine
   To sociablenesse, a name profane;
Or sinne, by tempting, or, not daring that,   65
   By wishing, though they never told her what.
Thus might'st thou'have slain more soules, had'st thou not crost
   Thy selfe, and to triumph, thine army lost.

Yet though these wayes be lost, thou hast left one,
    Which is, immoderate griefe that she is gone.   70
But we may scape that sinne, yet weepe as much,
    Our teares are due, because we are not such.
Some teares, that knot of friends, her death must cost,
    Because the chaine is broke, though no linke lost.

Elegie. Death

Language thou art too narrow, and too weake
    To ease us now; great sorrow cannot speake;
If we could sigh out accents, and weepe words,
    Griefe weares, and lessens, that tears breath affords.
Sad hearts, the lesse they seeme the more they are,   5
    (So guiltiest men stand mutest at the barre)
Not that they know not, feele not their estate,
    But extreme sense hath made them desperate.
Sorrow, to whom we owe all that we bee;
    Tyrant, in the fift and greatest Monarchy,   10
Was't, that she did possesse all hearts before,
    Thou hast kil'd her, to make thy Empire more?
Knew'st thou some would, that knew her not, lament,
    As in a deluge perish th'innocent?
Was't not enough to have that palace wonne,   15
    But thou must raze it too, that was undone?
Had'st thou staid there, and look'd out at her eyes,
    All had ador'd thee that now from thee flies,
For they let out more light, then they tooke in,
    They told not when, but did the day beginne.   20
She was too Saphirine, and cleare for thee;
    Clay, flint, and jeat now thy fit dwellings be;
Alas, shee was too pure, but not too weake;
    Who e'r saw Christall Ordinance but would break?
And if wee be thy conquest, by her fall   25
    Th'hast lost thy end, for in her perish all;
Or if we live, we live but to rebell,
    They know her better now, that knew her well.
If we should vapour out, and pine, and die;
    Since, shee first went, that were not miserie.   30

Shee chang'd our world with hers; now she is gone,
   Mirth and prosperity is oppression;
For of all morall vertues she was all,
   The Ethicks speake of vertues Cardinall.
Her soule was Paradise; the Cherubin   35
   Set to keepe it was grace, that kept out sinne.
Shee had no more then let in death, for wee
   All reape consumption from one fruitfull tree.
God tooke her hence, lest some of us should love
   Her, like that plant, him and his lawes above,   40
And when wee teares, hee mercy shed in this,
   To raise our mindes to heaven where now she is;
Who if her vertues would have let her stay
   Wee'had had a Saint, have now a holiday.
Her heart was that strange bush, where, sacred fire,   45
   Religion, did not consume, but'inspire
Such piety, so chast use of Gods day,
   That what we turne to *feast*, she turn'd to *pray*,
And did prefigure here, in devout tast,
   The rest of her high Sabaoth, which shall last.   50
Angels did hand her up, who next God dwell,
   (For she was of that order whence most fell)
Her body left with us, lest some had said,
   Shee could not die, except they saw her dead;
For from lesse vertue, and lesse beautiousnesse,   55
   The Gentiles fram'd them Gods and Goddesses.
The ravenous earth that now wooes her to be
   Earth too, will be a *Lemnia;* and the tree
That wraps that christall in a wooden Tombe,
   Shall be tooke up spruce, fill'd with diamond;   60
And we her sad glad friends all beare a part
   Of griefe, for all would waste a Stoicks heart.

Elegie on the L. C.

Sorrow, who to this house scarce knew the way:
Is, Oh, heire of it, our All is his prey.
This strange chance claimes strange wonder, and to us
Nothing can be so strange, as to weepe thus.

'Tis well his lifes loud speaking workes deserve,   5
And give praise too, our cold tongues could not serve:
'Tis well, hee kept teares from our eyes before,
That to fit this deepe ill, we might have store.
Oh, if a sweet briar, climbe up by'a tree,
If to a paradise that transplanted bee,   10
Or fell'd, and burnt for holy sacrifice,
Yet, that must wither, which by it did rise,
As we for him dead: though no familie
Ere rigg'd a soule for heavens discoverie
With whom more Venturers more boldly dare   15
Venture their states, with him in joy to share.
Wee lose what all friends lov'd, him; he gaines now
But life by death, which worst foes would allow,
If hee could have foes, in whose practise grew
All vertues, whose names subtile Schoolmen knew.   20
What ease, can hope that wee shall see'him, beget,
When wee must die first, and cannot dye yet?
His children are his pictures, Oh they bee
Pictures of him dead, senselesse, cold as he.
Here needs no marble Tombe, since hee is gone,   25
He, and about him, his, are turn'd to stone.

An hymne to the Saints, and to Marquesse Hamylton
To Sir Robert Carr

SIR,

*I presume you rather try what you can doe in me, then what I
can doe in verse; you know my uttermost when it was best, and
even then I did best when I had least truth for my subjects. In
this present case there is so much truth as it defeats all Poetry.
Call therefore this paper by what name you will, and, if it bee
not worthy of him, nor of you, nor of mee, smother it, and bee
that the sacrifice. If you had commanded mee to have embraced
the obligation with more alacrity; But, I thanke you that would
command me that which I was loath to doe, for, even that hath
given a tincture of merit to the obedience of*

*Your poore friend and
servant in Christ Jesus
J. D.*

Whether that soule which now comes up to you
Fill any former ranke or make a new;
Whether it take a name nam'd there before,
Or be a name it selfe, and *order* more
Then was in heaven till now; (for may not hee   5
Bee so, if every severall Angell bee
A *kind* alone?) What ever order grow
Greater by him in heaven, wee doe not so.
One of your orders growes by his accesse;
But, by his losse grow all our *orders* lesse;   10
The name of *Father, Master, Friend,* the name
Of *Subject* and of *Prince,* in one are lame;
Faire mirth is dampt, and conversation black,
The *household* widdow'd, and the *garter* slack;
The *Chappell* wants an eare, *Councell* a tongue;   15
Story, a theame; and *Musicke* lacks a song;
Blest *order* that hath him! the losse of him
Gangreend all *Orders* here; all lost a limbe.
Never made body such hast to confesse
What a soule was; All former comelinesse   20
Fled, in a minute, when the soule was gone,
And, having lost that beauty, would have none;
So fell our *Monasteries,* in one instant growne
Not to lesse houses, but, to heapes of stone;
So sent this body that faire forme it wore,   25
Unto the spheare of formes, and doth (before
His soule shall fill up his sepulchrall stone,)
Anticipate a Resurrection;
For, as in his fame, now, his soule is here,
So, in the forme thereof his bodie's there.   30
And if, faire soule, not with first *Innocents*
Thy station be, but with the *Penitents,*
(And, who shall dare to aske then when I am
Dy'd scarlet in the blood of that pure Lambe,
Whether that colour, which is scarlet then,   35
Were black or white before in eyes of men?)
When thou rememb'rest what sins thou didst finde
Amongst those many friends now left behinde,
And seest such sinners as they are, with thee
Got thither by repentance, Let it bee   40

Got thither by repentance, Let it bee   40
Thy wish to wish all there, to wish them cleane;
Wish *him* a *David, her* a *Magdalen.*

Epitaph on Himself

To the Countesse of Bedford

MADAME,
That I might make your Cabinet my tombe,
And for my fame which I love next my soule,
Next to my soule provide the happiest roome,
    Admit to that place this last funerall Scrowle.
        Others by Wills give Legacies, but I   5
        Dying, of you doe beg a Legacie.

Omnibus

My fortune and my will this custome breake,
When we are senselesse grown to make stones speak,
Though no stone tell thee what I was, yet thou
In my graves inside see what thou art now:
Yet th'art not yet so good; till us death lay   5
To ripe and mellow there, w'are stubborne clay,
Parents make us earth, and soules dignifie
Us to be glasse, here to grow gold we lie;
Whilst in our soules sinne bred and pampered is,
Our soules become worme-eaten Carkasses;   10
So we our selves miraculously destroy.
Here bodies with lesse miracle enjoy
Such priviledges, enabled here to scale
Heaven, when the Trumpets ayre shall them exhale.
Heare this, and mend thy selfe, and thou mendst me,   15
By making me being dead, doe good to thee,
    And thinke me well compos'd, that I could now
    A last-sicke houre to syllables allow.

INFINITATI SACRUM

16. Augusti 1601
METEMPSYCHOSIS
Poema Satyricon

Epistle

OTHERS at the Porches and entries of their Buildings set their Armes; I, my picture; if any colours can deliver a minde so plaine, and flat, and through light as mine. Naturally at a new Author, I doubt, and sticke, and doe not say quickly, good. I censure much and taxe; And this liberty costs mee more then others, by how much my owne things are worse then others. Yet I would not be so rebellious against my selfe, as not to doe it, since I love it; nor so unjust to others, to do it *sine talione*. As long as I give them as good hold upon mee, they must pardon mee my bitings. I forbid no reprehender, but him that like the Trent Councell forbids not bookes, but Authors, damning what ever such a name hath or shall write. None writes so ill, that he gives not some thing exemplary, to follow, or flie. Now when I beginne this booke, I have no purpose to come into any mans debt; how my stocke will hold out I know not; perchance waste, perchance increase in use; if I doe borrow any thing of Antiquitie, besides that I make account that I pay it to posterity, with as much and as good: You shall still finde mee to acknowledge it, and to thanke not him onely that hath digg'd out treasure for mee, but that hath lighted mee a candle to the place. All which I will bid you remember, (for I will have no such Readers as I can teach) is, that the Pithagorian doctrine doth not onely carry one soule from man to man, nor man to beast, but indifferently to plants also: and therefore you must not grudge to finde the same soule in an Emperour, in a Post-horse, and in a Mucheron, since no unreadinesse in the soule, but an indisposition in the organs workes this. And therefore though this soule could not move when it was a Melon, yet it may remember, and now tell mee, at what lascivious banquet it was serv'd. And though it could not speake, when it was a spider, yet it can remember, and now tell me, who used it for poyson to attaine dignitie. How ever the bodies have dull'd her other faculties, her memory hath ever been her owne, which makes me so seriously deliver you by her relation all her passages from her first making when shee was that apple which Eve eate, to this time when shee is hee, whose life you shall finde in the end of this booke.

The Progresse of the Soule

First Song

I

I Sing the progresse of a deathlesse soule,
Whom Fate, which God made, but doth not controule,
Plac'd in most shapes; all times before the law
Yoak'd us, and when, and since, in this I sing.
And the great world to his aged evening;   5
From infant morne, through manly noone I draw.
What the gold Chaldee, or silver Persian saw,
Greeke brasse, or Roman iron, is in this one;
A worke t'outweare *Seths* pillars, bricke and stone,
      And (holy writt excepted) made to yeeld to none.   10

II

Thee, eye of heaven, this great Soule envies not,
By thy male force, is all wee have, begot.
In the first East, thou now beginst to shine,
Suck'st early balme, and Iland spices there,
And wilt anon in thy loose-rein'd careere   15
At Tagus, Po, Sene, Thames, and Danow dine,
And see at night thy Westerne land of Myne,
Yet hast thou not more nations seene then shee,
That before thee, one day beganne to bee,
      And thy fraile light being quench'd, shall long,   20
            long out live thee.

III

Nor, holy *Janus* in whose soveraigne boate
The Church, and all the Monarchies did floate;
That swimming Colledge, and free Hospitall
Of all mankinde, that cage and vivarie
Of fowles, and beasts, in whose wombe, Destinie   25
Us, and our latest nephewes did install
(From thence are all deriv'd, that fill this All,)
Did'st thou *in* that great stewardship embarke
So diverse shapes into that floating parke,
      As have beene moved, and inform'd by this heavenly sparke.

IV

Great Destiny the Commissary of God,
That hast mark'd out a path and period
For every thing; who, where wee of-spring tooke,
Our wayes and ends seest at one instant; Thou
Knot of all causes, thou whose changelesse brow   35
Ne'r smiles nor frownes, O vouch thou safe to looke
And shew my story, in thy eternall booke:
That (if my prayer be fit) I may'understand
So much my selfe, as to know with what hand,
    How scant, or liberall this my lifes race is spand.   40

V

To my sixe lustres almost now outwore,
Except thy booke owe mee so many more,
Except my legend be free from the letts
Of steepe ambition, sleepie povertie,
Spirit-quenching sicknesse, dull captivitie,   45
Distracting businesse, and from beauties nets,
And all that calls from this, and to others whets,
O let me not launch out, but let mee save
Th'expense of braine and spirit; that my grave
    His right and due, a whole unwasted man may have.   50

VI

But if my dayes be long, and good enough,
In vaine this sea shall enlarge, or enrough
It selfe; for I will through the wave, and fome,
And shall, in sad lone wayes a lively spright,
Make my darke heavy Poëm light, and light.   55
For though through many streights, and lands I roame,
I launch at paradise, and I saile towards home;
The course I there began, shall here be staid,
Sailes hoised there, stroke here, and anchors laid
    In Thames, which were at Tigrys, and Euphrates waide.

VII

For the great soule which here amongst us now
Doth dwell, and moves that hand, and tongue, and brow,
Which, as the Moone the sea, moves us; to heare
Whose story, with long patience you will long;
(For 'tis the crowne, and last straine of my song)   65
This soule to whom *Luther,* and *Mahomet* were
Prisons of flesh; this soule which oft did teare,
And mend the wracks of th'Empire, and late Rome,
And liv'd when every great change did come,
  Had first in paradise, a low, but fatall roome.   70

VIII

Yet no low roome, nor then the greatest, lesse,
If (as devout and sharpe men fitly guesse)
That Crosse, our joy, and griefe, where nailes did tye
That All, which alwayes was all, every where;
Which could not sinne, and yet all sinnes did beare;   75
Which could not die, yet could not chuse but die;
Stood in the selfe same roome in Calvarie,
Where first grew the forbidden learned tree,
For on that tree hung in security
  This Soule, made by the Makers will from pulling free.   80

IX

Prince of the orchard, faire as dawning morne,
Fenc'd with the law, and ripe as soone as borne
That apple grew, which this Soule did enlive,
Till the then climing serpent, that now creeps
For that offence, for which all mankinde weepes,   85
Tooke it, and t'her whom the first man did wive
(Whom and her race, only forbiddings drive)
He gave it, she t'her husband, both did eate;
So perished the eaters, and the meate:
  And wee (for treason taints the blood) thence die and sweat.

X

Man all at once was there by woman slaine,
And one by one we'are here slaine o'er againe
By them. The mother poison'd the well-head,
The daughters here corrupt us, Rivolets;
No smalnesse scapes, no greatnesse breaks their nets;   95
She thrust us out, and by them we are led
Astray, from turning to whence we are fled.
Were prisoners Judges, 'twould seeme rigorous,
Shee sinn'd, we beare; part of our paine is, thus
   To love them, whose fault to this painfull love yoak'd us.

XI

So fast in us doth this corruption grow,
That now wee dare aske why wee should be so.
Would God (disputes the curious Rebell) make
A law, and would not have it kept? Or can
His creatures will, crosse his? Of every man   105
For one, will God (and be just) vengeance take?
Who sinn'd? t'was not forbidden to the snake
Nor her, who was not then made; nor is't writ
That Adam cropt, or knew the apple; yet
   The worme and she, and he, and wee endure for it.   110

XII

But snatch mee heavenly Spirit from this vaine
Reckoning their vanities, lesse is their gaine
Then hazard still, to meditate on ill,
Though with good minde; their reasons, like those toyes
Of glassie bubbles, which the gamesome boyes   115
Stretch to so nice a thinnes through a quill
That they themselves breake, doe themselves spill:
Arguing is heretiques game, and Exercise
As wrastlers, perfects them; Not liberties
   Of speech, but silence; hands, not tongues, end heresies.

XIII

Just in that instant when the serpents gripe,
Broke the slight veines, and tender conduit-pipe,
Through which this soule from the trees root did draw
Life, and growth to this apple, fled away
This loose soule, old, one and another day.   125
As lightning, which one scarce dares say, he saw,
'Tis so soone gone, (and better proofe the law
Of sense, then faith requires) swiftly she flew
To a darke and foggie Plot; Her, her fates threw
    There through th'earths pores, and in a Plant   130
        hous'd her anew.

XIV

The plant thus abled, to it selfe did force
A place, where no place was; by natures course
As aire from water, water fleets away
From thicker bodies, by this root throng'd so
His spungie confines gave him place to grow: 135
Just as in our streets, when the people stay
To see the Prince, and have so fill'd the way
That weesels scarce could passe, when she comes nere
They throng and cleave up, and a passage cleare,
    As if, for that time, their round bodies flatned were.   140

XV

His right arme he thrust out towards the East,
West-ward his left; th'ends did themselves digest
Into ten lesser strings, these fingers were:
And as a slumberer stretching on his bed,
This way he this, and that way scattered   145
His other legge, which feet with toes upbeare.
Grew on his middle parts, the first day, haire,
To show, that in loves businesse hee should still
A dealer bee, and be us'd well, or ill:
    His apples kindle, his leaves, force of conception kill.   150

XVI

A mouth, but dumbe, he hath; blinde eyes, deafe eares,
And to his shoulders dangle subtile haires;
A young *Colossus* there hee stands upright,
And as that ground by him were conquered
A leafie garland weares he on his head   155
Enchas'd with little fruits, so red and bright
That for them you would call your Loves lips white;
So, of a lone unhaunted place possest,
Did this soules second Inne, built by the guest,
   This living buried man, this quiet mandrake, rest.   160

XVII

No lustfull woman came this plant to grieve,
But 'twas because there was none yet but Eve:
And she (with other purpose) kill'd it quite;
Her sinne had now brought in infirmities,
And so her cradled child, the moist red eyes   165
Had never shut, nor slept since it saw light;
Poppie she knew, she knew the mandrakes might,
And tore up both, and so coold her childs blood;
Unvirtuous weeds might long unvex'd have stood;
   But hee's short liv'd, that with his death can doe most good.

XVIII

To an unfetterd soules quick nimble hast
Are falling stars, and hearts thoughts, but slow pac'd:
Thinner then burnt aire flies this soule, and she
Whom foure new comming, and foure parting Suns
Had found, and left the Mandrakes tenant, runnes   175
Thoughtlesse of change, when her firme destiny
Confin'd, and enjayld her, that seem'd so free,
Into a small blew shell, the which a poore
Warme bird orespread, and sat still evermore,
   Till her inclos'd child kickt, and pick'd it selfe a dore.

XIX

Outcrept a sparrow, this soules moving Inne,
On whose raw armes stiffe feathers now begin,
As childrens teeth through gummes, to breake with paine,
His flesh is jelly yet, and his bones threds,
All a new downy mantle overspreads,   185
A mouth he opes, which would as much containe
As his late house, and the first houre speaks plaine,
And chirps alowd for meat. Meat fit for men
His father steales for him, and so feeds then
    One, that within a moneth, will beate him from his hen.

XX

In this worlds youth wise nature did make hast,
Things ripened sooner, and did longer last;
Already this hot cocke, in bush and tree,
In field and tent, oreflutters his next hen;
He asks her not, who did so last, nor when,   195
Nor if his sister, or his neece shee be;
Nor doth she pule for his inconstancie
If in her sight he change, nor doth refuse
The next that calls; both liberty doe use;
    Where store is of both kindes, both kindes may freely chuse.

XXI

Men, till they tooke laws which made freedome lesse,
Their daughters, and their sisters did ingresse;
Till now unlawfull, therefore ill, 'twas not.
So jolly, that it can move, this soule is,
The body so free of his kindnesses,   205
That selfe-preserving it hath now forgot,
And slackneth so the soules, and bodies knot,
Which temperance streightens; freely on his she friends
He blood, and spirit, pith, and marrow spends,
    Ill steward of himself, himselfe in three yeares ends.

XXII

Else might he long have liv'd; man did not know
Of gummie blood, which doth in holly grow,
How to make bird-lime, nor how to deceive
With faind calls, hid nets, or enwrapping snare,
The free inhabitants of the Plyant aire.   215
Man to beget, and woman to conceive
Askt not of rootes, nor of cock-sparrowes, leave:
Yet chuseth hee, though none of these he feares,
Pleasantly three, then streightned twenty yeares
 To live; and to encrease his race, himselfe outweares.   220

XXIII

This cole with overblowing quench'd and dead,
The Soule from her too active organs fled
T'a brooke. A female fishes sandie Roe
With the males jelly, newly lev'ned was,
For they had intertouch'd as they did passe,   225
And one of those small bodies, fitted so,
This soule inform'd, and abled it to rowe
It selfe with finnie oares, which she did fit:
Her scales seem'd yet of parchment, and as yet
 Perchance a fish, but by no name you could call it.   230

XXIV

When goodly, like a ship in her full trim,
A swan, so white that you may unto him
Compare all whitenesse, but himselfe to none,
Glided along, and as he glided watch'd,
And with his arched necke this poore fish catch'd.   235
It mov'd with state, as if to looke upon
Low things it scorn'd, and yet before that one
Could thinke he sought it, he had swallow'd cleare
This, and much such, and unblam'd devour'd there
 All, but who too swift, too great, or well armed were.   240

XXV

Now swome a prison in a prison put,
And now this Soule in double walls was shut,
Till melted with the Swans digestive fire,
She left her house the fish, and vapour'd forth;
Fate not affording bodies of more worth   245
For her as yet, bids her againe retire
T'another fish, to any new desire
Made a new prey; For, he that can to none
Resistance make, nor complaint, sure is gone.
    Weaknesse invites, but silence feasts oppression.   250

XXVI

Pace with her native streame, this fish doth keepe,
And journeyes with her, towards the glassie deepe,
But oft retarded, once with a hidden net
Though with greate windowes, for when Need first taught
These tricks to catch food, then they were not wrought   255
As now, with curious greedinesse to let
None scape, but few, and fit for use, to get,
As, in this trap a ravenous pike was tane,
Who, though himselfe distrest, would faine have slain
    This wretch; So hardly are ill habits left again.   260

XXVII

Here by her smallnesse shee two deaths orepast,
Once innocence scap'd, and left the oppressor fast.
The net through-swome, she keepes the liquid path,
And whether she leape up sometimes to breath
And suck in aire, or finde it underneath,   265
Or working parts like mills or limbecks hath
To make the water thinne, and airelike faith
Cares not; but safe the Place she's come unto
Where fresh, with salt waves meet, and what to doe
    She knowes not, but betweene both makes a boord or two.

XXVIII

So farre from hiding her guests, water is,
That she showes them in bigger quantities
Then they are. Thus doubtfull of her way,
For game and not for hunger a sea Pie
Spied through this traiterous spectacle, from high,   275
The seely fish where it disputing lay,
And t'end her doubts and her, beares her away:
Exalted she'is, but to the exalters good,
As are by great ones, men which lowly stood.
    It's rais'd, to be the Raisers instrument and food.   280

XXIX

Is any kinde subject to rape like fish?
Ill unto man, they neither doe, nor wish:
Fishers they kill not, nor with noise awake,
They doe not hunt, nor strive to make a prey
Of beasts, nor their yong sonnes to beare away;   285
Foules they pursue not, nor do undertake
To spoile the nests industrious birds do make;
Yet them all these unkinde kinds feed upon,
To kill them is an occupation,
    And lawes make Fasts, and Lents for their destruction.

XXX

A sudden stiffe land-winde in that selfe houre
To sea-ward forc'd this bird, that did devour
The fish; he cares not, for with ease he flies,
Fat gluttonies best orator: at last
So long hee hath flowen, and hath flowen so fast   295
That many leagues at sea, now tir'd hee lyes,
And with his prey, that till then languisht, dies:
The soules no longer foes, two wayes did erre,
The fish I follow, and keepe no calender
    Of the other; he lives yet in some great officer.   300

XXXI

Into an embrion fish, our Soule is throwne,
And in due time throwne out againe, and growne
To such vastnesse as, if unmanacled
From Greece, Morea were, and that by some
Earthquake unrooted, loose Morea swome,   305
Or seas from Africks body had severed
And torne the hopefull Promontories head,
This fish would seeme these, and, when all hopes faile,
A great ship overset, or without saile
   Hulling, might (when this was a whelp) be like this whale

XXXII

At every stroake his brazen finnes do take,
More circles in the broken sea they make
Then cannons voices, when the aire they teare:
His ribs are pillars, and his high arch'd roofe
Of barke that blunts best steele, is thunder-proofe: 315
Swimme in him swallow'd Dolphins, without feare,
And feele no sides, as if his vast wombe were
Some Inland sea, and ever as hee went
Hee spouted rivers up, as if he ment
   To joyne our seas, with seas above the firmament.   320

XXXIII

He hunts not fish, but as an officer,
Stayes in his court, at his owne net, and there
All suitors of all sorts themselves enthrall;
So on his backe lyes this whale wantoning,
And in his gulfe-like throat, sucks every thing   325
That passeth neare. Fish chaseth fish, and all,
Flyer and follower, in this whirlepoole fall;
O might not states of more equality
Consist? and is it of necessity
   That thousand guiltlesse smals, to make one great, must die?

XXXIV

Now drinkes he up seas, and he eates up flocks,
He justles Ilands, and he shakes firme rockes.
Now in a roomefull house this Soule doth float,
And like a Prince she sends her faculties
To all her limbes, distant as Provinces.   335
The Sunne hath twenty times both crab and goate
Parched, since first lanch'd forth this living boate;
'Tis greatest now, and to destruction
Nearest; There's no pause at perfection;
   Greatnesse a period hath, but hath no station.   340

XXXV

Two little fishes whom hee never harm'd,
Nor fed on their kinde, two not throughly arm'd
With hope that they could kill him, nor could doe
Good to themselves by his death (they did not eate
His flesh, nor suck those oyles, which thence outstreat) 345
Conspir'd against him, and it might undoe
The plot of all, that the plotters were two,
But that they fishes were, and could not speake.
How shall a Tyran wise strong projects breake,
   If wreches can on them the common anger wreake?   350

XXXVI

The flaile-finn'd Thresher, and steel-beak'd Sword-fish
Onely attempt to doe, what all doe wish.
The Thresher backs him, and to beate begins;
The sluggard Whale yeelds to oppression,
And t'hide himselfe from shame and danger, downe   355
Begins to sinke; the Swordfish upward spins,
And gores him with his beake; his staffe-like finnes,
So well the one, his sword the other plyes,
That now a scoffe, and prey, this tyran dyes,
   And (his owne dole) feeds with himselfe all companies.

XXXVII

Who will revenge his death? or who will call
Those to account, that thought, and wrought his fall?
The heires of slaine kings, wee see are often so
Transported with the joy of what they get,
That they, revenge and obsequies forget,   365
Nor will against such men the people goe,
Because h'is now dead, to whom they should show
Love in that act; Some kings by vice being growne
So needy of subjects love, that of their own
    They thinke they lose, if love be to the dead Prince shown.

XXXVIII

This Soule, now free from prison, and passion,
Hath yet a little indignation
That so small hammers should so soone downe beat
So great a castle. And having for her house
Got the streight cloyster of a wreched mouse   375
(As basest men that have not what to eate
Nor enjoy ought, doe farre more hate the great
Then they, who good repos'd estates possesse)
This Soule, late taught that great things might by lesse
    Be slain, to gallant mischiefe doth herselfe addresse.   380

XXXIX

Natures great master-peece, an Elephant,
The onely harmlesse great thing; the giant
Of beasts; who thought, no more had gone, to make one wise
But to be just, and thankfull, loth to offend,
(Yet nature hath given him no knees to bend)   385
Himselfe he up-props, on himselfe relies,
And foe to none, suspects no enemies,
Still sleeping stood; vex't not his fantasie
Blacke dreames; like an unbent bow, carelesly
    His sinewy Proboscis did remisly lie: 390

XL

In which as in a gallery this mouse
Walk'd, and surveid the roomes of this vast house,
And to the braine, the soules bedchamber, went,
And gnaw'd the life cords there; Like a whole towne
Cleane undermin'd, the slaine beast tumbled downe;   395
With him the murtherer dies, whom envy sent
To kill, not scape, (for, only hee that ment
To die, did ever kill a man of better roome,)
And thus he made his foe, his prey, and tombe:
    Who cares not to turn back, may any whither come.   400

XLI

Next, hous'd this Soule a Wolves yet unborne whelp,
Till the best midwife, Nature, gave it helpe,
To issue. It could kill, as soone as goe.
Abel, as white, and milde as his sheepe were,
(Who, in that trade, of Church, and kingdomes, there   405
Was the first type) was still infested soe,
With this wolfe, that it bred his losse and woe;
And yet his bitch, his sentinell attends
The flocke so neere, so well warnes and defends,
    T'hat the wolfe, (hopelesse else) to corrupt her, intends.

XLII

Hee tooke a course, which since, succesfully,
Great men have often taken, to espie
The counsels, or to breake the plots of foes.
To Abels tent he stealeth in the darke,
On whose skirts the bitch slept; ere she could barke,   415
Attach'd her with streight gripes, yet hee call'd those,
Embracements of love; to loves worke he goes,
Where deeds move more then words; nor doth she show,
Nor must resist, nor needs hee streighten so
    His prey, for, were shee loose, she would nor barke, nor goe.

XLIII

Hee hath engag'd her; his, she wholy bides;
Who not her owne, none others secrets hides.
If to the flocke he come, and Abell there,
She faines hoarse barkings, but she biteth not,
Her faith is quite, but not her love forgot.   425
At last a trap, of which some every where
Abell had plac'd, ends all his losse, and feare,
By the Wolves death; and now just time it was
That a quicke soule should give life to that masse
   Of blood in Abels bitch, and thither this did passe.   430

XLIV

Some have their wives, their sisters some begot,
But in the lives of Emperours you shall not
Reade of a lust the which may equall this;
This wolfe begot himselfe, and finished
What he began alive, when hee was dead;   435
Sonne to himselfe, and father too, hee is
A ridling lust, for which Schoolemen would misse
A proper name. The whelpe of both these lay
In Abels tent, and with soft Moaba,
   His sister, being yong, it us'd to sport and play.   440

XLV

Hee soone for her too harsh, and churlish grew,
And Abell (the dam dead) would use this new
For the field. Being of two kindes thus made,
He, as his dam, from sheepe drove wolves away,
And as his Sire, he made them his owne prey.   445
Five yeares he liv'd, and cosened with his trade,
Then hopelesse that his faults were hid, betraid
Himselfe by flight, and by all followed,
From dogges, a wolfe; from wolves, a dogge he fled;
   And, like a spie to both sides false, he perished.   450

XLVI

It quickned next a toyfull Ape, and so
Gamesome it was, that it might freely goe
From tent to tent, and with the children play.
His organs now so like theirs hee doth finde,
That why he cannot laugh, and speake his minde,   455
He wonders. Much with all, most he doth stay
With Adams fift daughter *Siphatecia,*
Doth gaze on her, and, where she passeth, passe,
Gathers her fruits, and tumbles on the grasse,
   And wisest of that kinde, the first true lover was.   460

XLVII

He was the first that more desir'd to have
One then another; first that ere did crave
Love by mute signes, and had no power to speake;
First that could make love faces, or could doe
The valters sombersalts, or us'd to wooe   465
With hoiting gambolls, his owne bones to breake
To make his mistresse merry; or to wreake
Her anger on himselfe. Sinnes against kinde
They easily doe, that can let feed their minde
   With outward beauty; beauty they in boyes and
      beasts do find.

XLVIII

By this misled, too low things men have prov'd,
And too high; beasts and angels have beene lov'd.
This Ape, though else through-vaine, in this was wise,
He reach'd at things too high, but open way
There was, and he knew not she would say nay;   475
His toyes prevaile not, likelier meanes he tries,
He gazeth on her face with teare-shot eyes,
And up lifts subtly with his russet pawe
Her kidskinne apron without feare or awe
   Of nature; nature hath no gaole, though shee hath law.

XLIX

First she was silly and knew not what he ment.
That vertue, by his touches, chaft and spent,
Succeeds an itchie warmth, that melts her quite;
She knew not first, nowe cares not what he doth,
And willing halfe and more, more then halfe loth,   485
She neither puls nor pushes, but outright
Now cries, and now repents; when *Tethlemite*
Her brother, entred, and a great stone threw
After the Ape, who, thus prevented, flew.
    This house thus batter'd downe, the Soule possest a new.

L

And whether by this change she lose or win,
She comes out next, where the Ape would have gone in.
Adam and *Eve* had mingled bloods, and now
Like Chimiques equall fires, her temperate wombe
Had stew'd and form'd it: and part did become   495
A spungie liver, that did richly allow,
Like a free conduit, on a high hils brow,
Life-keeping moisture unto every part;
Part hardned it selfe to a thicker heart,
    Whose busie furnaces lifes spirits do impart.   500

LI

Another part became the well of sense,
The tender well-arm'd feeling braine, from whence,
Those sinowie strings which do our bodies tie,
Are raveld out; and fast there by one end,
Did this Soule limbes, these limbes a soule attend;   505
And now they joyn'd: keeping some quality
Of every past shape, she knew treachery,
Rapine, deceit, and lust, and ills enow
To be a woman. *Themech* she is now,
    Sister and wife to *Caine, Caine* that first did plow.   510

LII

Who ere thou beest that read'st this sullen Writ,
Which just so much courts thee, as thou dost it,
Let me arrest thy thoughts; wonder with mee,
Why plowing, building, ruling and the rest,
Or most of those arts, whence our lives are blest,   515
By cursed *Cains* race invented be,
And blest *Seth* vext us with Astronomie.
Ther's nothing simply good, nor ill alone,
Of every quality Comparison
   The onely measure is, and judge, Opinion.   520

    The end of the Progresse of the Soule.

DIVINE POEMS

To E. of D. with Six Holy Sonnets

See Sir, how as the Suns hot Masculine flame
    Begets strange creatures on Niles durty slime,
    In me, your fatherly yet lusty Ryme
(For, these songs are their fruits) have wrought the same;
But though the ingendring force from whence they came   5
    Bee strong enough, and nature doe admit
    Seaven to be borne at once, I send as yet
But six; they say, the seaventh hath still some maime.
    I choose your judgement, which the same degree
    Doth with her sister, your invention, hold,   10
As fire these drossie Rymes to purifie,
    Or as Elixar, to change them to gold;
You are that Alchimist which alwaies had
Wit, whose one spark could make good things of bad.

To the Lady Magdalen Herbert: of St. Mary Magdalen

    Her of your name, whose fair inheritance
        Bethina was, and jointure Magdalo:
    An active faith so highly did advance,
        That she once knew, more than the Church did know,
    The Resurrection; so much good there is   5
        Deliver'd of her, that some Fathers be
    Loth to believe one Woman could do this;
        But, think these Magdalens were two or three.
    Increase their number, Lady, and their fame:
        To their Devotion, add your Innocence;   10
    Take so much of th'example, as of the name;
        The latter half; and in some recompence
    That they did harbour Christ himself, a Guest,
        Harbour these Hymns, to his dear name addrest.

                                J. D.

HOLY SONNETS

La Corona

Deigne at my hands this crown of prayer and praise,
Weav'd in my low devout melancholie,
Thou which of good, hast, yea art treasury,
All changing unchang'd Antient of dayes;
But doe not, with a vile crowne of fraile bayes,   5
Reward my muses white sincerity,
But what thy thorny crowne gain'd, that give mee,
A crowne of Glory, which doth power alwayes;
The ends crowne our workes, but thou crown'st our ends,
For, at our end begins our endlesse rest;   10
The first last end, now zealously possest,
With a strong sober thirst, my soule attends.
'Tis time that heart and voice be lifted high,
Salvation to all that will is nigh.

Annunciation

Salvation to all that will is nigh;
That All, which alwayes is All every where
Which cannot sinne, and yet all sinnes must beare,
Which cannot die, yet cannot chuse but die,
Loe, faithfull Virgin, yeelds himselfe to lye   5
In prison, in thy wombe; and though he there
Can take no sinne, nor thou give, yet he'will weare
Taken from thence, flesh, which deaths force may trie.
Ere by the spheares time was created, thou
Wast in his minde, who is thy Sonne, and Brother;   10
Whom thou conceiv'st, conceiv'd; yea thou art now
Thy Makers maker, and thy Fathers mother;
Thou'hast light in darke; and shutst in little roome,
Immensity cloysterd in thy deare wombe.

Nativitie

Immensitie cloysterd in thy deare wombe,
Now leaves his welbelov'd imprisonment,
There he hath made himselfe to his intent
Weake enough, now into our world to come;
But Oh, for thee, for him, hath th'Inne no roome?   5
Yet lay him in this stall, and from the Orient,
Starres, and wisemen will travell to prevent
Th'effect of *Herods* jealous generall doome.
Seest thou, my Soule, with thy faiths eyes, how he
Which fils all place, yet none holds him, doth lye?   10
Was not his pity towards thee wondrous high,
That would have need to be pittied by thee?
Kisse him, and with him into Egypt goe,
With his kinde mother, who partakes thy woe.

Temple

With his kinde mother who partakes thy woe,
Joseph turne backe; see where your child doth sit,
Blowing, yea blowing out those sparks of wit,
Which himselfe on the Doctors did bestow;
The Word but lately could not speake, and loe,   5
It sodenly speakes wonders, whence comes it,
That all which was, and all which should be writ,
A shallow seeming child, should deeply know?
His Godhead was not soule to his manhood,
Nor had time mellowed him to this ripenesse,   10
But as for one which hath a long taske, 'tis good,
With the Sunne to beginne his businesse,
He in his ages morning thus began
By miracles exceeding power of man.

Crucifying

By *miracles exceeding power of man,*
Hee faith in some, envie in some begat,
For, what weake spirits admire, ambitious, hate;
In both affections many to him ran,
But Oh ! the worst are most, they will and can,   5
Alas, and do, unto the immaculate,
Whose creature Fate is, now prescribe a Fate,
Measuring selfe-lifes infinity to'a span,
Nay to an inch. Loe, where condemned hee
Beares his owne crosse, with paine, yet by and by   10
When it beares him, he must beare more and die.
Now thou art lifted up, draw mee to thee,
And at thy death giving such liberall dole,
Moyst, with one drop of thy blood, my dry soule.

Resurrection

Moyst with one drop of thy blood, my dry soule
Shall (though she now be in extreme degree
Too stony hard, and yet too fleshly,) bee
Freed by that drop, from being starv'd, hard, or foule,
And life, by this death abled, shall controule   5
Death, whom thy death slue; nor shall to mee
Feare of first or last death, bring miserie,
If in thy little booke my name thou enroule,
Flesh in that long sleep is not putrified,
But made that there, of which, and for which 'twas;   10
Nor can by other meanes be glorified.
May then sinnes sleep, and deaths soone from me passe,
That wak't from both, I againe risen may
Salute the last, and everlasting day.

Ascention

Salute the last and everlasting day,
Joy at the uprising of this Sunne, and Sonne,
Yee whose just teares, or tribulation
Have purely washt, or burnt your drossie clay;
Behold the Highest, parting hence away,   5
Lightens the darke clouds, which hee treads upon,
Nor doth hee by ascending, show alone,
But first hee, and hee first enters the way.
O strong Ramme, which hast batter'd heaven for mee,
Mild Lambe, which with thy blood, hast mark'd the path; 10
Bright Torch, which shin'st, that I the way may see
Oh, with thy owne blood quench thy owne just wrath,
And if thy holy Spirit, my Muse did raise,
Deigne at my hands this crowne of prayer and praise.

Holy Sonnets
I
Thou hast made me, And shall thy worke decay?
Repaire me now, for now mine end doth haste,
I runne to death, and death meets me as fast,
And all my pleasures are like yesterday;
I dare not move my dimme eyes any way,   5
Despaire behind, and death before doth cast
Such terrour, and my feeble flesh doth waste
By sinne in it, which it t'wards hell doth weigh;
Onely thou art above, and when towards thee
By thy leave I can looke, I rise againe;   10
But our old subtle foe so tempteth me,
That not one houre my selfe I can sustaine;
Thy Grace may wing me to prevent his art,
And thou like Adamant draw mine iron heart.

II

As due by many titles I resigne
My selfe to thee, O God, first I was made
By thee, and for thee, and when I was decay'd
Thy blood bought that, the which before was thine;
I am thy sonne, made with thy selfe to shine,   5
Thy servant, whose paines thou hast still repaid,
Thy sheepe, thine Image, and, till I betray'd
My selfe, a temple of thy Spirit divine;
Why doth the devill then usurpe on mee?
Why doth he steale, nay ravish that's thy right?   10
Except thou rise and for thine owne worke fight,
Oh I shall soone despaire, when I doe see
That thou lov'st mankind well, yet wilt'not chuse me.
And Satan hates mee, yet is loth to lose mee.

III

O might those sighes and teares returne againe
Into my breast and eyes, which I have spent,
That I might in this holy discontent
Mourne with some fruit, as I have mourn'd in vaine;
In mine Idolatry what showres of raine   5
Mine eyes did waste? what griefs my heart did rent?
That sufferance was my sinne; now I repent;
'Cause I did suffer I must suffer paine.
Th'hydroptique drunkard, and night-scouting thiefe,
The itchy Lecher, and selfe tickling proud   10
Have the remembrance of past joyes, for reliefe
Of comming ills. To (poore) me is allow'd
No ease; for, long, yet vehement griefe hath beene
Th'effect and cause, the punishment and sinne.

IV

Oh my blacke Soule! now thou art summoned
By sicknesse, deaths herald, and champion;
Thou art like a pilgrim, which abroad hath done
Treason, and durst not turne to whence hee is fled,
Or like a thiefe, which till deaths doome be read,   5
Wisheth himselfe delivered from prison;

But damn'd and hal'd to execution,
Wisheth that still he might be imprisoned.
Yet grace, if thou repent, thou canst not lacke;
But who shall give thee that grace to beginne?   10
Oh make thy selfe with holy mourning blacke,
And red with blushing, as thou art with sinne;
Or wash thee in Christs blood, which hath this might
That being red, it dyes red soules to white.

V

I am a little world made cunningly
Of Elements, and an Angelike spright,
But black sinne hath betraid to endlesse night
My worlds both parts, and (oh) both parts must die.
You which beyond that heaven which was most high   5
Have found new sphears, and of new lands can write,
Powre new seas in mine eyes, that so I might
Drowne my world with my weeping earnestly,
Or wash it, if it must be drown'd no more:
But oh it must be burnt ! alas the fire   10
Of lust and envie have burnt it heretofore,
And made it fouler; Let their flames retire,
And burne me oh Lord, with a fiery zeale
Of thee and thy house, which doth in eating heale.

VI

This is my playes last scene, here heavens appoint
My pilgrimages last mile; and my race
Idly, yet quickly runne, hath this last pace,
My spans last inch, my minutes latest point,
And gluttonous death, will instantly unjoynt   5
My body, and soule, and I shall sleepe a space,
But my'ever-waking part shall see that face,
Whose feare already shakes my every joynt:
Then, as my soule, to'heaven her first seate, takes flight,
And earth-borne body, in the earth shall dwell,   10
So, fall my sinnes, that all may have their right,
To where they'are bred, and would presse me, to hell.
Impute me righteous, thus purg'd of evill,
For thus I leave the world, the flesh, the devill.

VII

At the round earths imagin'd corners, blow
Your trumpets, Angells, and arise, arise
From death, you numberlesse infinities
Of soules, and to your scattred bodies goe,
All whom the flood did, and fire shall o'erthrow,   5
All whom warre, dearth, age, agues, tyrannies,
Despaire, law, chance, hath slaine, and you whose eyes,
Shall behold God, and never tast deaths woe.
But let them sleepe, Lord, and mee mourne a space,
For, if above all these, my sinnes abound,   10
'Tis late to aske abundance of thy grace,
When wee are there; here on this lowly ground,
Teach mee how to repent; for that's as good
As if thou'hadst seal'd my pardon, with thy blood.

VIII

If faithfull soules be alike glorifi'd
As Angels, then my fathers soule doth see,
And adds this even to full felicitie,
That valiantly I hels wide mouth o'rstride:
But if our mindes to these soules be descry'd   5
By circumstances, and by signes that be
Apparent in us, not immediately,
How shall my mindes white truth by them be try'd?
They see idolatrous lovers weepe and mourne,
And vile blasphemous Conjurers to call   10
On Jesus name, and Pharisaicall
Dissemblers feigne devotion. Then turne
O pensive soule, to God, for he knowes best
Thy true griefe, for he put it in my breast.

IX

If poysonous mineralls, and if that tree,
Whose fruit threw death on else immortall us,
If lecherous goats, if serpents envious
Cannot be damn'd; Alas; why should I bee?
Why should intent or reason, borne in mee,   5
Make sinnes, else equall, in mee more heinous?

And mercy being easie, and glorious
To God; in his sterne wrath, why threatens hee?
But who am I, that dare dispute with thee
O God? Oh! of thine onely worthy blood,   10
And my teares, make a heavenly Lethean flood,
And drowne in it my sinnes blacke memorie;
That thou remember them, some claime as debt,
I thinke it mercy, if thou wilt forget.

                              X

Death be not proud, though some have called thee
Mighty and dreadfull, for, thou art not soe,
For, those, whom thou think'st, thou dost overthrow,
Die not, poore death, nor yet canst thou kill mee.
From rest and sleepe, which but thy pictures bee,   5
Much pleasure, then from thee, much more must flow,
And soonest our best men with thee doe goe,
Rest of their bones, and soules deliverie.
Thou art slave to Fate, Chance, kings, and desperate men,
And dost with poyson, warre, and sicknesse dwell,   10
And poppie, or charmes can make us sleepe as well,
And better then thy stroake; why swell'st thou then?
One short sleepe past, wee wake eternally,
And death shall be no more; death, thou shalt die.

                             XI

Spit in my face you Jewes, and pierce my side,
Buffet, and scoffe, scourge and crucifie mee,
For I have sinn'd, and sinn'd, and onely hee,
Who could do no iniquitie, hath dyed:
But by my death can not be satisfied   5
My sinnes, which passe the Jewes impiety:
They kill'd once an inglorious man, but I
Crucifie him daily, being now glorified.
Oh let mee then, his strange love still admire:
Kings pardon, but he bore our punishment.   10
And *Jacob* came cloth'd in vile harsh attire
But to supplant, and with gainfull intent:
God cloth'd himselfe in vile mans flesh, that so
Hee might be weake enough to suffer woe.

XII

Why are wee by all creatures waited on?
Why doe the prodigall elements supply
Life and food to mee, being more pure then I,
Simple, and further from corruption?
Why brook'st thou, ignorant horse, subjection?   5
Why dost thou bull, and bore so seelily
Dissemble weaknesse, and by'one mans stroke die,
Whose whole kinde, you might swallow and feed upon?
Weaker I am, woe is mee, and worse then you,
You have not sinn'd, nor need be timorous.   10
But wonder at a greater wonder, for to us
Created nature doth these things subdue,
But their Creator, whom sin, nor nature tyed,
For us, his Creatures, and his foes, hath dyed.

XIII

What if this present were the worlds last night?
Marke in my heart, O Soule, where thou dost dwell,
The picture of Christ crucified, and tell
Whether that countenance can thee affright,
Teares in his eyes quench the amasing light,   5
Blood fills his frownes, which from his pierc'd head fell.
And can that tongue adjudge thee unto hell,
Which pray'd forgivenesse for his foes fierce spight?
No, no; but as in my idolatrie
I said to all my profane mistresses,   10
Beauty, of pitty, foulnesse onely is
A signe of rigour: so I say to thee,
To wicked spirits are horrid shapes assign'd,
This beauteous forme assures a pitious minde.

XIV

Batter my heart, three person'd God; for, you
As yet but knocke, breathe, shine, and seeke to mend;
That I may rise, and stand, o'erthrow mee,'and bend
Your force, to breake, blowe, burn and make me new.
I, like an usurpt towne, to'another due,   5
Labour to'admit you, but Oh, to no end,

Reason your viceroy in mee, mee should defend,
But is captiv'd, and proves weake or untrue.
Yet dearely'I love you,'and would be loved faine,
But am betroth'd unto your enemie: 10
Divorce mee,'untie, or breake that knot againe,
Take mee to you, imprison mee, for I
Except you'enthrall mee, never shall be free,
Nor ever chast, except you ravish mee.

XV

Wilt thou love God, as he thee! then digest,
My Soule, this wholsome meditation,
How God the Spirit, by Angels waited on
In heaven, doth make his Temple in thy brest.
The Father having begot a Sonne most blest,   5
And still begetting, (for he ne'r begonne)
Hath deign'd to chuse thee by adoption,
Coheire to'his glory,'and Sabbaths endlesse rest.
And as a robb'd man, which by search doth finde
His stolne stuffe sold, must lose or buy'it againe: 10
The Sonne of glory came downe, and was slaine,
Us whom he'had made, and Satan stolne, to unbinde.
Twas much, that man was made like God before,
But, that God should be made like man, much more.

XVI

Father, part of his double interest
Unto thy kingdome, thy Sonne gives to mee,
His joynture in the knottie Trinitie
Hee keepes, and gives to me his deaths conquest.
This Lambe, whose death, with life the world hath blest,   5
Was from the worlds beginning slaine, and he
Hath made two Wills, which with the Legacie
Of his and thy kingdome, doe thy Sonnes invest.
Yet such are thy laws, that men argue yet
Whether a man those statutes can fulfill;   10
None doth; but all-healing grace and spirit
Revive againe what law and letter kill.
Thy lawes abridgement, and thy last command
Is all but love; Oh let this last Will stand !

XVII

Since she whom I lov'd hath payd her last debt
To Nature, and to hers, and my good is dead,
And her Soule early into heaven ravished,
Wholly on heavenly things my mind is sett.
Here the admyring her my mind did whett   5
To seeke thee God; so streames do shew their head;
But though I have found thee, and thou my thirst hast fed,
A holy thirsty dropsy melts mee yett.
But why should I begg more Love, when as thou
Dost wooe my soule for hers; offring all thine: 10
And dost not only feare least I allow
My Love to Saints and Angels, things divine,
But in thy tender jealosy dost doubt
Least the World, Fleshe, yea Devill putt thee out.

XVIII

Show me deare Christ, thy spouse, so bright and clear.
What! is it She, which on the other shore
Goes richly painted? or which rob'd and tore
Laments and mournes in Germany and here?
Sleepes she a thousand, then peepes up one yeare?   5
Is she selfe truth and errs? now new, now outwore?
Doth she, and did she, and shall she evermore
On one, on seaven, or on no hill appeare?
Dwells she with us, or like adventuring knights
First travaile we to seeke and then make Love?   10
Betray kind husband thy spouse to our sights,
And let myne amorous soule court thy mild Dove,
Who is most trew, and pleasing to thee, then
When she'is embrac'd and open to most men.

XIX

Oh, to vex me, contraryes meet in one:
Inconstancy unnaturally hath begott
A constant habit; that when I would not
I change in vowes, and in devotione.
As humorous is my contritione   5
As my prophane Love, and as soone forgott:

As ridlingly distemper'd, cold and hott,
As praying, as mute; as infinite, as none.
I durst not view heaven yesterday; and to day
In prayers, and flattering speaches I court God;   10
To morrow I quake with true feare of his rod.
So my devout fitts come and go away
Like a fantastique Ague: save that here
Those are my best dayes, when I shake with feare.

The Crosse

Since Christ embrac'd the Crosse it selfe, dare I
His image, th'image of his Crosse deny?
Would I have profit by the sacrifice,
And dare the chosen Altar to despise?
It bore all other sinnes, but is it fit   5
That it should beare the sinne of scorning it?
Who from the picture would avert his eye,
How would he flye his paines, who there did dye?
From mee, no Pulpit, nor misgrounded law,
Nor scandall taken, shall this Crosse withdraw,   10
It shall not, for it cannot; for, the losse
Of this Crosse, were to mee another Crosse;
Better were worse, for, no affliction,
No Crosse is so extreme, as to have none.
Who can blot out the Crosse, which th'instrument   15
Of God, dew'd on mee in the Sacrament?
Who can deny mee power, and liberty
To stretch mine armes, and mine owne Crosse to be?
Swimme, and at every stroake, thou art thy Crosse;
The Mast and yard make one, where seas do tosse;   20
Looke downe, thou spiest out Crosses in small things;
Looke up, thou seest birds rais'd on crossed wings;
All the Globes frame, and spheares, is nothing else
But the Meridians crossing Parallels.
Materiall Crosses then, good physicke bee,   25
But yet spirituall have chiefe dignity.
These for extracted chimique medicine serve,
And cure much better, and as well preserve;

Then are you your own physicke, or need none,
When Still'd, or purg'd by tribulation. 30
For when that Crosse ungrudg'd, unto you stickes,
Then are you to your selfe, a Crucifixe.
As perchance, Carvers do not faces make,
But that away, which hid them there, do take;
Let Crosses, soe, take what hid Christ in thee, 35
And be his image, or not his, but hee.
But, as oft Alchimists doe coyners prove,
So may a selfe-dispising, get selfe-love,
And then as worst surfets, of best meates bee,
Soe is pride, issued from humility, 40
For, 'tis no child, but monster; therefore Crosse
Your joy in crosses, else, 'tis double losse.
And crosse thy senses, else, both they, and thou
Must perish soone, and to destruction bowe.
For if the'eye seeke good objects, and will take 45
No crosse from bad, wee cannot scape a snake.
So with harsh, hard, sowre, stinking, crosse the rest,
Make them indifferent all; call nothing best.
But most the eye needs crossing, that can rome,
And move; To th'other th'objects must come home. 50
And crosse thy heart: for that in man alone
Points downewards, and hath palpitation.
Crosse those dejections, when it downeward tends,
And when it to forbidden heights pretends.
And as the braine through bony walls doth vent 55
By sutures, which a Crosses forme present,
So when thy braine workes, ere thou utter it,
Crosse and correct concupiscence of witt.
Be covetous of Crosses, let none fall.
Crosse no man else, but crosse thy selfe in all. 60
Then doth the Crosse of Christ worke fruitfully
Within our hearts, when wee love harmlessly
That Crosses pictures much, and with more care
That Crosses children, which our Crosses are.

Resurrection, imperfect

Sleep sleep old Sun, thou canst not have repast
As yet, the wound thou took'st on friday last;
Sleepe then, and rest; The world may beare thy stay,
A better Sun rose before thee to day,
Who, not content to'enlighten all that dwell   5
On the earths face, as thou, enlightned hell,
And made the darke fires languish in that vale,
As, at thy presence here, our fires grow pale.
Whose body having walk'd on earth, and now
Hasting to Heaven, would, that he might allow   10
Himselfe unto all stations, and fill all,
For these three daies become a minerall;
Hee was all gold when he lay downe, but rose
All tincture, and doth not alone dispose
Leaden and iron wills to good, but is   15
Of power to make even sinfull flesh like his.
Had one of those, whose credulous pietie
Thought, that a Soule one might discerne and see
Goe from a body,'at this sepulcher been,
And, issuing from the sheet, this body seen,   20
He would have justly thought this body a soule,
If not of any man, yet of the whole.
             Desunt cætera.

The Annuntiation and Passion

Tamely, fraile body,'abstaine to day; to day
My soule eates twice, Christ hither and away.
Shee sees him man, so like God made in this,
That of them both a circle embleme is,
Whose first and last concurre; this doubtfull day   5
Of feast or fast, Christ came, and went away.
Shee sees him nothing twice at once, who'is all;
Shee sees a Cedar plant it selfe, and fall,
Her Maker put to making, and the head
Of life, at once, not yet alive, yet dead.   10
She sees at once the virgin mother stay

Reclus'd at home, Publique at Golgotha;
Sad and rejoyc'd shee's seen at once, and seen
At almost fiftie, and at scarce fifteene.
At once a Sonne is promis'd her, and gone,   15
Gabriell gives Christ to her, He her to John;
Not fully a mother, Shee's in Orbitie,
At once receiver and the legacie.
All this, and all betweene, this day hath showne,
Th'Abridgement of Christs story, which makes one   20
(As in plaine Maps, the furthest West is East)
Of the'Angels *Ave,*'and *Consummatum est.*
How well the Church, Gods Court of faculties
Deales, in some times, and seldome joyning these !
As by the selfe-fix'd Pole wee never doe   25
Direct our course, but the next starre thereto,
Which showes where the'other is, and which we say
(Because it strayes not farre) doth never stray;
So God by his Church, neerest to him, wee know,
And stand firme, if wee by her motion goe;   30
His Spirit, as his fiery Pillar doth
Leade, and his Church, as cloud; to one end both.
This Church, by letting these daies joyne, hath shown
Death and conception in mankinde is one;
Or 'twas in him the same humility,   35
That he would be a man, and leave to be:
Or as creation he hath made, as God,
With the last judgement, but one period,
His imitating Spouse would joyne in one
Manhoods extremes: He shall come, he is gone: 40
Or as though one blood drop, which thence did fall,
Accepted, would have serv'd, he yet shed all;
So though the least of his paines, deeds, or words,
Would busie a life, she all this day affords;
This treasure then, in grosse, my Soule uplay,   45
And in my life retaile it every day.

Good Friday, 1613. Riding Westward

Let mans Soule be a Spheare, and then, in this,
The intelligence that moves, devotion is,
And as the other Spheares, by being growne
Subject to forraigne motions, lose their owne,
And being by others hurried every day,   5
Scarce in a yeare their naturall forme obey:
Pleasure or businesse, so, our Soules admit
For their first mover, and are whirld by it.
Hence is't, that I am carryed towards the West
This day, when my Soules forme bends toward the East.   10
There I should see a Sunne, by rising set,
And by that setting endlesse day beget;
But that Christ on this Crosse, did rise and fall,
Sinne had eternally benighted all.
Yet dare I'almost be glad, I do not see   15
That spectacle of too much weight for mee.
Who sees Gods face, that is selfe life, must dye;
What a death were it then to see God dye?
It made his owne Lieutenant Nature shrinke,
It made his footstoole crack, and the Sunne winke.   20
Could I behold those hands which span the Poles,
And turne all spheares at once, peirc'd with those holes?
Could I behold that endlesse height which is
Zenith to us, and our Antipodes,
Humbled below us? or that blood which is   25
The seat of all our Soules, if not of his,
Made durt of dust, or that flesh which was worne
By God, for his apparell, rag'd, and torne?
If on these things I durst not looke, durst I
Upon his miserable mother cast mine eye,   30
Who was Gods partner here, and furnish'd thus
Halfe of that Sacrifice, which ransom'd us?
Though these things, as I ride, be from mine eye,
They'are present yet unto my memory,
For that looks towards them; and thou look'st towards mee,
O Saviour, as thou hang'st upon the tree;
I turne my backe to thee, but to receive
Corrections, till thy mercies bid thee leave.

O thinke mee worth thine anger, punish mee,
Burne off my rusts, and my deformity,   40
Restore thine Image, so much, by thy grace,
That thou may'st know mee, and I'll turne my face.

The Litanie

I
The Father

Father of Heaven, and him, by whom
It, and us for it, and all else, for us
   Thou madest, and govern'st ever, come
And re-create mee, now growne ruinous:
      My heart is by dejection, clay,   5
      And by selfe-murder, red.
From this red earth, O Father, purge away
All vicious tinctures, that new fashioned
I may rise up from death, before I'am dead.

II
The Sonne

O Sonne of God, who seeing two things,   10
Sinne, and death crept in, which were never made,
   By bearing one, tryed'st with what stings
The other could thine heritage invade;
      O be thou nail'd unto my heart,
      And crucified againe,   15
Part not from it, though it from thee would part,
But let it be, by applying so thy paine,
Drown'd in thy blood, and in thy passion slaine.

III
The Holy Ghost

O Holy Ghost, whose temple I
Am, but of mudde walls, and condensed dust,   20
   And being sacrilegiously
Halfe wasted with youths fires, of pride and lust,
      Must with new stormes be weatherbeat;

Double in my heart thy flame,
Which let devout sad teares intend; and let   25
(Though this glasse lanthorne, flesh, do suffer maime)
Fire, Sacrifice, Priest, Altar be the same.

IV
The Trinity
O Blessed glorious Trinity,
Bones to Philosophy, but milke to faith,
Which, as wise serpents, diversly   30
Most slipperinesse, yet most entanglings hath
As you distinguish'd undistinct
By power, love, knowledge bee,
Give mee a such selfe different instinct
Of these; let all mee elemented bee,   35
Of power, to love, to know, you unnumbered three.

V
The Virgin Mary
For that faire blessed Mother-maid,
Whose flesh redeem'd us; That she-Cherubin,
Which unlock'd Paradise, and made
One claime for innocence, and disseiz'd sinne,   40
Whose wombe was a strange heav'n, for there
God cloath'd himselfe, and grew,
Our zealous thankes wee poure. As her deeds were
Our helpes, so are her prayers; nor can she sue
In vaine, who hath such titles unto you.   45

VI
The Angels
And since this life our nonage is,
And wee in Wardship to thine Angels be,
Native in heavens faire Palaces,
Where we shall be but denizen'd by thee,
As th'earth conceiving by the Sunne,   50
Yeelds faire diversitie,
Yet never knowes which course that light doth run,
So let mee study, that mine actions bee
Worthy their sight, though blinde in how they see.

VII

The Patriarches

And let thy Patriarches Desire   55
(Those great Grandfathers of thy Church, which saw
   More in the cloud, then wee in fire,
Whom Nature clear'd more, then us Grace and Law,
     And now in Heaven still pray, that wee
      May use our new helpes right,)   60
Be satisfy'd, and fructifie in mee;
Let not my minde be blinder by more light
Nor Faith, by Reason added, lose her sight.

VIII

The Prophets

Thy Eagle-sighted Prophets too,
Which were thy Churches Organs, and did sound   65
   That harmony, which made of two
One law, and did unite, but not confound;
     Those heavenly Poëts which did see
     Thy will, and it expresse
In rythmique feet, in common pray for mee,   70
That I by them excuse not my excesse
In seeking secrets, or Poëtiquenesse.

IX

The Apostles

And thy illustrious Zodiacke
Of twelve Apostles, which ingirt this All,
   (From whom whosoever do not take   75
Their light, to darke deep pits, throw downe, and fall,)
     As through their prayers, thou'hast let mee know
     That their bookes are divine;
May they pray still, and be heard, that I goe
Th'old broad way in applying; O decline   80
Mee, when my comment would make thy word mine.

X
The Martyrs

And since thou so desirously
Did'st long to die, that long before thou could'st,
 And long since thou no more couldst dye,
Thou in thy scatter'd mystique body wouldst   85
   In Abel dye, and ever since
   In thine; let their blood come
To begge for us, a discreet patience
Of death, or of worse life: for Oh, to some
Not to be Martyrs, is a martyrdome.   90

XI
The Confessors

Therefore with thee triumpheth there
A Virgin Squadron of white Confessors,
 Whose bloods betroth'd, not marryed were,
Tender'd, not taken by those Ravishers:
   They know, and pray, that wee may know, 95
   In every Christian
Hourly tempestuous persecutions grow;
Tentations martyr us alive; A man
Is to himselfe a Dioclesian.

XII
The Virgins

The cold white snowie Nunnery,   100
Which, as thy mother, their high Abbesse, sent
 Their bodies backe againe to thee,
As thou hadst lent them, cleane and innocent,
   Though they have not obtain'd of thee,
   That or thy Church, or I,   105
Should keep, as they, our first integrity;
Divorce thou sinne in us, or bid it die,
And call chast widowhead Virginitie.

XIII

The Doctors

Thy sacred Academie above
Of Doctors, whose paines have unclasp'd, and taught   110
   Both bookes of life to us (for love
To know thy Scriptures tells us, we are wrote
         In thy other booke) pray for us there
         That what they have misdone
Or mis-said, wee to that may not adhere;   115
Their zeale may be our sinne. Lord let us runne
Meane waies, and call them stars, but not the Sunne.

XIV

And whil'st this universall Quire,
That Church in triumph, this in warfare here,
   Warm'd with one all-partaking fire   120
Of love, that none be lost, which cost thee deare,
         Prayes ceaslesly,'and thou hearken too,
         (Since to be gratious
Our taske is treble, to pray, beare, and doe)
Heare this prayer Lord: O Lord deliver us   125
From trusting in those prayers, though powr'd out thus.

XV

From being anxious, or secure,
Dead clods of sadnesse, or light squibs of mirth,
   From thinking, that great courts immure
All, or no happinesse, or that this earth   130
         Is only for our prison fram'd,
         Or that thou art covetous
To them whom thou lovest, or that they are maim'd
From reaching this worlds sweet, who seek thee thus,
With all their might, Good Lord deliver us.   135

XVI

From needing danger, to bee good,
From owing thee yesterdaies teares to day,
   From trusting so much to thy blood,
That in that hope, wee wound our soule away,

From bribing thee with Almes, to excuse   140
   Some sinne more burdenous,
From light affecting, in religion, newes,
From thinking us all soule, neglecting thus
Our mutuall duties, Lord deliver us.

XVII

  From tempting Satan to tempt us,   145
By our connivence, or slack companie,
   From measuring ill by vitious,
Neglecting to choake sins spawne, Vanitie,
    From indiscreet humilitie,
     Which might be scandalous,   150
And cast reproach on Christianitie,
From being spies, or to spies pervious,
From thirst, or scorne of fame, deliver us.

XVIII

  Deliver us for thy descent
Into the Virgin, whose wombe was a place   155
   Of middle kind; and thou being sent
To'ungratious us, staid'st at her full of grace;
    And through thy poore birth, where first thou
    Glorifiedst Povertie,
And yet soone after riches didst allow,   160
By accepting Kings gifts in the Epiphanie,
Deliver, and make us, to both waies free.

XIX

  And through that bitter agonie,
Which is still the agonie of pious wits,
   Disputing what distorted thee,   165
And interrupted evennesse, with fits;
    And through thy free confession
    Though thereby they were then
Made blind, so that thou might'st from them have gone,
Good Lord deliver us, and teach us when   170
Wee may not, and we may blinde unjust men.

XX

Through thy submitting all, to blowes
Thy face, thy clothes to spoile; thy fame to scorne,
   All waies, which rage, or Justice knowes,
And by which thou could'st shew, that thou wast born;   175
      And through thy gallant humblenesse
      Which thou in death did'st shew,
Dying before thy soule they could expresse,
Deliver us from death, by dying so,
To this world, ere this world doe bid us goe.   180

XXI

When senses, which thy souldiers are,
Wee arme against thee, and they fight for sinne,
   When want, sent but to tame, doth warre
And worke despaire a breach to enter in,
      When plenty, Gods image, and seale   185
      Makes us Idolatrous,
And love it, not him, whom it should reveale,
When wee are mov'd to seeme religious
Only to vent wit, Lord deliver us.

XXII

In Churches, when the'infirmitie   190
Of him which speakes, diminishes the Word,
   When Magistrates doe mis-apply
To us, as we judge, lay or ghostly sword,
      When plague, which is thine Angell, raignes,
      Or wars, thy Champions, swaie,   195
When Heresie, thy second deluge, gaines;
In th'houre of death, the'Eve of last judgement day,
Deliver us from the sinister way.

XXIII

Heare us, O heare us Lord; to thee
A sinner is more musique, when he prayes,   200
    Then spheares, or Angels praises bee,
In Panegyrique Allelujaes;
            Heare us, for till thou heare us, Lord
            We know not what to say;
Thine eare to'our sighes, teares, thoughts gives voice and word.
O Thou who Satan heard'st in Jobs sicke day,
Heare thy selfe now, for thou in us dost pray.

XXIV

That wee may change to evennesse
This intermitting aguish Pietie;
    That snatching cramps of wickednesse   210
And Apoplexies of fast sin, may die;
            That musique of thy promises,
            Not threats in Thunder may
Awaken us to our just offices;
What in thy booke, thou dost, or creatures say,   215
That we may heare, Lord heare us, when wee pray.

XXV

That our eares sicknesse wee may cure,
And rectifie those Labyrinths aright;
    That wee, by harkning, not procure
Our praise, nor others dispraise so invite;   220
            That wee get not a slipperinesse
            And senslesly decline,
From hearing bold wits jeast at Kings excesse,
To'admit the like of majestie divine;
That we may locke our eares, Lord open thine.   225

XXVI

That living law, the Magistrate,
Which to give us, and make us physicke, doth
   Our vices often aggravate,
That Preachers taxing sinne, before her growth,
      That Satan, and invenom'd men   230
        Which well, if we starve, dine,
When they doe most accuse us, may see then
Us, to amendment, heare them; thee decline:
That we may open our eares, Lord lock thine.

XXVII

That learning, thine Ambassador,   235
From thine allegeance wee never tempt,
   That beauty, paradises flower
For physicke made, from poyson be exempt,
      That wit, borne apt high good to doe,
        By dwelling lazily   240
On Natures nothing, be not nothing too,
That our affections kill us not, nor dye,
Heare us, weake ecchoes, O thou eare, and cry.

XXVIII

Sonne of God heare us, and since thou
By taking our blood, owest it us againe,   245
   Gaine to thy self, or us allow;
And let not both us and thy selfe be slaine;
      O Lambe of God, which took'st our sinne
        Which could not stick to thee,
O let it not returne to us againe,   250
But Patient and Physition being free,
As sinne is nothing, let it no where be.

Upon the Translation of the Psalmes by Sir Philip Sydney, and the Countesse of Pembroke his Sister

Eternall God, (for whom who ever dare
Seeke new expressions, doe the Circle square,
And thrust into strait corners of poore wit
Thee, who art cornerlesse and infinite)
I would but blesse thy Name, not name thee now;   5
(And thy gifts are as infinite as thou:)
Fixe we our prayses therefore on this one,
That, as thy blessed Spirit fell upon
These Psalmes first Author in a cloven tongue;
(For 'twas a double power by which he sung   10
The highest matter in the noblest forme;)
So thou hast cleft that spirit, to performe
That worke againe, and shed it, here, upon
Two, by their bloods, and by thy Spirit one;
A Brother and a Sister, made by thee   15
The Organ, where thou art the Harmony.
Two that make one *John Baptists* holy voyce,
And who that Psalme, *Now let the Iles rejoyce*,
Have both translated, and apply'd it too,
Both told us what, and taught us how to doe.   20
They shew us Ilanders our joy, our King,
They tell us *why*, and teach us *how* to sing;
Make all this All, three Quires, heaven, earth, and sphears;
The first, Heaven, hath a song, but no man heares,
The Spheares have Musick, but they have no tongue,   25
Their harmony is rather danc'd than sung;
But our third Quire, to which the first gives eare,
(For, Angels learne by what the Church does here)
This Quire hath all. The Organist is hee
Who hath tun'd God and Man, the Organ we: 30
The songs are these, which heavens high holy Muse
Whisper'd to *David, David* to the Jewes:
And *Davids* Successors, in holy zeale,
In formes of joy and art doe re-reveale
To us so sweetly and sincerely too,   35
That I must not rejoyce as I would doe
When I behold that these Psalmes are become

So well attyr'd abroad, so ill at home,
So well in Chambers, in thy Church so ill,
As I can scarce call that reform'd untill   40
This be reform'd; Would a whole State present
A lesser gift than some one man hath sent?
And shall our Church, unto our Spouse and King
More hoarse, more harsh than any other, sing?
For *that* we pray, we praise thy name for *this,*   45
Which, by this *Moses* and this *Miriam,* is
Already done; and as those Psalmes we call
(Though some have other Authors) *Davids* all:
So though some have, some may some Psalmes translate,
We thy Sydnean Psalmes shall celebrate,   50
And, till we come th'Extemporall song to sing,
(Learn'd the first hower, that we see the King,
Who hath translated those translators) may
These their sweet learned labours, all the way
Be as our tuning; that, when hence we part,   55
We may fall in with them, and sing our part.

To Mr Tilman after he had taken orders

Thou, whose diviner soule hath caus'd thee now
To put thy hand unto the holy Plough,
Making Lay-scornings of the Ministry,
Not an impediment, but victory;
What bringst thou home with thee? how is thy mind   5
Affected since the vintage? Dost thou finde
New thoughts and stirrings in thee? and as Steele
Toucht with a Loadstone, dost new motions feele?
Or, as a Ship after much paine and care,
For Iron and Cloth brings home rich Indian ware,   10
Hast thou thus traffiqu'd, but with farre more gaine
Of noble goods, and with lesse time and paine?
Thou art the same materials, as before,
Onely the stampe is changed; but no more.
And as new crowned Kings alter the face,   15
But not the monies substance; so hath grace

Chang'd onely Gods old Image by Creation,
To Christs new stampe, at this thy Coronation;
Or, as we paint Angels with wings, because
They beare Gods message, and proclaime his lawes,   20
Since thou must doe the like, and so must move,
Art thou new feather'd with cœlestiall love?
Deare, tell me where thy purchase lies, and shew
What thy advantage is above, below.
But if thy gainings doe surmount expression,   25
Why doth the foolish world scorne that profession,
Whose joyes passe speech? Why do they think unfit
That Gentry should joyne families with it?
As if their day were onely to be spent
In dressing, Mistressing and complement;   30
Alas poore joyes, but poorer men, whose trust
Seemes richly placed in sublimed dust;
(For, such are cloathes and beauty, which though gay,
Are, at the best, but of sublimed clay.)
Let then the world thy calling disrespect,   35
But goe thou on, and pitty their neglect.
What function is so noble, as to bee
Embassadour to God and destinie?
To open life, to give kingdomes to more
Than Kings give dignities; to keepe heavens doore?   40
Maries prerogative was to beare Christ, so
'Tis preachers to convey him, for they doe
As Angels out of clouds, from Pulpits speake;
And blesse the poore beneath, the lame, the weake.
If then th'Astronomers, whereas they spie   45
A new-found Starre, their Opticks magnifie,
How brave are those, who with their Engine, can
Bring man to heaven, and heaven againe to man?
These are thy titles and preheminences,
In whom must meet Gods graces, mens offences,   50
And so the heavens which beget all things here,
And the earth our mother, which these things doth beare,
Both these in thee, are in thy Calling knit,
And make thee now a blest Hermaphrodite.

A Hymne to Christ, at the Authors
last going into Germany

In what torne ship soever I embarke,
That ship shall be my embleme of thy Arke;
What sea soever swallow mee, that flood
Shall be to mee an embleme of thy blood;
Though thou with clouds of anger do disguise   5
Thy face; yet through that maske I know those eyes,
　　Which, though they turne away sometimes,
　　　　They never will despise.

I sacrifice this Iland unto thee,
And all whom I lov'd there, and who lov'd mee;   10
When I have put our seas twixt them and mee,
Put thou thy sea betwixt my sinnes and thee.
As the trees sap doth seeke the root below
In winter, in my winter now I goe,
　　Where none but thee, th'Eternall root   15
　　　　Of true Love I may know.

Nor thou nor thy religion dost controule,
The amorousnesse of an harmonious Soule,
But thou would'st have that love thy selfe: As thou
Art jealous, Lord, so I am jealous now,   20
Thou lov'st not, till from loving more, thou free
My soule: Who ever gives, takes libertie:
　　O, if thou car'st not whom I love
　　　　Alas, thou lov'st not mee.

Seale then this bill of my Divorce to All,   25
On whom those fainter beames of love did fall;
Marry those loves, which in youth scattered bee
On Fame, Wit, Hopes (false mistresses) to thee.
Churches are best for Prayer, that have least light:
To see God only, I goe out of sight: 30
　　And to scape stormy dayes, I chuse
　　　　An Everlasting night.

The Lamentations of Jeremy,
for the most part according to Tremelius

CHAPTER I

1 How sits this citie, late most populous,
    Thus solitary, and like a widdow thus!
Amplest of Nations, Queene of Provinces
    She was, who now thus tributary is!

2 Still in the night shee weepes, and her teares fall   5
    Downe by her cheekes along, and none of all
Her lovers comfort her; Perfidiously
    Her friends have dealt, and now are enemie.

3 Unto great bondage, and afflictions
    Juda is captive led; Those nations   10
With whom shee dwells, no place of rest afford,
    In streights shee meets her Persecutors sword.

4 Emptie are the gates of Sion, and her waies
    Mourne, because none come to her solemne dayes.
Her Priests doe groane, her maides are comfortlesse,   15
    And shee's unto her selfe a bitternesse.

5 Her foes are growne her head, and live at Peace,
    Because when her transgressions did increase,
The Lord strooke her with sadnesse: Th'enemie
    Doth drive her children to captivitie.   20

6 From Sions daughter is all beauty gone,
    Like Harts, which seeke for Pasture, and find none,
Her Princes are, and now before the foe
    Which still pursues them, without strength they go.

7 Now in her daies of Teares, Jerusalem   25
    (Her men slaine by the foe, none succouring them)
Remembers what of old, shee esteemed most,
    Whilest her foes laugh at her, for what she hath lost.

8   Jerusalem hath sinn'd, therefore is shee
                Remov'd, as women in uncleannesse bee;   30
            Who honor'd, scorne her, for her foulnesse they
                Have seene; her selfe doth groane, and turne away.

9   Her foulnesse in her skirts was seene, yet she
                Remembred not her end; Miraculously
            Therefore shee fell, none comforting: Behold   35
                O Lord my affliction, for the Foe growes bold.

10   Upon all things where her delight hath beene,
                The foe hath stretch'd his hand, for shee hath seene
            Heathen, whom thou command'st, should not doe so,
                Into her holy Sanctuary goe.   40

11   And all her people groane, and seeke for bread;
                And they have given, only to be fed,
            All precious things, wherein their pleasure lay:
                How cheape I'am growne, O Lord, behold, and weigh.

12   All this concernes not you, who passe by mee,   45
                O see, and marke if any sorrow bee
            Like to my sorrow, which Jehova hath
                Done to mee in the day of his fierce wrath?

13   That fire, which by himselfe is governed
                He hath cast from heaven on my bones, and spred 50
            A net before my feet, and mee o'rthrowne,
                And made me languish all the day alone.

14   His hand hath of my sinnes framed a yoake
                Which wreath'd, and cast upon my neck, hath broke
            My strength. The Lord unto those enemies   55
                Hath given mee, from whom I cannot rise.

15   He under foot hath troden in my sight
                My strong men; He did company invite
            To breake my young men; he the winepresse hath
                Trod upon Juda's daughter in his wrath.   60

16   For these things doe I weepe, mine eye, mine eye
          Casts water out; For he which should be nigh
      To comfort mee, is now departed farre;
          The foe prevailes, forlorne my children are.

17   There's none, though *Sion* do stretch out her hand,   65
          To comfort her, it is the Lords command
      That *Jacobs* foes girt him. Jerusalem
          Is as an uncleane woman amongst them.

18   But yet the Lord is just, and righteous still,
          I have rebell'd against his holy will;   70
      O heare all people, and my sorrow see,
          My maides, my young men in captivitie.

19   I called for my *lovers* then, but they
          Deceiv'd mee, and my Priests, and Elders lay
      Dead in the citie; for they sought for meat   75
          Which should refresh their soules, they could not get.

20   Because I am in streights, *Jehova* see
          My heart o'rturn'd, my bowells muddy bee,
      Because I have rebell'd so much, as fast
          The sword without, as death within, doth wast.   80

21   Of all which heare I mourne, none comforts mee,
          My foes have heard my griefe, and glad they be,
      That thou hast done it; But thy promis'd day
          Will come, when, as I suffer, so shall they.

22   Let all their wickednesse appeare to thee,   85
          Doe unto them, as thou hast done to mee,
      For all my sinnes: The sighs which I have had
          Are very many, and my heart is sad.

CHAPTER II

1   How over Sions daughter hath God hung
        His wraths thicke cloud! and from heaven hath flung 90
     To earth the beauty of *Israel,* and hath
        Forgot his foot-stoole in the day of wrath!

2   The Lord unsparingly hath swallowed
        All Jacobs dwellings, and demolished
     To ground the strengths of *Juda,* and prophan'd   95
        The Princes of the Kingdome, and the land.

3   In heat of wrath, the horne of *Israel* hee
        Hath cleane cut off, and lest the enemie
     Be hindred, his right hand he doth retire,
        But is towards *Jacob,* All-devouring fire.   100

4   Like to an enemie he bent his bow,
        His right hand was in posture of a foe,
     To kill what *Sions* daughter did desire,
        'Gainst whom his wrath, he poured forth, like fire.

5   For like an enemie *Jehova* is,   105
        Devouring *Israel,* and his Palaces,
     Destroying holds, giving additions
        To *Juda's* daughters lamentations.

6   Like to a garden hedge he hath cast down
        The place where was his congregation,   110
     And *Sions* feasts and sabbaths are forgot;
        Her King, her Priest, his wrath regardeth not.

7   The Lord forsakes his Altar, and detests
        His Sanctuary, and in the foes hand rests
     His Palace, and the walls, in which their cries   115
        Are heard, as in the true solemnities.

8   The Lord hath cast a line, so to confound
        And levell *Sions* walls unto the ground;
     He drawes not back his hand, which doth oreturne
        The wall, and Rampart, which together mourne.   120

9   Their gates are sunke into the ground, and hee
         Hath broke the barres; their King and Princes bee
     Amongst the heathen, without law, nor there
         Unto their Prophets doth the Lord appeare.

10   There *Sions Elders* on the ground are plac'd,   125
         And silence keepe; Dust on their heads they cast,
     In sackcloth have they girt themselves, and low
         The Virgins towards ground, their heads do throw.

11   My bowells are growne muddy, and mine eyes
         Are faint with weeping: and my liver lies   130
     Pour'd out upon the ground, for miserie
         That sucking children in the streets doe die.

12   When they had cryed unto their Mothers, where
         Shall we have bread, and drinke? they fainted there,
     And in the streets like wounded persons lay   135
         Till 'twixt their mothers breasts they went away.

13   *Daughter Jerusalem,* Oh what may bee
         A witnesse, or comparison for thee?
     Sion, to ease thee, what shall I name like thee?
         Thy breach is like the sea, what help can bee?   140

14   For thee vaine foolish things thy Prophets sought,
         Thee, thine iniquities they have not taught,
     Which might disturne thy bondage: but for thee
         False burthens, and false causes they would see.

15   The passengers doe clap their hands, and hisse,   145
         And wag their head at thee, and say, Is this
     That citie, which so many men did call
         Joy of the earth, and perfectest of all?

16   Thy foes doe gape upon thee, and they hisse,
         And gnash their teeth, and say, Devoure wee this, 150
     For this is certainly the day which wee
         Expected, and which now we finde, and see.

17   The Lord hath done that which he purposed,
            Fulfill'd his word of old determined;
        He hath throwne downe, and not spar'd, and thy foe 155
            Made glad above thee, and advanc'd him so.

18   But now, their hearts against the Lord do call,
            Therefore, O walls of *Sion,* let teares fall
        Downe like a river, day and night; take thee
            No rest, but let thine eye incessant be.   160

19   Arise, cry in the night, poure, for thy sinnes,
            Thy heart, like water, when the watch begins;
        Lift up thy hands to God, lest children dye,
            Which, faint for hunger, in the streets doe lye.

20   Behold O Lord, consider unto whom   165
            Thou hast done this; what, shall the women come
        To eate their children of a spanne? shall thy
            Prophet and Priest be slaine in Sanctuary?

21   On ground in streets, the yong and old do lye,
            My virgins and yong men by sword do dye;   170
        Them in the day of thy wrath thou hast slaine,
            Nothing did thee from killing them containe.

22   As to a solemne feast, all whom I fear'd
            Thou call'st about mee; when thy wrath appear'd,
        None did remaine or scape, for those which I   175
            Brought up, did perish by mine enemie.

CHAPTER III

1   I am the man which have affliction seene,
            Under the rod of Gods wrath having beene,
2   He hath led mee to darknesse, not to light,
3   And against mee all day, his hand doth fight.   180

4	Hee hath broke my bones,worne out my flesh and skinne,
5	Built up against mee; and hath girt mee in
6	With hemlocke, and with labour; and set mee
	In darke, as they who dead for ever bee.

7	Hee hath hedg'd me lest I scape, and added more	185
	To my steele fetters, heavier then before.	
8	When I crie out, he out shuts my prayer: And hath	
9	Stop'd with hewn stone my way, and turn'd my path.	

10	And like a Lion hid in secrecie,	
	Or Beare which lyes in wait, he was to mee.	190
11	He stops my way, teares me, made desolate,	
12	And hee makes mee the marke he shooteth at.	

13	Hee made the children of his quiver passe	
14	Into my reines, I with my people was	
	All the day long, a song and mockery.	195
15	Hee hath fill'd mee with bitternesse, and he	

16	Hath made me drunke with wormewood. He hath burst	
	My teeth with stones, and covered mee with dust;	
17	And thus my Soule farre off from peace was set,	
	And my prosperity I did forget.	200

18	My strength, my hope (unto my selfe I said)
	Which from the Lord should come, is perished.
19	But when my mournings I do thinke upon,
	My wormwood, hemlocke, and affliction,

20	My Soule is humbled in remembring this;	205
21	My heart considers, therefore, hope there is.	
22	'Tis Gods great mercy we'are not utterly	
	Consum'd, for his compassions do not die;	

23	For every morning they renewed bee,	
	For great, O Lord, is thy fidelity.	210
24	The Lord is, saith my Soule, my portion,	
	And therefore in him will I hope alone.	

25   The Lord is good to them, who on him relie,
            And to the Soule that seeks him earnestly.
26   It is both good to trust, and to attend   215
            (The Lords salvation) unto the end:

27   'Tis good for one his yoake in youth to beare;
28   He sits alone. and doth all speech forbeare,
29   Because he hath borne it. And his mouth he layes
            Deepe in the dust, yet then in hope he stayes.   220

30   He gives his cheekes to whosoever will
            Strike him, and so he is reproched still.
31   For, not for ever doth the Lord forsake,
32   But when he'hath strucke with sadnes, hee doth take

        Compassion, as his mercy'is infinite;   225
33   Nor is it with his heart, that he doth smite;
34   That underfoot the prisoners stamped bee,
35   That a mans right the Judge himselfe doth see

36   To be wrung from him, That he subverted is
            In his just cause; the Lord allowes not this.   230
37   Who then will say, that ought doth come to passe,
            But that which by the Lord commanded was?

38   Both good and evill from his mouth proceeds;
39   Why then grieves any man for his misdeeds?
40   Turne wee to God, by trying out our wayes;   235
41   To him in heaven, our hands with hearts upraise.

42   Wee have rebell'd, and falne away from thee,
43   Thou pardon'st not; Usest no clemencie;
        Pursuest us, kill'st us, coverest us with wrath,
44   Cover'st thy selfe with clouds, that our prayer hath

45   No power to passe. And thou hast made us fall
            As refuse, and off-scouring to them all.
46, 47 All our foes gape at us. Feare and a snare
            With ruine, and with waste, upon us are.

48	With watry rivers doth mine eye oreflow	245
	For ruine of my peoples daughter so;	
49	Mine eye doth drop downe teares incessantly,	
50	Untill the Lord looke downe from heaven to see.	

51	And for my citys daughters sake, mine eye	
52	Doth breake mine heart. Causles mine enemy,	250
53	Like a bird chac'd me. In a dungeon	
	They have shut my life, and cast on me a stone.	

54	Waters flow'd o'r my head, then thought I, I am	
55	Destroy'd; I called Lord, upon thy name	
56	Out of the pit. And thou my voice didst heare;	255
	Oh from my sigh, and crye, stop not thine eare.	

57	Then when I call'd upon thee, thou drew'st nere	
	Unto mee, and said'st unto mee, do not feare.	
58	Thou Lord my Soules cause handled hast, and thou	
59	Rescud'st my life. O Lord do thou judge now,	260

60	Thou heardst my wrong. Their vengeance all they have wrought;	
61	How they reproach'd, thou hast heard, and what they thought,	
62	What their lips uttered, which against me rose,	
	And what was ever whisper'd by my foes.	

63	I am their song, whether they rise or sit,	265
64	Give them rewards Lord, for their working fit,	
65, 66	Sorrow of heart, thy curse. And with thy might	
	Follow, and from under heaven destroy them quite.	

CHAPTER IV

1	How is the gold become so dimme? How is	
	Purest and finest gold thus chang'd to this?	270
	The stones which were stones of the Sanctuary,	
	Scattered in corners of each street do lye.	

2   The pretious sonnes of Sion, which should bee
               Valued at purest gold, how do wee see
           Low rated now, as earthen Pitchers, stand,   275
               Which are the worke of a poore Potters hand.

3   Even the Sea-calfes draw their brests, and give
               Sucke to their young; my peoples daughters live,
           By reason of the foes great cruelnesse,
               As do the Owles in the vast Wildernesse.   280

4   And when the sucking child doth strive to draw,
               His tongue for thirst cleaves to his upper jaw.
           And when for bread the little children crye,
               There is no man that doth them satisfie.

5   They which before were delicately fed,   285
               Now in the streets forlorne have perished,
           And they which ever were in scarlet cloath'd,
               Sit and embrace the dunghills which they loath'd.

6   The daughters of my people have sinned more,
               Then did the towne of *Sodome* sinne before;   290
           Which being at once destroy'd, there did remaine
               No hands amongst them, to vexe them againe.

7   But heretofore purer her Nazarite
               Was then the snow, and milke was not so white;
           As carbuncles did their pure bodies shine,   295
               And all their polish'dnesse was Saphirine.

8   They are darker now then blacknes, none can know
               Them by the face, as through the streets they goe,
           For now their skin doth cleave unto the bone,
               And withered, is like to dry wood growne.   300

9   Better by sword then famine 'tis to dye;
               And better through pierc'd, then through penury.
10   Women by nature pitifull, have eate
               Their children drest with their owne hands for meat.

11   *Jehova* here fully accomplish'd hath   305
         His indignation, and powr'd forth his wrath,
     Kindled a fire in *Sion,* which hath power
         To eate, and her foundations to devour.

12   Nor would the Kings of the earth, nor all which live
         In the inhabitable world beleeve,   310
     That any adversary, any foe
         Into *Jerusalem* should enter so.

13   For the Priests sins, and Prophets, which have shed
         Blood in the streets, and the just murthered:
14   Which when those men, whom they made blinde, did stray
         Thorough the streets, defiled by the way

     With blood, the which impossible it was
         Their garments should scape touching, as they passe,
15   Would cry aloud, depart defiled men,
         Depart, depart, and touch us not; and then   320

     They fled, and strayd, and with the *Gentiles* were,
         Yet told their friends, they should not long dwell there;
16   For this they are scattered by Jehovahs face
         Who never will regard them more; No grace

     Unto their old men shall the foe afford,   325
         Nor, that they are Priests, redeeme them from the sword.
17   And wee as yet, for all these miseries
         Desiring our vaine helpe, consume our eyes:

     And such a nation as cannot save,
         We in desire and speculation have.   330
18   They hunt our steps, that in the streets wee feare
         To goe: our end is now approached neere,

     Our dayes accomplish'd are, this the last day.
19   Eagles of heaven are not so swift as they
         Which follow us, o'r mountaine tops they flye   335
     At us, and for us in the desart lye.

20 The annointed Lord, breath of our nostrils, hee
    Of whom we said, under his shadow, wee
   Shall with more ease under the Heathen dwell,
    Into the pit which these men digged, fell.   340

21 Rejoyce O *Edoms daughter,* joyfull bee
    Thou which inhabitst Huz, for unto thee
   This cup shall passe, and thou with drunkennesse
    Shalt fill thy selfe, and shew thy nakednesse.

22 And then thy sinnes O *Sion,* shall be spent,   345
    The Lord will not leave thee in banishment.
   Thy sinnes O *Edoms daughter,* hee will see,
    And for them, pay thee with captivitie.

CHAPTER V

1 Remember, O Lord, what is fallen on us;
    See, and marke how we are reproached thus,   350
2 For unto strangers our possession
    Is turn'd, our houses unto Aliens gone,

3 Our mothers are become as widowes, wee
    As Orphans all, and without father be;
4 Waters which are our owne, wee drunke, and pay, 355
    And upon our owne wood a price they lay.

5 Our persecutors on our necks do sit,
    They make us travaile, and not intermit,
6 We stretch our hands unto th'*Egyptians*
    To get us bread; and to the *Assyrians.*   360

7 Our Fathers did these sinnes, and are no more,
    But wee do beare the sinnes they did before.
8 They are but servants, which do rule us thus,
    Yet from their hands none would deliver us.

9   With danger of our life our bread wee gat;   365
         For in the wildernesse, the sword did wait.

10   The tempests of this famine wee liv'd in,
         Black as an Oven colour'd had our skinne:

11   In *Judaes* cities they the maids abus'd
         By force, and so women in *Sion* us'd.   370

12   The Princes with their hands they hung; no grace
         Nor honour gave they to the Elders face.

13   Unto the mill our yong men carried are,
         And children fell under the wood they bare.

14   Elders, the gates; youth did their songs forbeare,   375
15   Gone was our joy; our dancings, mournings were.

16   Now is the crowne falne from our head; and woe
         Be unto us, because we'have sinned so.

17   For this our hearts do languish, and for this
         Over our eyes a cloudy dimnesse is.   380

18   Because mount *Sion* desolate doth lye,
         And foxes there do goe at libertie:

19   But thou O Lord art ever, and thy throne
         From generation, to generation.

20   Why should'st thou forget us eternally?   385
         Or leave us thus long in this misery?

21   Restore us Lord to thee, that so we may
         Returne, and as of old, renew our day.

22   For oughtest thou, O Lord, despise us thus,
         And to be utterly enrag'd at us?   390

Hymne to God my God, in my Sicknesse

Since I am comming to that Holy roome,
   Where, with thy Quire of Saints for evermore,
I shall be made thy Musique; As I come
   I tune the Instrument here at the dore,
   And what I must doe then, thinke here before.   5

Whilst my Physitians by their love are growne
   Cosmographers, and I their Mapp, who lie
Flat on this bed, that by them may be showne
   That this is my South-west discoverie
   Per fretum febris, by these streights to die,   10

I joy, that in these straits, I see my West;
   For, though theire currants yeeld returne to none,
What shall my West hurt me? As West and East
   In all flatt Maps (and I am one) are one,
   So death doth touch the Resurrection.   15

Is the Pacifique Sea my home? Or are
   The Easterne riches? Is *Jerusalem?*
Anyan, and *Magellan,* and *Gibraltare,*
   All streights, and none but streights, are wayes to them,
   Whether where *Japhet* dwelt, or *Cham,* or *Sem.*   20

We thinke that *Paradise* and *Calvarie,*
   Christs Crosse, and *Adams* tree, stood in one place;
Looke Lord, and finde both *Adams* met in me;
   As the first *Adams* sweat surrounds my face,
   May the last *Adams* blood my soule embrace.   25

So, in his purple wrapp'd receive mee Lord,
   By these his thornes give me his other Crowne;
And as to others soules I preach'd thy word,
   Be this my Text, my Sermon to mine owne,
   Therfore that he may raise the Lord throws down.   30

A Hymne to God the Father

I

Wilt thou forgive that sinne where I begunne,
  Which was my sin, though it were done before?
Wilt thou forgive that sinne; through which I runne,
  And do run still: though still I do deplore?
    When thou hast done, thou hast not done,   5
      For, I have more.

II

Wilt thou forgive that sinne which I have wonne
  Others to sinne? and, made my sinne their doore?
Wilt thou forgive that sinne which I did shunne
  A yeare, or two: but wallowed in, a score?   10
    When thou hast done, thou hast not done,
      For I have more.

III

I have a sinne of feare, that when I have spunne
  My last thred, I shall perish on the shore;
But sweare by thy selfe, that at my death thy sonne   15
  Shall shine as he shines now, and heretofore;
    And, having done that, Thou hast done,
      I feare no more.

INDEX OF POEM TITLES

INDEX OF FIRST LINES